D1174202

SONGS OF THE CHURCH

SONGS
OF THE CHURCH

Walter E. Yoder, Editor

HERALD PRESS
SCOTTDALE, PENNSYLVANIA

First Printing, 1953
Second Printing, 1959
Third Printing, 1963

PRINTED IN U·S·A·

Introduction

The true children of God are happy; their constant joy is maintained by the very nature of the experience of their salvation. God's pardon of sin, the new birth in Christ, the gift of the Spirit, and the other countless blessings of the Christian life are signal occasions for sincere song.

The true children of God must sing; their God-given voices will throb with praise, thanksgiving, aspiration, consecration, and the commitments of discipleship. They regard the privilege of singing in worship as a birthright of Christianity and one of the most potential factors in spiritual worship.

The Mennonite Church of today has a rich heritage in choral, congregational music. Few groups of organized Christians have promoted and utilized congregational singing in worship as has our church in the past. This fact must not become an occasion for pride and praise of denomination, but it should serve as a small tribute to the fidelity and foresight of our godly founders who realized the true worth of music sung by the entire congregation. It is expected of us, we who constitute the church of today, to carry on and further develop the resources in church music to which we have fallen heir. This, we believe, is the basic reason for the production of a new collection of good music for our congregations.

The publication of this new book, **Songs of the Church,** represents a large measure of hard work on the part of the General Conference Music Committee. As a committee, we have made extensive surveys in church music materials with especial consideration for new and virtuous textual and musical settings. Much prayer and concern for the future welfare of our church music has prevailed.

The editor, Walter E. Yoder, Music Department Head, Goshen College, Goshen, Indiana, and chairman of the committee, has done a most creditable job in bringing suggestions to the committee and in making the final arrangements and decisions for the book's production.

Songs of the Church has a number of distinctive features which I feel will commend it to our assemblies. A wide range in textual topics, musical settings which span more than four centuries from the Reformation chorale to the present, recommended chorus selections, and the inclusion of responsive readings are being provided. In this book we are making available to our people some of the fine, old German chorales which were given up when we accepted English as our language. American Mennonite hymnody is featured by including selections from **The Harmonia Sacra** and from some current composers within the church. Many standard hymns are included, as well as some of the better Gospel songs of the past and present.

The General Conference Music Committee is composed of Walter E. Yoder, chairman, J. Mark Stauffer, secretary, John P. Duerksen, Paul Erb, and Chester K. Lehman. We send this new publication out on wings borne by prayer and expectancy. We can attest to the blessing of the Lord on the work thus far and we have faith to believe that His continued blessing will attend this book as it finds place in our worship assemblies. We sincerely hope and pray that **Songs of the Church** will serve to strengthen congregational singing by adding new inspiration and meaning to our worship experience through music.

—J. Mark Stauffer.

Contents

Songs of the Church

* * *

I Will Sing Praises unto the Lord 1

LA PREE L. M.

Warren La Pree

Omer S. Garber, 1950

1. All peo - ple that on earth do dwell; Him serve with
2. Sing to the Lord with cheer - ful voice, Come ye be -
3. O en - ter then His gates with praise, Praise, laud, and
fear, His praise forth tell: With - out our aid He
fore Him and re - joice; The Lord, ye know, is
bless His name al - ways; His mer - cy is for -
doth us make, And for His sheep He doth us take.
God in - deed, We are His folk, He doth us feed.
ev - er sure, And shall from age to age en - dure.

2 Around the Throne of God in Heaven

GLORY C. M. Ref.

Anne Shepherd, 1809-1857 Henry E. Mathews, c. 1853

1. A - round the throne of God in heav'n Thou-sands of chil - dren stand,
2. What brought them to that world a - bove, That heav'n so bright and fair,
3. On earth they sought the Sav-iour's grace, On earth they loved His name;

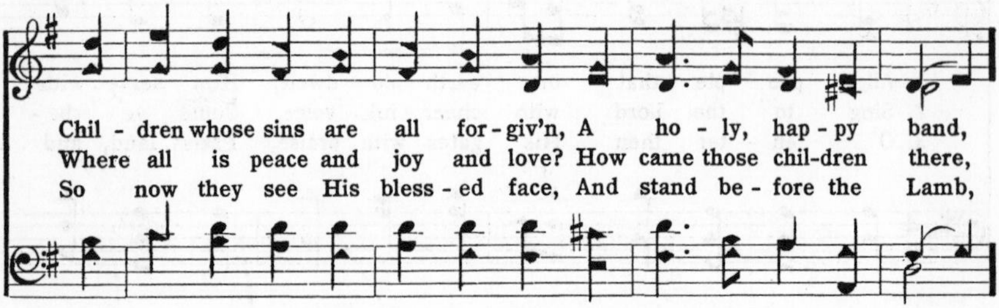

Chil - dren whose sins are all for - giv'n, A ho - ly, hap - py band,
Where all is peace and joy and love? How came those chil-dren there,
So now they see His bless - ed face, And stand be - fore the Lamb,

REFRAIN

Sing-ing "Glo - ry, glo - ry, Glo - ry be to God on high!" A-men.

3 Heaven and Earth, the Sea and Air

GOTT SEI DANK 7. 7. 7. 7.

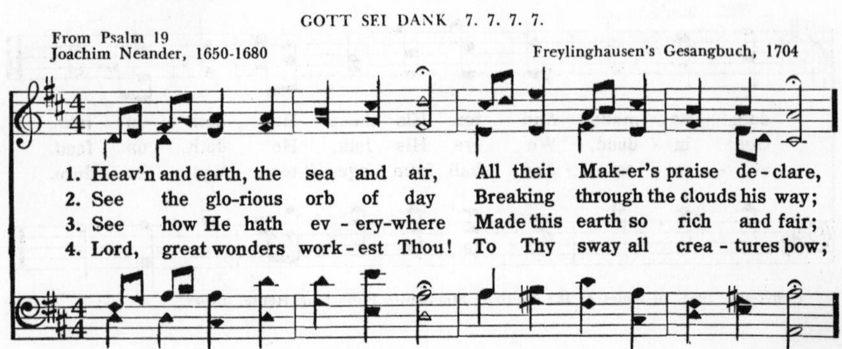
From Psalm 19
Joachim Neander, 1650-1680
Freylinghausen's Gesangbuch, 1704
1. Heav'n and earth, the sea and air, All their Mak-er's praise de - clare,
2. See the glo-rious orb of day Breaking through the clouds his way;
3. See how He hath ev - ery-where Made this earth so rich and fair;
4. Lord, great wonders work - est Thou! To Thy sway all crea - tures bow;

Wake, my soul, a - wake and sing: Now thy grate-ful prais-es bring.
Moon and stars with sil - v'ry light Praise Him through the si - lent night.
Hill and vale and fruit - ful land, All things liv - ing, show His hand.
Write Thou deep-ly in my heart What I am, and what Thou art. A-men.
Holy, Lord God of Sabaoth
4
SANCTUS
Harmonia Sacra
Ho - ly, ho - ly, ho - ly, Lord God of Sab - a - oth.
Heav'n and earth are full of the maj - es - ty of Thy glo - ry.
Glo - ry be to Thee, Glo - ry be to Thee,
Glo - ry be to Thee Glo - ry be to
Glo - ry be to Thee, To Thee, O Lord most high.
Thee

5 All Praise to Him Who Reigns Above

BLESSED NAME C. M. Ref.

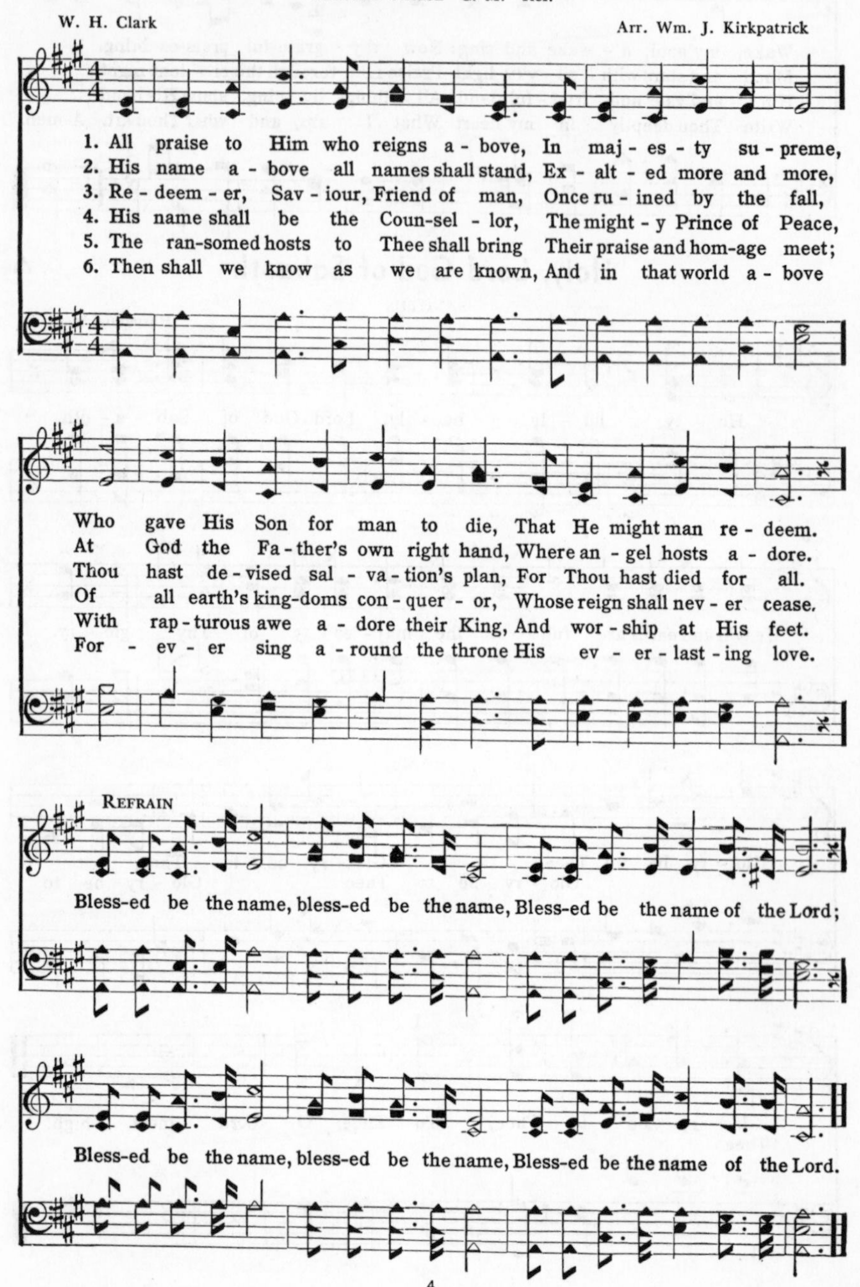
W. H. Clark
Arr. Wm. J. Kirkpatrick
1. All praise to Him who reigns a - bove, In maj - es - ty su - preme,
2. His name a - bove all names shall stand, Ex - alt - ed more and more,
3. Re - deem - er, Sav - iour, Friend of man, Once ru - ined by the fall,
4. His name shall be the Coun-sel - lor, The might - y Prince of Peace,
5. The ran-somed hosts to Thee shall bring Their praise and hom-age meet;
6. Then shall we know as we are known, And in that world a - bove
Who gave His Son for man to die, That He might man re - deem.
At God the Fa - ther's own right hand, Where an - gel hosts a - dore.
Thou hast de - vised sal - va - tion's plan, For Thou hast died for all.
Of all earth's king-doms con - quer - or, Whose reign shall nev - er cease.
With rap - turous awe a - dore their King, And wor - ship at His feet.
For - ev - er sing a - round the throne His ev - er - last - ing love.
Refrain
Bless-ed be the name, bless-ed be the name, Bless-ed be the name of the Lord;
Bless-ed be the name, bless-ed be the name, Bless-ed be the name of the Lord.

All Hail the Power of Jesus' Name

6

DIADEM C. M. Ref.
E. Perronet
James Ellor
1. All hail the pow'r of Je - sus' name! Let an - gels pros - trate fall,
2. Ye cho - sen seed of Is - rael's race, Ye ransomed from the fall,
3. Let ev - ery kin - dred, ev - ery tribe, On this ter - res - trial ball,
4. O that with yon - der sa - cred throng We at His feet may fall,
Let an - gels pros - trate fall; Bring forth the roy - al di - a - dem,
Ye ran - somed from the fall, Hail Him who saves you by His grace,
On this ter - res - trial ball, To Him all maj - es - ty as - cribe,
We at His feet may fall! We'll join the ev - er - last - ing song,
And crown . . . . Him, Crown Him,
And crown Him, crown Him, crown Him, And crown Him Lord of
And crown . . . . Him, Crown Him,
And crown Him, crown Him, crown Him, Crown . . . .
crown Him, crown Him;
all, crown Him; And crown Him Lord of all! A - men.
crown . . . . Him;
. . . . Him; And crown Him Lord of all!

7 All Hail the Power of Jesus' Name

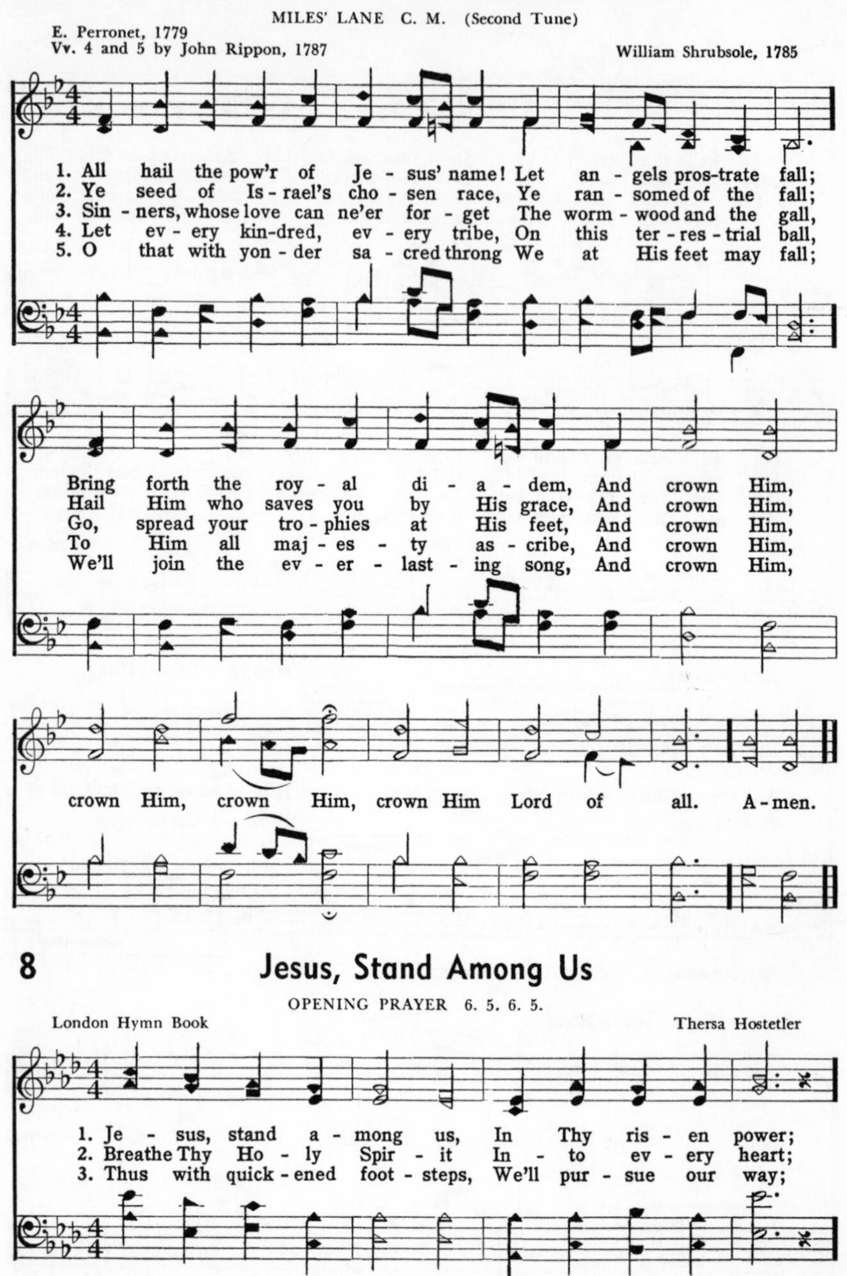
MILES' LANE C. M. (Second Tune)
E. Perronet, 1779
Vv. 4 and 5 by John Rippon, 1787
William Shrubsole, 1785
1. All hail the pow'r of Je - sus' name! Let an - gels pros-trate fall;
2. Ye seed of Is - rael's cho - sen race, Ye ran - somed of the fall;
3. Sin - ners, whose love can ne'er for - get The worm - wood and the gall,
4. Let ev - ery kin-dred, ev - ery tribe, On this ter - res - trial ball,
5. O that with yon - der sa - cred throng We at His feet may fall;
Bring forth the roy - al di - a - dem, And crown Him,
Hail Him who saves you by His grace, And crown Him,
Go, spread your tro - phies at His feet, And crown Him,
To Him all maj - es - ty as - cribe, And crown Him,
We'll join the ev - er - last - ing song, And crown Him,
crown Him, crown Him, crown Him Lord of all. A - men.
8
Jesus, Stand Among Us
OPENING PRAYER 6. 5. 6. 5.
London Hymn Book
Thersa Hostetler
1. Je - sus, stand a - mong us, In Thy ris - en power;
2. Breathe Thy Ho - ly Spir - it In - to ev - ery heart;
3. Thus with quick - ened foot - steps, We'll pur - sue our way;

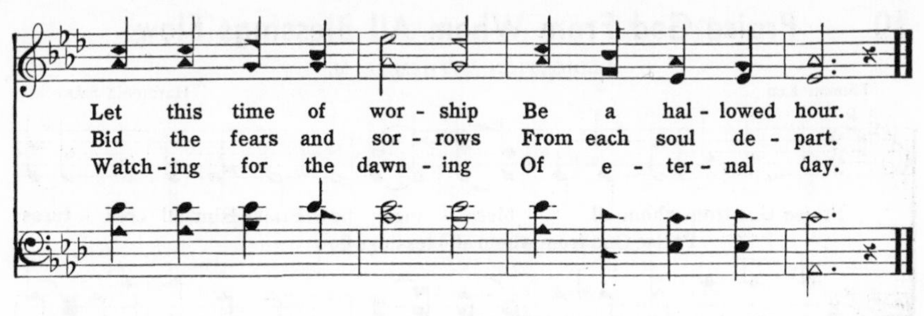

Let this time of wor - ship Be a hal - lowed hour.
Bid the fears and sor - rows From each soul de - part.
Watch - ing for the dawn - ing Of e - ter - nal day.

Holy God, We Praise Thy Name 9

GROSSER GOTT, WIR LOBEN DICH 7. 8. 7. 8. 7. 7.

Te Deum
Tr. Clarence Walworth, 1820-1900 — Katholisches Gesangbuch, Vienna, 1774

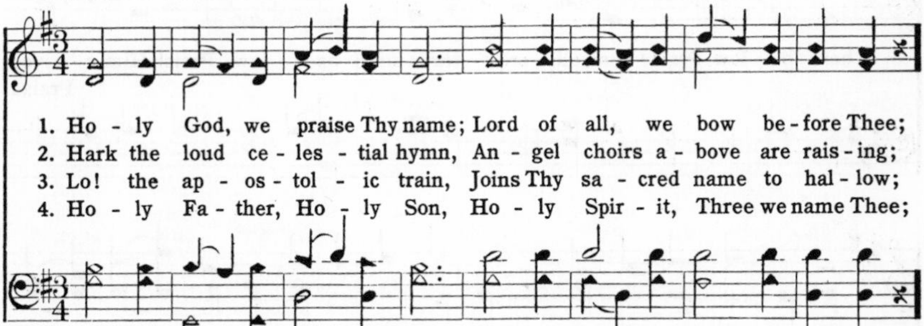

1. Ho - ly God, we praise Thy name; Lord of all, we bow be - fore Thee;
2. Hark the loud ce - les - tial hymn, An - gel choirs a - bove are rais - ing;
3. Lo! the ap - os - tol - ic train, Joins Thy sa - cred name to hal - low;
4. Ho - ly Fa - ther, Ho - ly Son, Ho - ly Spir - it, Three we name Thee;

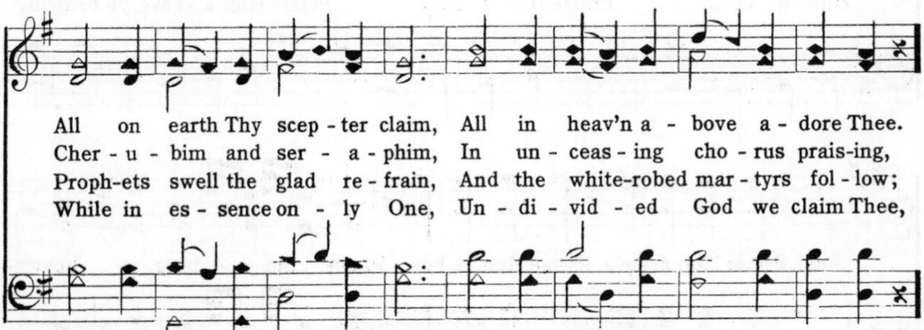

All on earth Thy scep - ter claim, All in heav'n a - bove a - dore Thee.
Cher - u - bim and ser - a - phim, In un - ceas - ing cho - rus prais-ing,
Proph-ets swell the glad re - frain, And the white-robed mar - tyrs fol - low;
While in es - sence on - ly One, Un - di - vid - ed God we claim Thee,

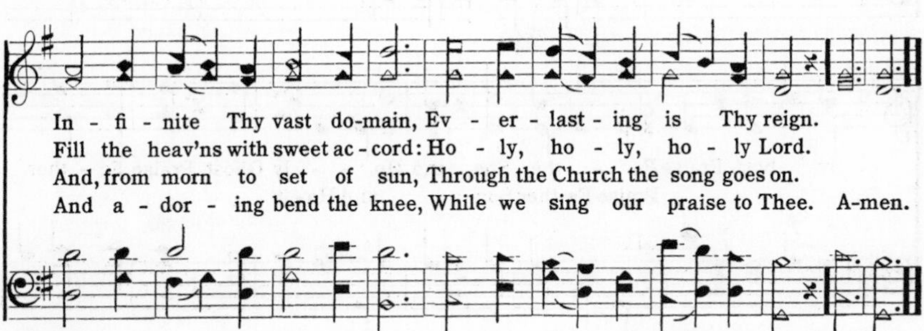

In - fi - nite Thy vast do-main, Ev - er - last - ing is Thy reign.
Fill the heav'ns with sweet ac - cord: Ho - ly, ho - ly, ho - ly Lord.
And, from morn to set of sun, Through the Church the song goes on.
And a - dor - ing bend the knee, While we sing our praise to Thee. A-men.

10 Praise God From Whom All Blessings Flow

DEDICATION ANTHEM L. M.

Thomas Ken

Harmonia Sacra

Son, and Ho-ly Ghost, Praise Fa-ther, Son, and Ho-ly Ghost.
Hal-le-lu-jah, hal-le-lu-jah, hal-le-lu-jah a-men, A-men,
Hal-le-lu-jah, hal-le-lu-jah, hal-le-lu-jah, hal-le-lu-jah,
Hal-le - lu-jah
hal-le-lu-jah, Hal-le-lu-jah, hal-le-lu-jah, hal-le-lu-jah,
a - men, A-men, Hal-le-lu-jah, a-men, Hal-le-lu-jah, a-men.

11 Christ Is Our Cornerstone

DARWALL 6. 6. 6. 6. 8. 8.

8th century. Tr. John Chandler, 1837

John Darwall, 1770

1. Christ is our Cor - ner - stone, On Him a - lone we build;
2. O then with hymns of praise These hal - lowed courts shall ring;
3. Here, gra - cious God, do Thou For ev - er - more draw nigh;
4. Here may we gain from Heaven The grace which we im - plore;
With His true saints a - lone The courts of heav'n are filled:
Our voic - es we will raise The Three in One to sing;
Ac - cept each faith - ful vow, And mark each sup - pliant sigh;
And may that grace, once given, Be with us ev - er - more,
On His great love our hopes we place Of
And thus pro - claim in joy - ful song Both
In co - pious shower on all who pray Each
Un - til that day when all the blest To
pres - ent grace and joys a - bove.
loud and long that glo - rious name.
ho - ly day Thy bless - ings pour!
end - less rest are called a - way! A - men.

Give Thanks to God

12

THANKS C. M. D.

Psalm 105

English

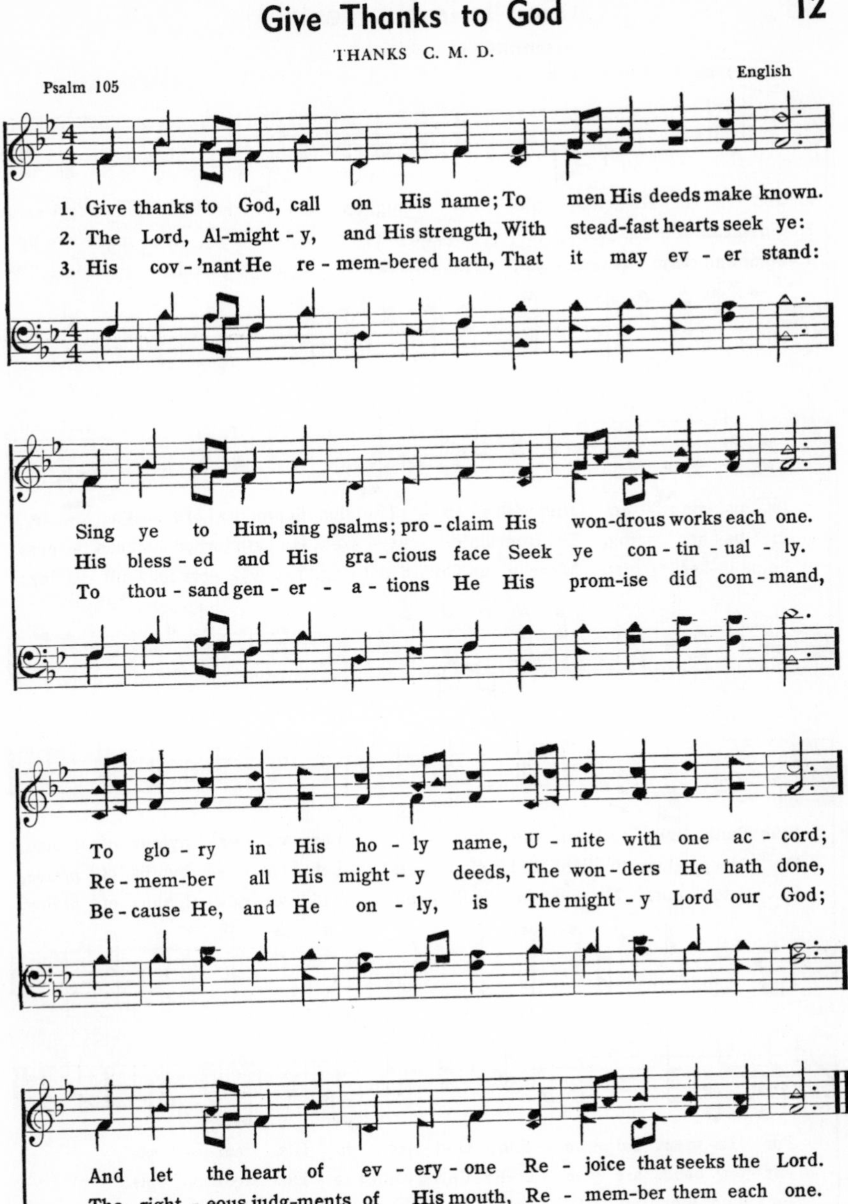
1. Give thanks to God, call on His name; To men His deeds make known.
2. The Lord, Al-might - y, and His strength, With stead-fast hearts seek ye:
3. His cov - 'nant He re - mem-bered hath, That it may ev - er stand:
Sing ye to Him, sing psalms; pro - claim His won-drous works each one.
His bless - ed and His gra - cious face Seek ye con - tin - ual - ly.
To thou - sand gen - er - a - tions He His prom-ise did com - mand,
To glo - ry in His ho - ly name, U - nite with one ac - cord;
Re - mem-ber all His might - y deeds, The won - ders He hath done,
Be - cause He, and He on - ly, is The might - y Lord our God;
And let the heart of ev - ery - one Re - joice that seeks the Lord.
The right - eous judg-ments of His mouth, Re - mem-ber them each one.
And His most right-eous judg-ments are In all the earth a - broad.

13 God Is in His Temple

GRONINGEN 6. 6. 8. 6. 6. 8. 6. 6. 6.

W. T. Matson | Joachim Neander

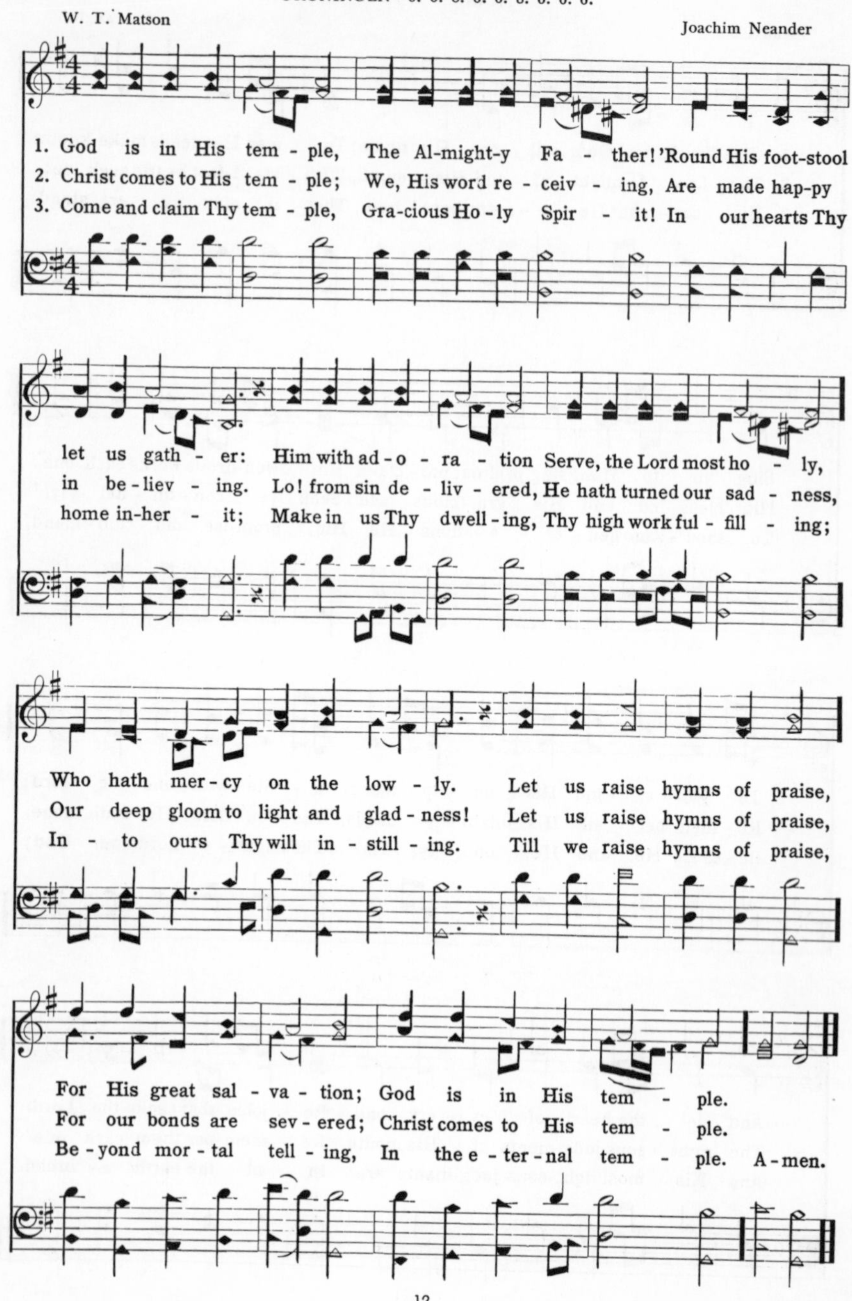
1. God is in His tem - ple, The Al-might-y Fa - ther! 'Round His foot-stool let us gath - er: Him with ad - o - ra - tion Serve, the Lord most ho - ly, Who hath mer - cy on the low - ly. Let us raise hymns of praise, For His great sal - va - tion; God is in His tem - ple.
2. Christ comes to His tem - ple; We, His word re - ceiv - ing, Are made hap-py in be - liev - ing. Lo! from sin de - liv - ered, He hath turned our sad - ness, Our deep gloom to light and glad - ness! Let us raise hymns of praise, For our bonds are sev - ered; Christ comes to His tem - ple.
3. Come and claim Thy tem - ple, Gra-cious Ho - ly Spir - it! In our hearts Thy home in-her - it; Make in us Thy dwell - ing, Thy high work ful - fill - ing; In - to ours Thy will in - still - ing. Till we raise hymns of praise, Be - yond mor - tal tell - ing, In the e - ter - nal tem - ple. A - men.

Holy Lord, Holy Lord 14

FAHRE FORT

Anonymous

Johann E. Schmidt, 1704

1. Ho - ly Lord, ho - ly Lord, Ho - ly and al - might - y Lord,
2. Thanks and praise, thanks and praise, Thanks and praise be ev - er Thine,
3. Lord, our God, Lord, our God, May Thy pre - cious sav - ing Word,

Thou, who, as the great Cre - a - tor, Art by all Thy works a - dored;
That Thy Word to us is giv - en, Teaching us with pow'r di - vine,
Till our race is here com-plet - ed, Light un - to our path af - ford;

Source of u - ni - ver - sal na - ture, And to man re -
That the Lord of earth and heav - en, Ev - er - last - ing
And, when in Thy pres - ence seat - ed, We to Thee will

deemed by Je - sus' blood, Sov - 'reign Good, Sov - 'reign Good.
life for us to gain, Once was slain, once was slain.
ren - der for Thy grace Cease - less praise, cease - less praise. A-men.

15 Hallelujah, Praise Jehovah

KIRKPATRICK 8. 7. 8. 7. D. Ref.

Psalm 148

Wm. J. Kirkpatrick

1. Hal - le - lu - jah, praise Je - ho - vah, From the heav-ens praise His name;
2. Let them prais - es give Je - ho - vah, They were made at His com-mand;
3. All ye fruit - ful trees and ce - dars, All ye hills and moun-tains high,
Praise Je - ho - vah in the high - est, All His an - gels praise pro - claim.
Them for - ev - er He es - tab - lished, His de - cree shall ev - er stand.
Creep - ing things, and beasts and cat - tle, Birds that in the heav - ens fly,
All His hosts, to - geth - er praise Him, Sun and moon and stars on high;
From the earth, O praise Je - ho - vah, All ye floods, ye drag - ons all,
Kings of earth, and all ye peo - ple, Princ - es great, earth's judges all;
Praise Him, O ye heav'ns of heav - ens, And ye floods a - bove the sky.
Fire and hail and storm and va - pors, Storm-y winds that hear His call,
Praise His name, young men and maid - ens, A - ged men, and chil - dren small.
Refrain
Let them prais - es give Je - ho - vah, For His name a - lone is high,
Let them prais-es

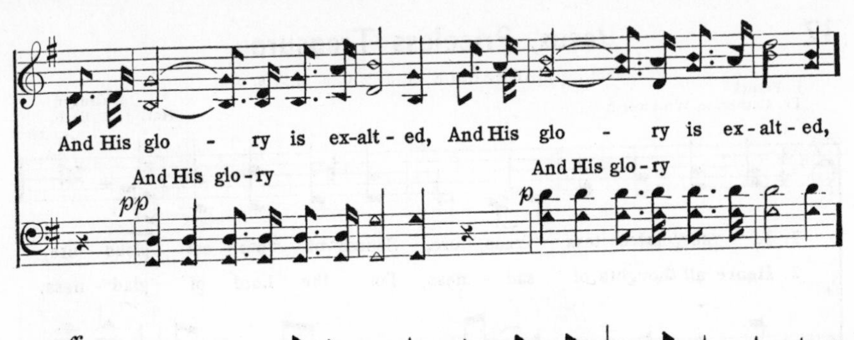

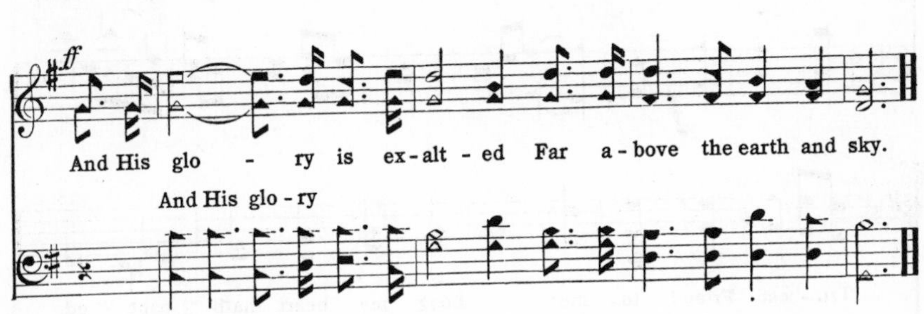

My God, How Endless Is Thy Love 16

NEWELL L. M.

Isaac Watts, 1719

Reuben Brooks, 1897

1. My God, how end-less is Thy love! Thy gifts are ev-ery eve-ning new;
2. Thou spread'st the cur-tain of the night, Great guar-dian of my sleep-ing hours;
3. I yield my powers to Thy com-mand, To Thee I con-se-crate my days;

And morn-ing mer-cies, from a-bove, Gent-ly dis-till, like ear-ly dew.
Thy sov'reign word re-stores the light, And quick-ens all my drow-sy powers.
Per-pet-ual bless-ings from Thy hand De-mand per-pet-ual songs of praise. A-men.

17 Jesus, Priceless Treasure

JESU, MEINE FREUDE 6. 6. 5. 6. 6. 5. 7. 8. 6.
J. Franck
Tr. Catherine Winkworth
J. Cruger
Har. J. S. Bach
1. Je - sus, price - less Treas - ure, Source of pur - est pleas - ure,
2. Hence all thoughts of sad - ness, For the Lord of glad - ness,
Tru - est Friend to me; Long my heart hath pant - ed,
Je - sus en - ters in: Those who love the Fa - ther,
Till it well - nigh faint - ed, Thirst-ing af - ter Thee.
Though the storms may gath - er, Still have peace with - in;
Thine I am, O spot - less Lamb, I will suf - fer
Yea, what - e'er we here must bear, Still in Thee lies

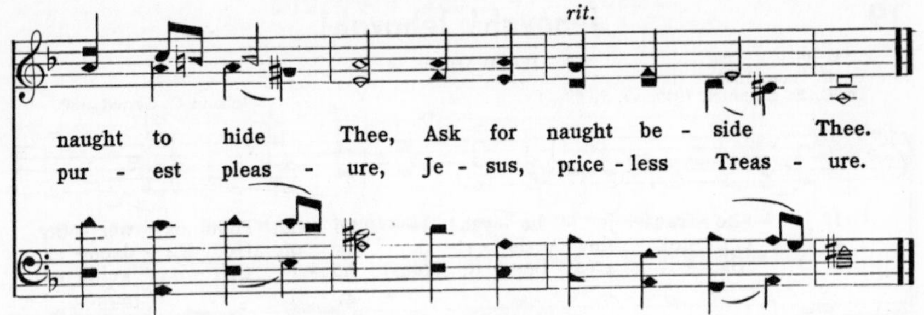
rit.
naught to hide Thee, Ask for naught be - side Thee.
pur - est pleas - ure, Je - sus, price - less Treas - ure.

In Thy Name, O Lord, Assembling 18

CORONAE 8. 7. 8. 7. 4. 7.

Thomas Kelly

William H. Monk

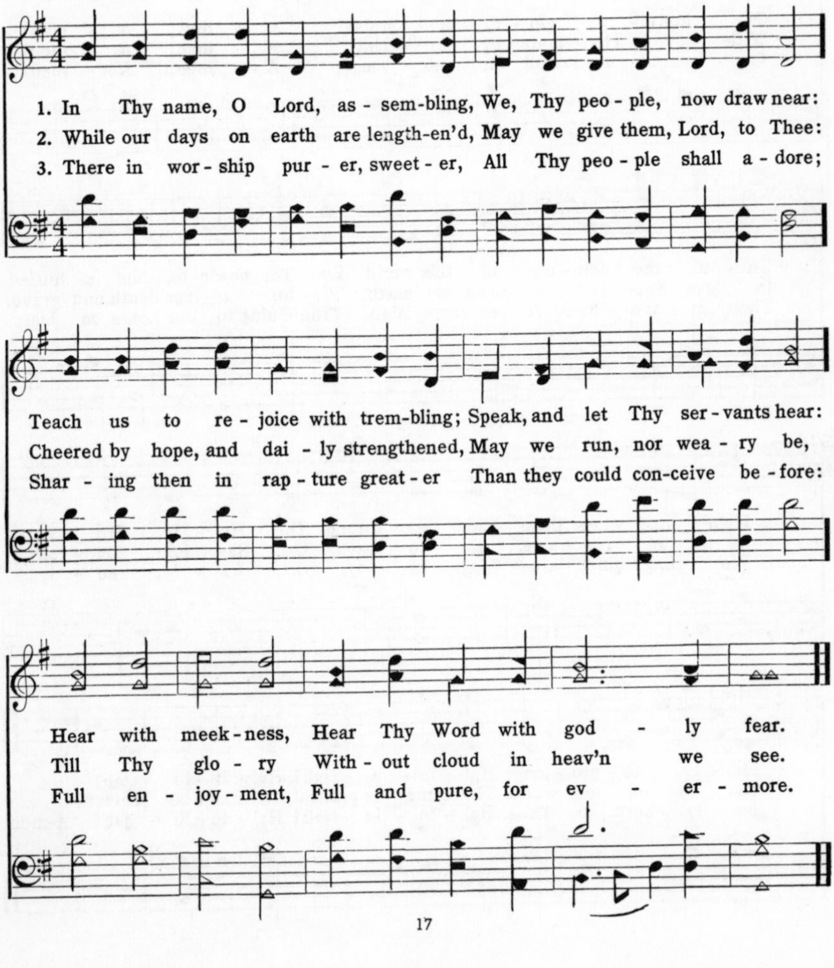

1. In Thy name, O Lord, as - sem - bling, We, Thy peo - ple, now draw near:
2. While our days on earth are length - en'd, May we give them, Lord, to Thee:
3. There in wor - ship pur - er, sweet - er, All Thy peo - ple shall a - dore;

Teach us to re - joice with trem - bling; Speak, and let Thy ser - vants hear:
Cheered by hope, and dai - ly strengthened, May we run, nor wea - ry be,
Shar - ing then in rap - ture great - er Than they could con - ceive be - fore:

Hear with meek - ness, Hear Thy Word with god - ly fear.
Till Thy glo - ry With - out cloud in heav'n we see.
Full en - joy - ment, Full and pure, for ev - er - more.

19 Jehovah! Jehovah!

G. K. Pfeffel, 1776
Tr. C. Haas, 1897, v. 1.
Tr. C. E. Krehbiel, 1939, vv. 2, 3.

JEHOVAH P. M.

Johann C. Gerold, 1800

1. Je - ho - vah! Je - ho - vah! Je - ho - vah! Thou art wor - thy
2. Sing prais - es, sing prais - es! O Son of God, Re - deem - er,
3. O Spir - it, great Spir - it, Most ho - ly Spir - it, guide us!
Of hon - or, glo - ry and praise! A - men, A - men!
With joy Thy prais - es we sing, A - men, A - men!
Thy name we laud in our song. A - men, A - men!
Un - til the tem - ple of this world By Thy pow'r to dust is hurled,
In love Thou cam - est down to earth, Vic - tor o - ver death and grave,
Thou art the Com - fort - er come nigh, True Guide to our home on high.
Help us when these halls we throng The Ho - ly, Ho - ly,
All to res - cue, all to save, O Sav - iour, Sav - iour,
We cling, quick-'ning Maj - es - ty, O ho - ly, ho - ly,
Ho - ly to pro - long, Hal - le - lu - jah! Hal - le - lu - jah!
Sav - iour of the world, Thy name be praised, Thy name be praised!
ho - ly Lord, to Thee. Hal - le - lu - jah! Hal - le - lu - jah! A-men.

Jesus, Thou Joy of Loving Hearts 

AVE COELORUM DOMINA L. M.

Bernard of Clairvaux — Josquin des Pres

1. Je - sus, Thou joy of lov - ing hearts! From the best
2. O Je - sus, ev - er with us stay; Chase the dark

Je - sus, Thou joy of lov - ing hearts! From the
O Je - sus, ev - er with us stay; Chase the

Je - sus, Thou joy of lov - ing hearts! From the best
O Je - sus, ev - er with us stay; Chase the dark

bliss that earth im - parts, We turn un - filled to Thee a -
night of sin a - way. Make all our mo - ments calm and

best bliss that earth im - parts, We turn un - filled to Thee
dark night of sin a - way. Make all our mo - ments calm

bliss that earth im - parts, We turn un - filled to Thee a -
night of sin a - way, Make all our mo - ments calm and

gain, O Fount of Life, Thou Light of men.
bright, Shed o'er the world Thy ho - ly light.

O Fount of Life,
Shed o'er the world

a - gain, O Fount of Life, Thou Light of men.
and bright, Shed o'er the world Thy ho - ly light.

gain, O Fount of Life, Thou Light of men.
bright, Shed o'er the world Thy ho - ly light.

21 Jesus, Wondrous Saviour!

McMASTER 8. 7. 8. 7. D.

D. A. McGregor

Thomas Hastings

1. Je - sus, won-drous Sav - iour! Christ, of kings the King!
2. All earth's flow - ing pleas - ures Were a win - try sea,
3. Life is death, if sev - ered From Thy throb - bing heart.
4. Je - sus! all per - fec - tions Rise and end in Thee;
An - gels fall be - fore Thee, Pros - trate, wor - ship - ing;
Heav'n it - self with - out Thee Dark as night would be.
Death with life a - bun - dant At Thy touch would start.
Bright - ness of God's glo - ry Thou, e - ter - nal - ly.
Fair - est they con - fess Thee In the heav'n a - bove.
Lamb of God! Thy glo - ry Is the light a - bove.
Worlds and men and an - gels All con - sist in Thee:
Fa - vored be - yond meas - ure They Thy face who see;
We would sing Thee fair - est Here in hymns of love.
Lamb of God! Thy glo - ry Is the life of love.
Yet Thou cam - est to us In hu - mil - i - ty.
May we, gra - cious Sav - iour, Share this ec - sta - sy.

O Come, Loud Anthems Let Us Sing 22

PSALTER C. M. Ref.

Tate and Brady, 1696 — Adapted from Haydn

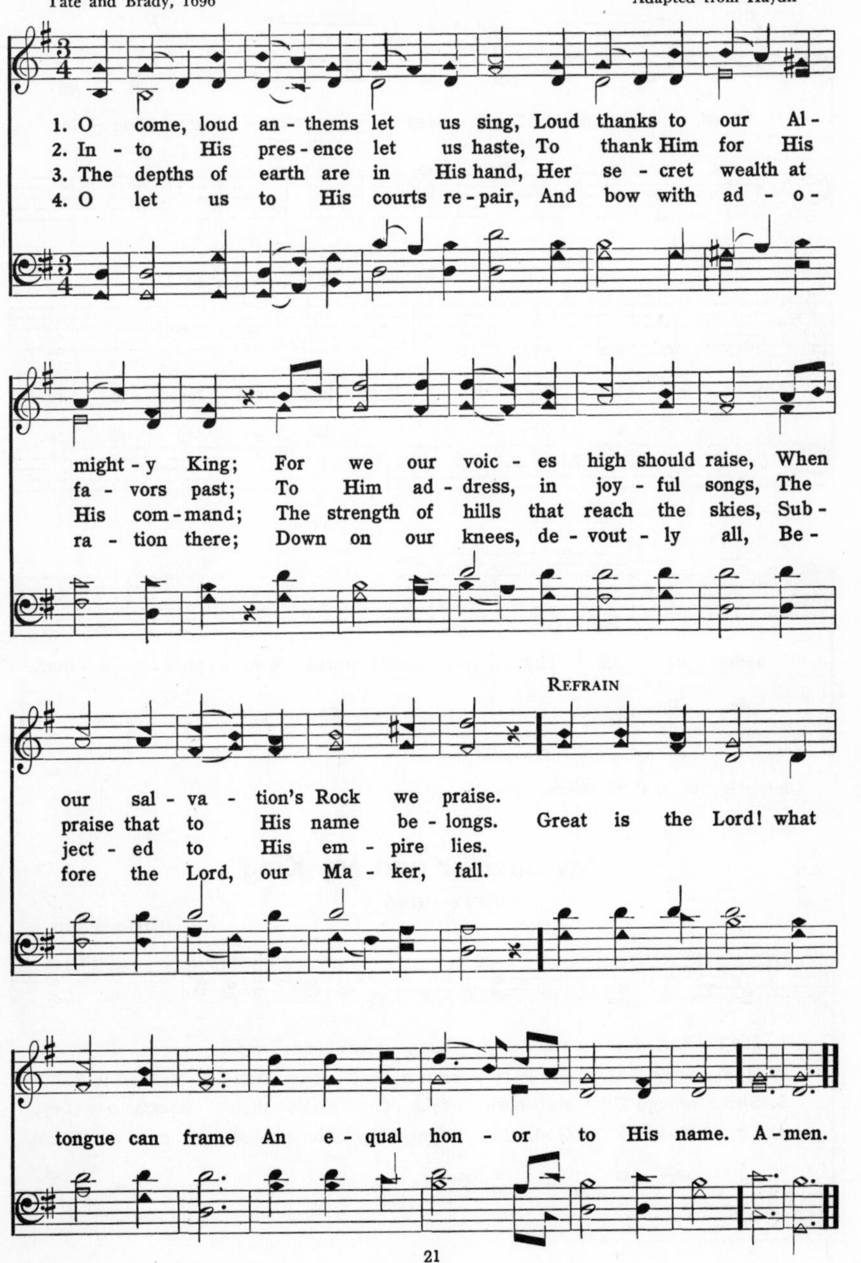
1. O come, loud an - thems let us sing, Loud thanks to our Al -
2. In - to His pres - ence let us haste, To thank Him for His
3. The depths of earth are in His hand, Her se - cret wealth at
4. O let us to His courts re - pair, And bow with ad - o -
might - y King; For we our voic - es high should raise, When
fa - vors past; To Him ad - dress, in joy - ful songs, The
His com - mand; The strength of hills that reach the skies, Sub -
ra - tion there; Down on our knees, de - vout - ly all, Be -
REFRAIN
our sal - va - tion's Rock we praise.
praise that to His name be - longs. Great is the Lord! what
ject - ed to His em - pire lies.
fore the Lord, our Ma - ker, fall.
tongue can frame An e - qual hon - or to His name. A - men.

23 Lord, I Seek Thee

HOOVER 8. 7. 8. 7.

C. G. Hoover

pp *p*

Lord, I seek Thee, heav - y la - den; Hum - bly
kneel - ing at Thy feet, Thou hast suf - fered to re -
deem us, All Thy gra - cious works com - plete. A - men.

24 My Saviour and My King

NINETY-THIRD S. M.

Harmonia Sacra

1. My Sav - iour and my King, Thy beau - ties are di - vine;
2. Now make Thy glo - ry known; Gird on Thy dread - ful sword
3. Strike through Thy stub-born foes, O make their hearts o - bey,
4. Thy laws, O God, are right, Thy throne shall ev - er stand,
3
3

28 O God, Thou Faithful God

O GOTT, DU FROMMER GOTT 6. 7. 6. 7. 6. 6. 6. 6.

John Heermann
Tr. Catherine Winkworth

Har. J. S. Bach

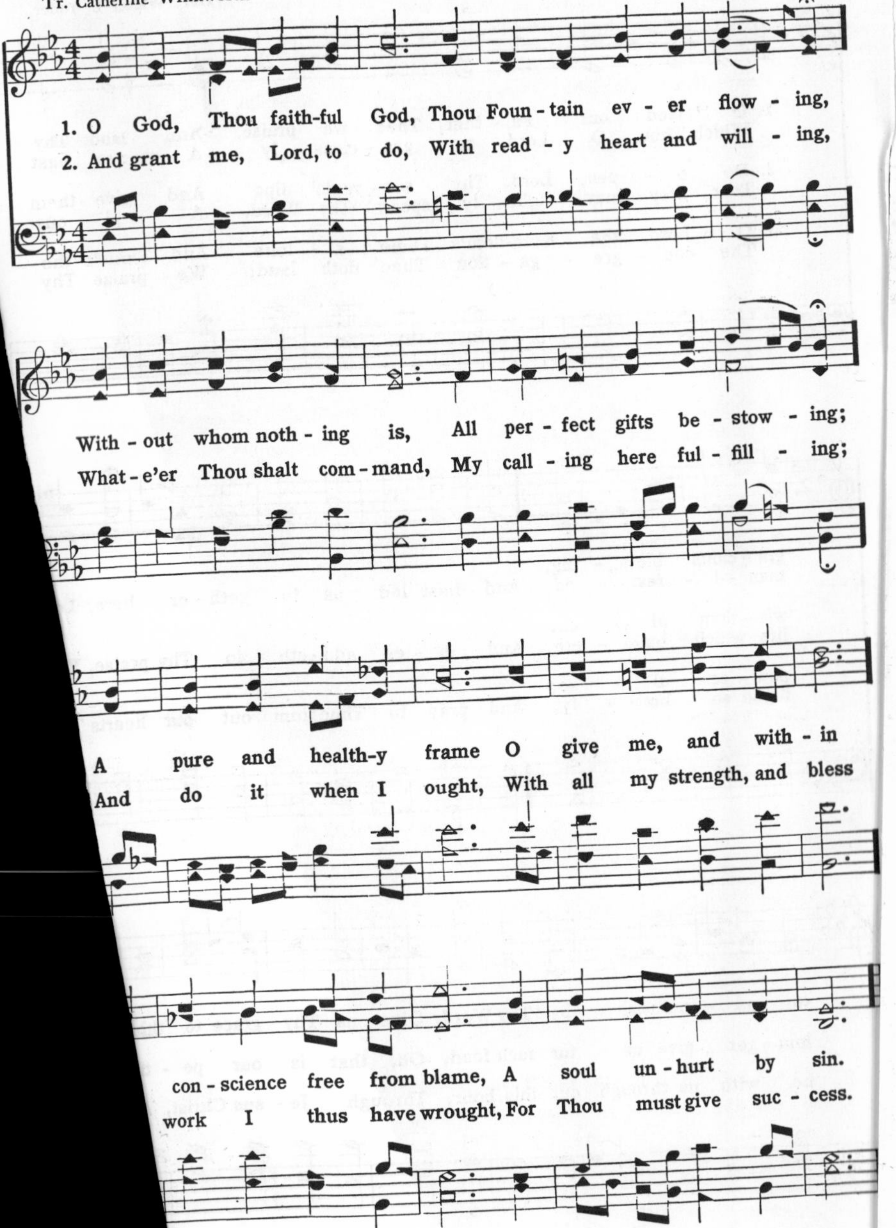

1. O God, Thou faith-ful God, Thou Foun-tain ev-er flow-ing, With-out whom noth-ing is, All per-fect gifts be-stow-ing; A pure and health-y frame O give me, and with-in con-science free from blame, A soul un-hurt by sin.

2. And grant me, Lord, to do, With read-y heart and will-ing, What-e'er Thou shalt com-mand, My call-ing here ful-fill-ing; And do it when I ought, With all my strength, and bless work I thus have wrought, For Thou must give suc-cess.

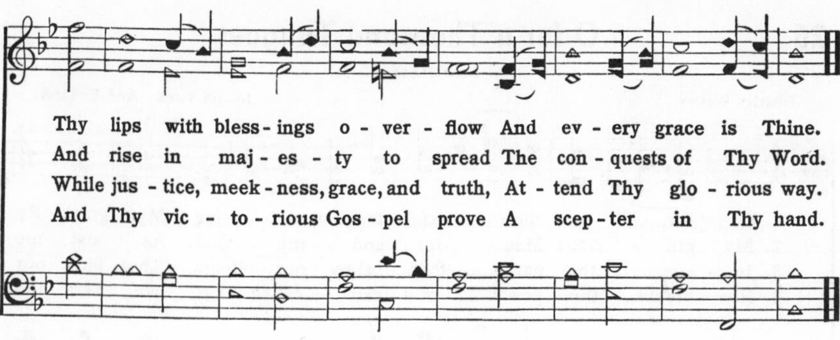
Thy lips with bless-ings o-ver-flow And ev-ery grace is Thine.
And rise in maj-es-ty to spread The con-quests of Thy Word.
While jus-tice, meek-ness, grace, and truth, At-tend Thy glo-rious way.
And Thy vic-to-rious Gos-pel prove A scep-ter in Thy hand.

Now to the King of Heaven 25

ST. JOHN 6. 6. 6. 6. 8. 8.
Isaac Watts, 1674-1748
Melody from the Parish Choir, 1851
Now to the King of heav'n Your cheer-ful voi-ces raise; To
Him be glo-ry giv'n, Pow'r, maj-es-ty and praise; Wide as He reigns His
name be sung By ev-ery tongue in end-less strains. A-men.

O for a Thousand Tongues

LINGHAM C. M.

Charles Wesley — Joseph Funk Arr. F. L. A.

1. O for.......... a thou - sand tongues to sing My great Re -
2. My gra - cious Mas - ter and my God, As - sist me
3. Je - sus,........ the name...... that calms our fears, That bids our
4. He breaks.... the pow'r...... of a can - celled sin, He sets the

deem - er's praise, My great...... Re - deem - er's praise; The glo - ries
to pro - claim, As - sist........... me to pro - claim, To spread thro'
sor - rows cease, That bids......... our sor - rows cease, 'Tis mu - sic
pris - 'ner free, He sets......... the pris - 'ner free; His blood can

of......... my God..... and King, The tri - umphs of, the tri - umphs of His grace,
all........ the earth.... a - broad, The hon - ors of, the hon - ors of Thy name,
in......... the sin - ner's ears, 'Tis life and health, 'tis life and health and peace,
make... the foul - est clean, His blood a - vails, His blood a - vails for me,

The tri - umphs of His grace,.... The tri - umphs of His grace.
The hon - ors of Thy name,.... The hon - ors of Thy name.
'Tis life and health and peace,...'Tis life........ and health and peace.
His blood a - vails for me,.......His blood..... a - vails for me.

O God Our Father, Thee We Praise

PRAISE SONG

Leonard Clock, 1590
Eng. Tr. J. C. Wenger

German Chorale
Har. Walter E. Yoder

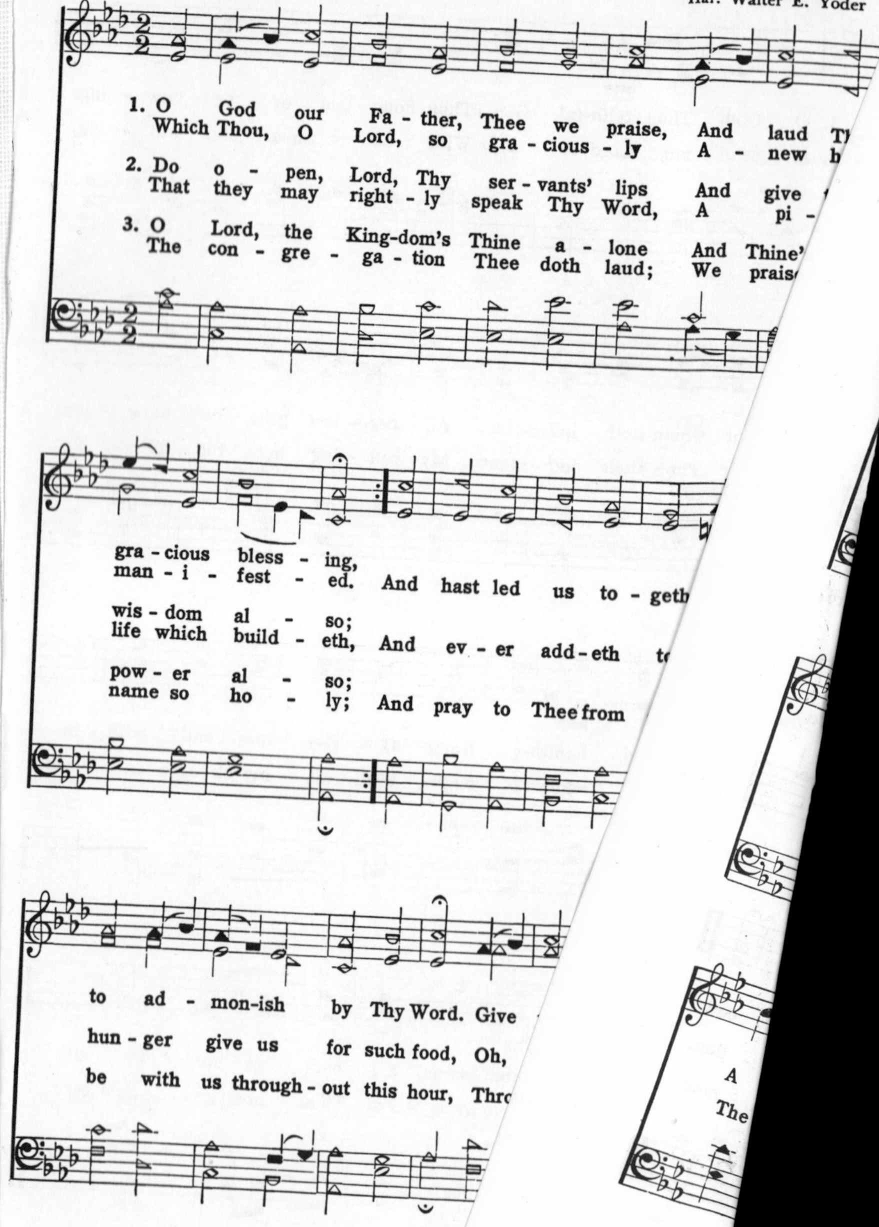

1. O God our Fa - ther, Thee we praise, And laud Th
Which Thou, O Lord, so gra - cious - ly A - new h
2. Do o - pen, Lord, Thy ser - vants' lips And give
That they may right - ly speak Thy Word, A pi -
3. O Lord, the King - dom's Thine a - lone And Thine'
The con - gre - ga - tion Thee doth laud; We prais

gra - cious bless - ing,
man - i - fest - ed. And hast led us to - geth
wis - dom al - so;
life which build - eth, And ev - er add - eth t
pow - er al - so;
name so ho - ly; And pray to Thee from

to ad - mon - ish by Thy Word. Give
hun - ger give us for such food, Oh,
be with us through - out this hour, Thr

A
The

Praise Him! Praise Him! 29

GOSPEL SONG P. M.

Fanny J. Crosby — Chester G. Allen

1. Praise Him! praise Him! Je-sus, our blessed Re - deem-er! Sing, O earth–His
2. Praise Him! praise Him! Je-sus, our blessed Re - deem-er! For our sins He
3. Praise Him! praise Him! Je-sus, our blessed Re - deem-er! Heav'nly por - tals
won - der - ful love pro - claim! Hail Him! Hail Him! high-est arch-an-gels in
suf - fered and bled and died; He our Rock, our hope of e - ter - nal sal -
loud with ho - san - nas ring! Je - sus, Sav - iour, reign-eth for - ev - er and
D. S.—Praise Him, Praise Him! tell of His ex - cel-lent
FINE
glo - ry; Strength and hon - or give to His ho - ly name! Like a Shep-herd,
va-tion, Hail Him! hail Him! Je - sus, the Cru - ci - fied. Sound His prais-es!
ev - er: Crown Him! crown Him! Prophet and Priest and King! Christ is com-ing!
great-ness, Praise Him! praise Him! ev - er in joy-ful song.
D. S.
Je-sus will guard His chil-dren, In His arms He car-ries them all day long;
Je-sus who bore our sor-rows, Love un-bound-ed, won-der-ful, deep and strong;
o - ver the world vic - to-rious, Pow'r and glo - ry un - to the Lord be - long;

30 O Maker of the Sea and Sky

MOZART L. M.

Henry Burton, 1905

From the Kyrie, Twelfth Mass, by Johann Mozart, 1756-1791

1. O Mak - er of the sea and sky, Whose word the storm - y winds ful - fill, On the wide o - cean Thou art nigh, Bid - ding these hearts of ours be still.
2. What if Thy foot - steps are not known? We know Thy way is in the sea; We trace the shad - ow of Thy throne, Con - stant a - mid in - con - stan - cy.
3. Thou bidd'st the north or south wind blow; The lone - ly sea - bird is Thy care; And in the clouds which come and go, We see Thy char - iots ev - ery - where.
4. The sun that lights the home - land dear Spreads the new morn - ing o'er the deep; And in the dark Thy stars ap - pear, Keep - ing their watch - es while we sleep.
5. And so, se - cure from all a - larms, Thy seas be - neath, Thy skies a - bove, Clasped in the ev - er - last - ing arms, We rest in Thine un - slum - bering love. A - men.

31 Songs of Praise the Angels Sang

INNOCENTS 7. 7. 7. 7.

Henry Pollard

1. Songs of praise the an - gels sang, Heav'n with al - le - lu - ias rang,
2. Songs of praise a - woke the morn When the Prince of Peace was born;
3. Heav'n and earth must pass a - way; Songs of praise shall crown that day:

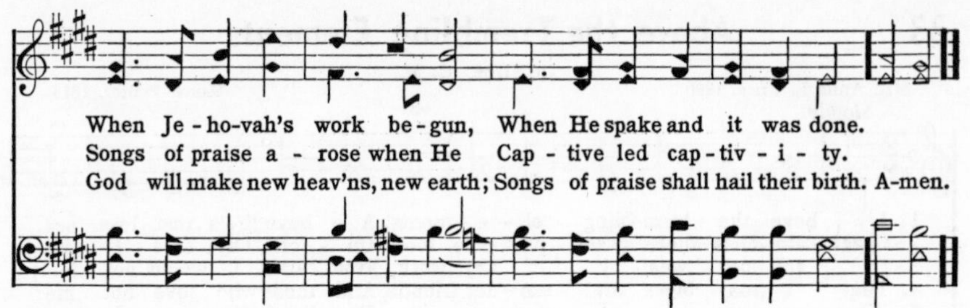
When Je-ho-vah's work be-gun, When He spake and it was done.
Songs of praise a - rose when He Cap - tive led cap-tiv - i - ty.
God will make new heav'ns, new earth; Songs of praise shall hail their birth. A-men.

Sing to the Great Jehovah's Praise 32

SAINTS C. M.

Charles Wesley

Ebenezer Beesley

1. Sing to the great Je-ho-vah's praise, All praise to Him be-longs;
2. His prov-i-dence has brought us through An-oth-er var-ious year;
3. Fa-ther, Thy mer-cies past we own, Thy still con-tin-ued care;
4. Our lips and lives shall glad-ly show The won-ders of Thy love,

Who kind-ly length-ens out our days, Who kind-ly
We all, with vows and an-thems new, We all, with
To Thee pre-sent-ing through Thy Son, To Thee pre-
While on in Je-sus' steps we go, While on in

length-ens out our days, De-mands our choic-est songs.
vows and an-thems new, Be-fore our God ap-pear.
sent-ing through Thy Son What-e'er we have or are.
Je-sus' steps we go To seek Thy face a-bove.

33 Above the Trembling Elements

DUNDEE C. M.

Mrs. Anna L. Price, 1890 — Scotch Psalter, 1615

Slowly

1. A - bove the trem-bling el - e - ments, A - bove life's rest - less sea,
2. Great calm-ness there, sweet pa-tience, too, Up - on Thy face I see;
3. I am not wea - ry of Thy work, From earth I would not flee;
4. That I may bless my ten - der friends, And those who love not me;
5. What - ev - er falls of good or ill, Thy hand, Thy care I see,
6. And when my eyes close for the last, Still this my prayer shall be—

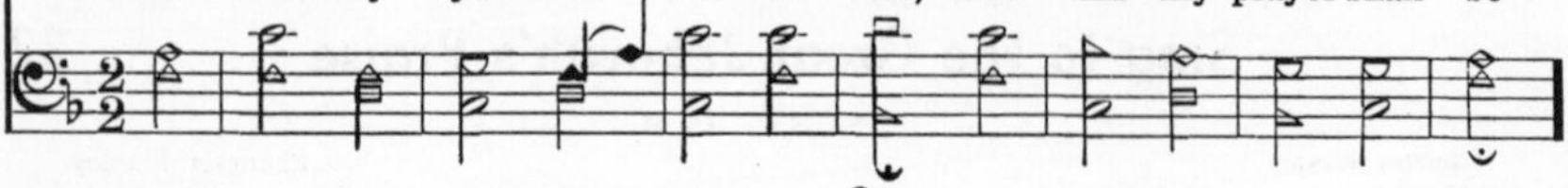

Dear Sav - iour, lift my spir - it up, Oh, lift me up to Thee!
I would be calm and pa - tient, Lord, Oh, lift me up to Thee!
But while I walk, and while I serve, Oh, lift me up to Thee!
Oh, lift me high a - bove my - self, Dear Je - sus, up to Thee!
And while these var - ied deal - ings pass, Oh, lift me up to Thee!
Dear Sav - iour, lift my spir - it up, And lift me up to Thee!

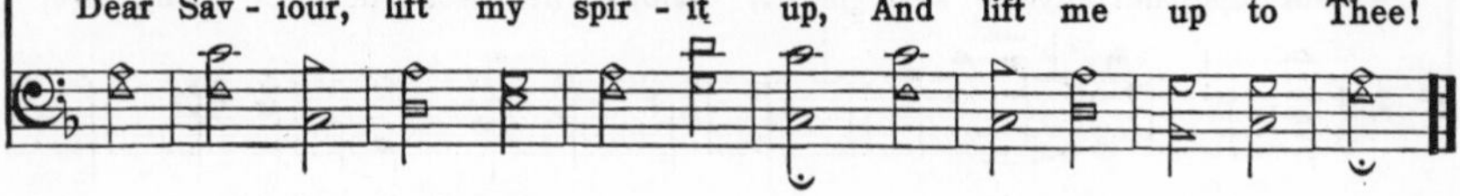

34 The Lord Hath Done Great Things for Us

PSALM 126 C. M.

Rollin Pease — Dwight Weldy

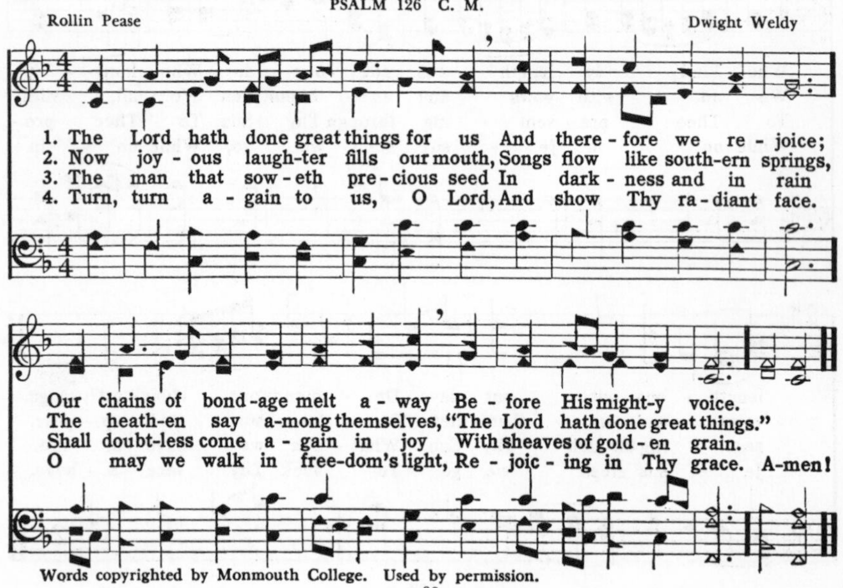
1. The Lord hath done great things for us And there - fore we re - joice;
2. Now joy - ous laugh - ter fills our mouth, Songs flow like south - ern springs,
3. The man that sow - eth pre - cious seed In dark - ness and in rain
4. Turn, turn a - gain to us, O Lord, And show Thy ra - diant face.
Our chains of bond - age melt a - way Be - fore His might - y voice.
The heath - en say a - mong themselves, "The Lord hath done great things."
Shall doubt - less come a - gain in joy With sheaves of gold - en grain.
O may we walk in free - dom's light, Re - joic - ing in Thy grace. A - men!

Before Jehovah's Awful Throne 35

WATTS L. M.

Isaac Watts, 1719 J. D. Brunk, 1910

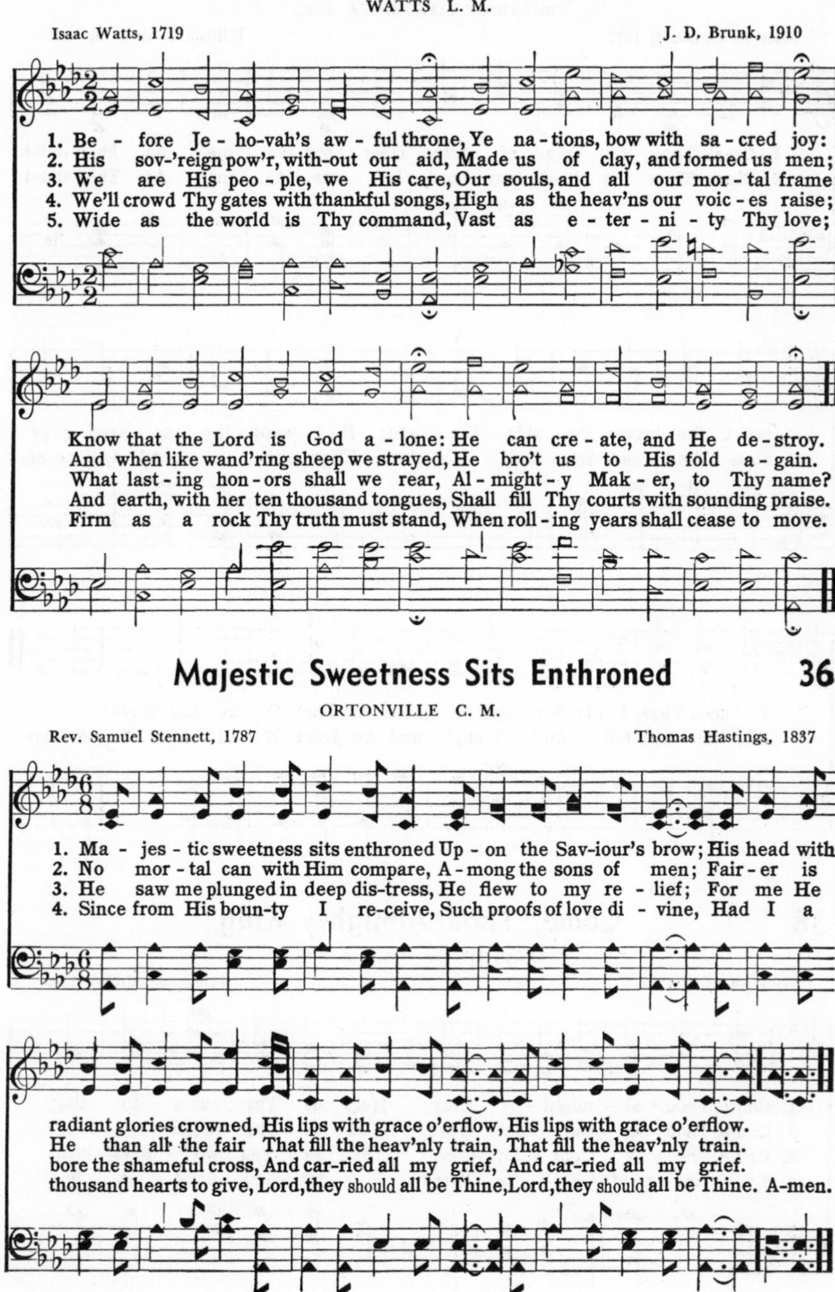
1. Be - fore Je - ho-vah's aw - ful throne, Ye na - tions, bow with sa - cred joy:
2. His sov-'reign pow'r, with-out our aid, Made us of clay, and formed us men;
3. We are His peo - ple, we His care, Our souls, and all our mor - tal frame;
4. We'll crowd Thy gates with thankful songs, High as the heav'ns our voic - es raise;
5. Wide as the world is Thy command, Vast as e - ter - ni - ty Thy love;
Know that the Lord is God a - lone: He can cre - ate, and He de - stroy.
And when like wand'ring sheep we strayed, He bro't us to His fold a - gain.
What last - ing hon - ors shall we rear, Al - might - y Mak - er, to Thy name?
And earth, with her ten thousand tongues, Shall fill Thy courts with sounding praise.
Firm as a rock Thy truth must stand, When roll - ing years shall cease to move.
Majestic Sweetness Sits Enthroned 36
ORTONVILLE C. M.
Rev. Samuel Stennett, 1787
Thomas Hastings, 1837
1. Ma - jes - tic sweetness sits enthroned Up - on the Sav-iour's brow; His head with
2. No mor - tal can with Him compare, A - mong the sons of men; Fair - er is
3. He saw me plunged in deep dis-tress, He flew to my re - lief; For me He
4. Since from His boun-ty I re-ceive, Such proofs of love di - vine, Had I a
radiant glories crowned, His lips with grace o'erflow, His lips with grace o'erflow.
He than all the fair That fill the heav'nly train, That fill the heav'nly train.
bore the shameful cross, And car-ried all my grief, And car-ried all my grief.
thousand hearts to give, Lord, they should all be Thine, Lord, they should all be Thine. A-men.

37 Break Thou the Bread of Life

BREAD OF LIFE 6. 4. 6. 4. D.

Mary A. Lathbury, 1877 — William F. Sherwin, 1877

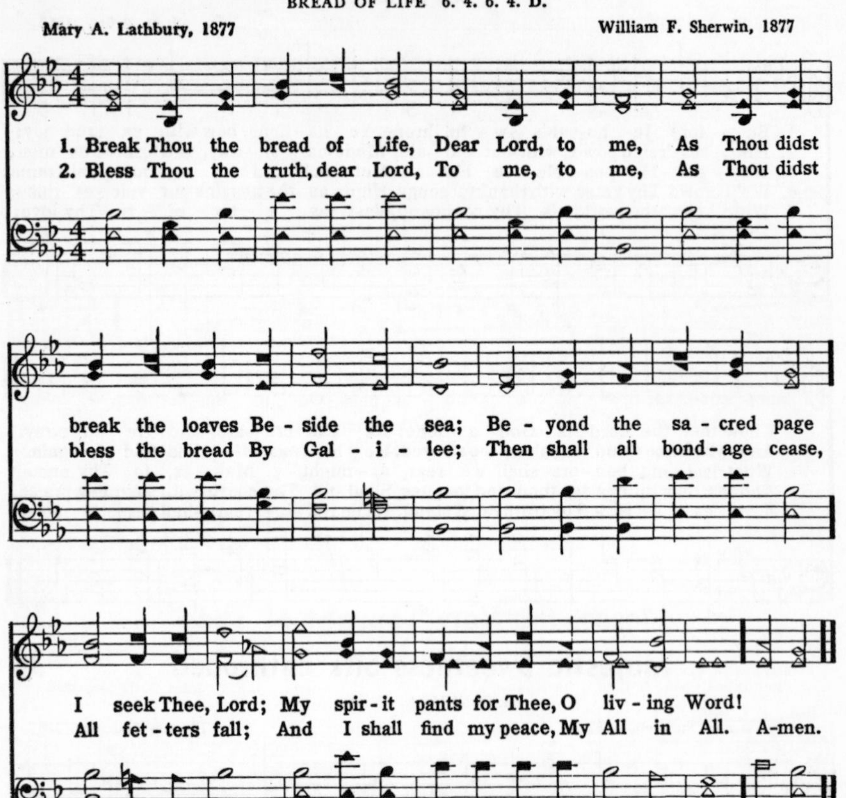

1. Break Thou the bread of Life, Dear Lord, to me, As Thou didst
2. Bless Thou the truth, dear Lord, To me, to me, As Thou didst
break the loaves Be - side the sea; Be - yond the sa - cred page
bless the bread By Gal - i - lee; Then shall all bond - age cease,
I seek Thee, Lord; My spir - it pants for Thee, O liv - ing Word!
All fet - ters fall; And I shall find my peace, My All in All. A-men.

38 Come, Thou Almighty King

ITALIAN HYMN 6. 6. 4. 6. 6. 6. 4

Anonymous, c. 1757 — Felice de Giardini, 1769

1. Come, Thou al - might - y King, Help us Thy name to sing,
2. Come, Thou in - car - nate Word, Gird on Thy might - y sword,
3. Come, ho - ly Com - fort - er, Thy sa - cred wit - ness bear
4. To the great One in Three E - ter - nal prais - es be

Help us to praise; Fa - ther, all glo - ri - ous, O'er all vic -
Our prayer at - tend; Come, and Thy peo - ple bless, And give Thy
In this glad hour; Thou, who al - might - y art, Now rule in
Hence ev - er - more; His sov - 'reign maj - es - ty May we in
to - ri - ous, Come, and reign o - ver us, An - cient of Days.
word suc - cess; Spir - it of ho - li - ness, On us de - scend.
ev - ery heart, And ne'er from us de - part, Spir - it of pow'r.
glo - ry see, And to e - ter - ni - ty Love and a - dore. A - men.

Jesus, the Very Thought of Thee 39

ST. AGNES C. M.

Bernard of Clairvaux, 1091-1153
Tr. Edward Caswall, 1849

John B. Dykes, 1866

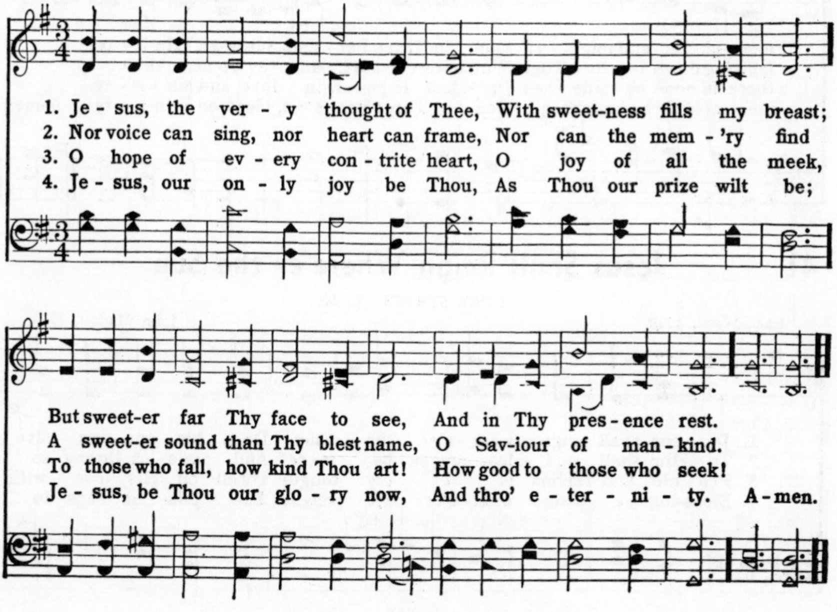

1. Je - sus, the ver - y thought of Thee, With sweet-ness fills my breast;
But sweet-er far Thy face to see, And in Thy pres - ence rest.

2. Nor voice can sing, nor heart can frame, Nor can the mem - 'ry find
A sweet-er sound than Thy blest name, O Sav-iour of man - kind.

3. O hope of ev - ery con - trite heart, O joy of all the meek,
To those who fall, how kind Thou art! How good to those who seek!

4. Je - sus, our on - ly joy be Thou, As Thou our prize wilt be;
Je - sus, be Thou our glo - ry now, And thro' e - ter - ni - ty. A - men.

40 Holy Holy, Holy

NICAEA 12. 13. 12. 10.

Reginald Heber — John B. Dykes

1. Ho - ly, ho - ly, ho - ly! Lord God Al - might - y! Ear - ly in the
2. Ho - ly, ho - ly, ho - ly! All the saints a - dore Thee, Cast-ing down their
3. Ho - ly, ho - ly, ho - ly! Tho' the darkness hide Thee, Tho' the eye of
4. Ho - ly, ho - ly, ho - ly! Lord God Al - might - y! All Thy work shall
morn - ing our song shall rise to Thee; Ho - ly, ho - ly, ho - ly!
gold-en crowns a - round the glass - y sea; Cher - u - bim and ser-a - phim
sin-ful man Thy glo - ry may not see, On - ly Thou art ho - ly;
praise Thy name, in earth, and sky, and sea; Ho - ly, ho - ly, ho - ly!
mer - ci - ful and might - y! God in Three Per - sons, bless-ed Trin-i - ty!
fall - ing down be - fore Thee, Which wert and art, and ev-er-more shalt be.
there is none be - side Thee Per - fect in power, in love, and pur - i - ty.
mer - ci - ful and might - y! God in Three Per - sons, bless-ed Trin-i - ty! A-men.

41 Jesus Shall Reign Where'er the Sun

DUKE STREET L. M.

Isaac Watts, 1719 — John Hatton, 1793

1. Je - sus shall reign wher - e'er the sun Does his suc - ces - sive
2. To Him shall end - less prayer be made, And prais - es throng to
3. Peo - ple and realms of ev - ery tongue Dwell on His love with
4. Bless-ings a - bound wher - e'er He reigns; The pris-'ner leaps to

jour - neys run; His king-dom stretch from shore to shore,
crown His head; His name, like sweet per - fume, shall rise
sweet - est song; And in - fant voic - es shall pro - claim
lose his chains, The wea - ry find e - ter - nal rest,
Till moons shall wax and wane no more.
With ev - ery morn - ing sac - ri - fice.
Their ear - ly bless - ings on His name.
And all the sons of want are blest. A - men.

Fairest Lord Jesus 42

CRUSADER'S HYMN

Münster, 1677
Translated about 1850

Silesian Folk Song
Arr. Richard S. Willis, 1850

1. Fair-est Lord Je - sus, Rul - er of all na - ture, O Thou of God and man the Son;
2. Fair are the meadows, Fair-er still the woodlands, Robed in the blooming garb of spring;
3. Fair is the sunshine, Fair-er still the moonlight, And all the twinkling, star-ry host;
Thee will I cher-ish, Thee will I hon-or, Thou, my soul's glory, joy and crown.
Je - sus is fair - er, Je - sus is pur- er, Who makes the woeful heart to sing.
Je-sus shines brighter, Je-sus shines purer Than all the angels heav'n can boast. A-men.

43 In Thy Holy Place We Bow

THY HOLY PLACE 7. 7. 7. 7. 7. 8. 7. 8. 7.

S. F. Coffman, 1901 — J. D. Brunk, 1911

m
1. In Thy ho - ly place we bow, Per-fumes sweet to heav - en rise,
2. Ho - ly light doth fill this place—Spir - it light our way to guide;
3. On Thy ho - ly bread we feed, Hun - ger nev - er more to know:
cres.
dim.
While our gold - en cens - ers glow With the fire of sac - ri - fice.
In the pres-ence of Thy face Sin and dark-ness ne'er can hide.
Thou sup - pli - est all our need; Fa - ther, whith - er shall we go?
p
cres.
Saints low bend - ing, prayers as - cend-ing, Ho - ly lips and hands im-plore;—
Heav-en's gleam-ing, full-ness stream-ing, Life and truth for man is found;
Ne'er for - sak - ing, here par - tak - ing Bread our souls to sat - is - fy;
m
cres.
dim.
Faith be - liev - ing and re - ceiv - ing Grace from Him whom we a - dore.
Light per - vad - ing, nev - er fad - ing, Light-ing all the world a - round.
Here a - bid - ing and con - fid - ing, We shall nev - er want nor die.

My Jesus, I Love Thee 44

GORDON 11. 11. 11. 11.

William Ralf Featherstone — Adoniram J. Gordon, 1836-1895

1. My Je - sus, I love Thee, I know Thou art mine,
2. I love Thee, be - cause Thou hast first lov - ed me,
3. I will love Thee in life, I will love Thee in death,
4. In man - sions of glo - ry and end - less de - light,
For Thee all the fol - lies of sin I re - sign;
And pur - chased my par - don on Cal - va - ry's tree;
And praise Thee as long as Thou lend - est me breath;
I'll ev - er a - dore Thee in heav - en so bright;
My gra - cious Re - deem - er, my Sav - iour art Thou;
I love Thee for wear - ing the thorns on Thy brow;
And say when the death - dew lies cold on my brow,
I'll sing with the glit - ter - ing crown on my brow,
If ev - er I loved Thee, my Je - sus, 'tis now. A-men.

45 O Worship the King, All-Glorious Above

LYONS 10. 10. 11. 11.

Robert Grant, 1833 — J. Michael Haydn, 1770

1. O wor - ship the King, all - glo - rious a - bove, O
2. O tell of His might, O sing of His grace, Whose
3. Thy boun - ti - ful care what tongue can re - cite? It
4. Frail chil - dren of dust, and fee - ble as frail, In
grate - ful - ly sing His pow'r and His love; Our
robe is the light, whose can - o - py space; His
breathes in the air, it shines in the light, It
Thee do we trust, nor find Thee to fail; Thy
Shield and De - fend - er, the An - cient of Days, Pa -
char - iots of wrath the deep thun - der - clouds form, And
streams from the hills, it de - scends to the plain, And
mer - cies how ten - der! how firm to the end! Our
vil - ioned in splen - dor, and gird - ed with praise.
dark is His path on the wings of the storm.
sweet - ly dis - tils in the dew and the rain.
Mak - er, De - fend - er, Re - deem - er, and Friend. A - men.

Therefore with Angels and Archangels 46

TERSANCTUS P. M.

Unknown

Therefore with angels and archangels, and with all the company of . . . heav'n
We laud and magnify Thy glorious . . . . name,

Ev - er - more prais - ing Thee, and say - ing, Ho - ly, Ho - ly,

Crescendo.

Ho - ly Lord God of Hosts;

f

Heav'n and earth are full of . . . Thy glo - ry:

p *Cres.*

Glo - ry be to Thee, O Lord, Most High.

f

A - men.

47 Wake the Song of Jubilee

AMBOY 7. 7. 7. 7. D.

Harmonia Sacra

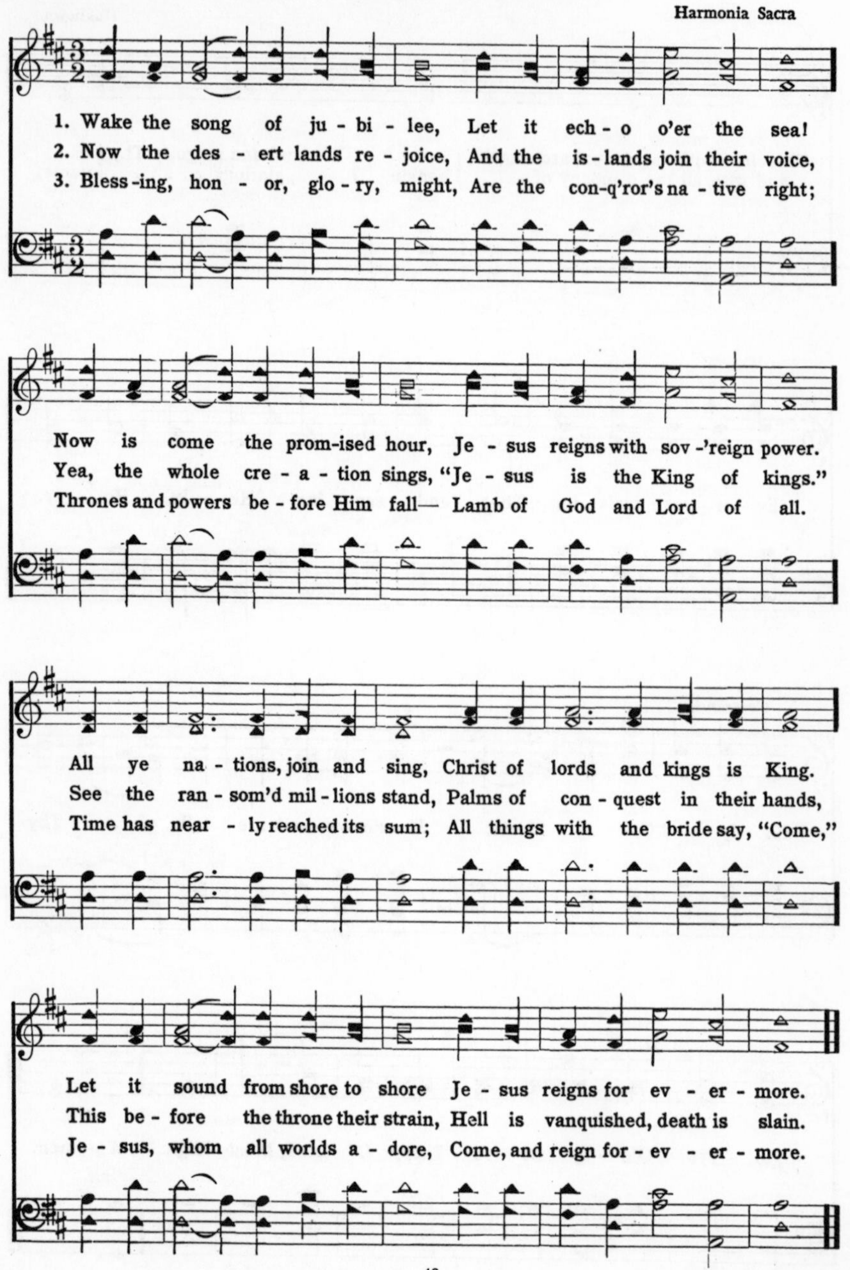
1. Wake the song of ju - bi - lee, Let it ech - o o'er the sea!
2. Now the des - ert lands re - joice, And the is - lands join their voice,
3. Bless-ing, hon - or, glo - ry, might, Are the con-q'ror's na - tive right;
Now is come the prom-ised hour, Je - sus reigns with sov -'reign power.
Yea, the whole cre - a - tion sings, "Je - sus is the King of kings."
Thrones and powers be - fore Him fall— Lamb of God and Lord of all.
All ye na - tions, join and sing, Christ of lords and kings is King.
See the ran - som'd mil - lions stand, Palms of con - quest in their hands,
Time has near - ly reached its sum; All things with the bride say, "Come,"
Let it sound from shore to shore Je - sus reigns for ev - er - more.
This be - fore the throne their strain, Hell is vanquished, death is slain.
Je - sus, whom all worlds a - dore, Come, and reign for - ev - er - more.

We Praise Thee, O God, Our Redeemer, Creator 48

KREMSER 12. 11. 12. 11.

Julia Bulkley Cady

Old Netherlands

1. We praise Thee, O God, our Re - deem - er, Cre - a - tor,
2. We wor - ship Thee, God of our fa - thers, we bless Thee;
3. With voi - ces u - nit - ed our prais - es we of - fer,
In grate - ful de - vo - tion our trib - ute we bring.
Thro' life's storm and tem - pest our Guide hast Thou been.
To Thee, great Je - ho - vah, glad an - thems we raise.
We lay it be - fore Thee, we kneel and a - dore Thee,
When per - ils o'er - take us, es - cape Thou wilt make us,
Thy strong arm will guide us, our God is be - side us,
We bless Thy ho - ly name, glad prais - es we sing.
And with Thy help, O Lord, our bat - tles we win.
To Thee, our great Re - deem - er, for - ev - er be praise.

49 Great God, Indulge

HAGERSTOWN L. M.
Isaac Watts
J. D. Brunk
1. Great God, in - dulge my hum - ble claim, Thou art my hope, my joy, my rest; The glo - ries that com - pose Thy name Stand all en - gaged to make me blest.
2. Thou great and good, Thou just and wise, Thou art my Fa - ther and my God; And I am Thine by sa - cred ties, Thy son, Thy serv - ant, bought with blood.
3. With read - y feet, I love t'ap - pear A - mong Thy saints, and seek Thy face; Oft have I seen Thy glo - ry there, And felt the pow'r of sov - 'reign grace.
4. I'll lift my hands, I'll raise my voice, While I have breath to pray or praise; This work shall make my heart re - joice, Thro' - out the rem - nant of my days.
50
O Praise Ye the Lord
LAUDE 10. 10. 11. 11.
O praise ye the Lord, Pre - pare your glad voice, His praise in the

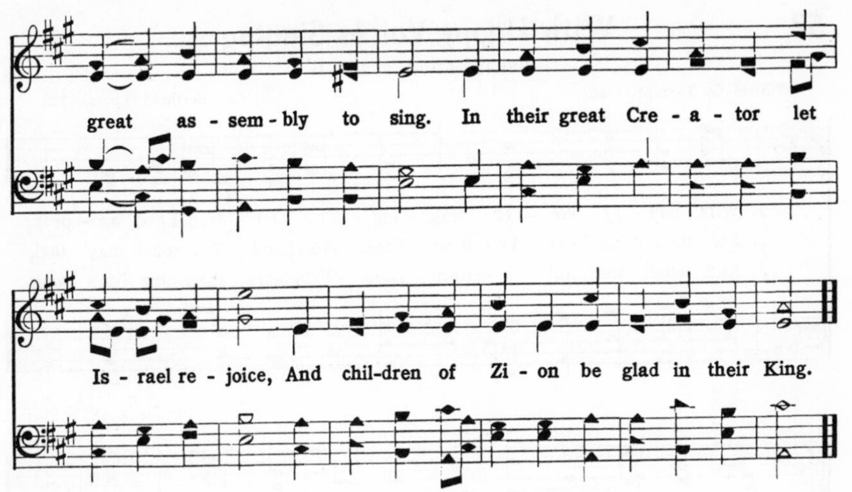
great as-sem-bly to sing. In their great Cre-a-tor let
Is-rael re-joice, And chil-dren of Zi-on be glad in their King.

Come, We Who Love the Lord 51

ST. THOMAS S. M.

Rev. Isaac Watts, 1709

Aaron Williams, 1760

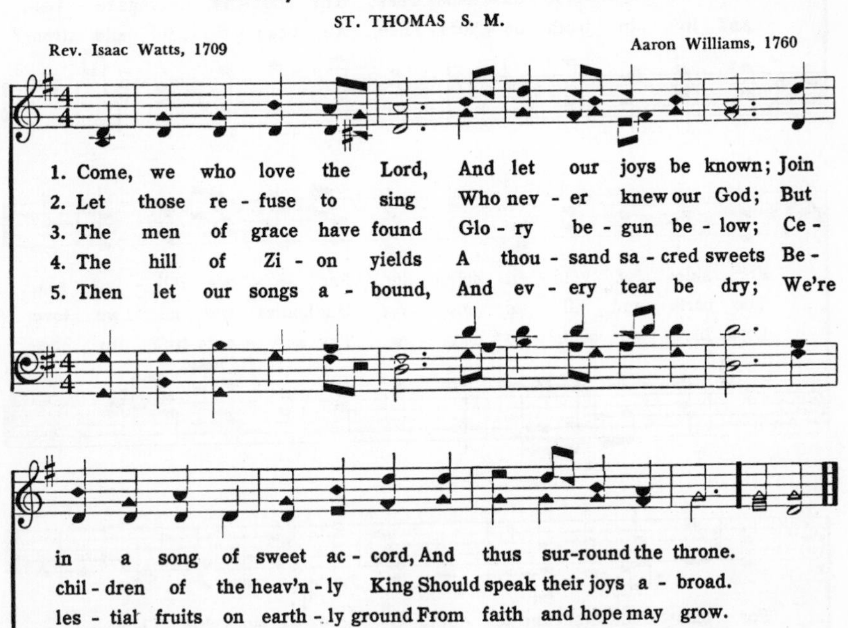
1. Come, we who love the Lord, And let our joys be known; Join
2. Let those re-fuse to sing Who nev-er knew our God; But
3. The men of grace have found Glo-ry be-gun be-low; Ce-
4. The hill of Zi-on yields A thou-sand sa-cred sweets Be-
5. Then let our songs a-bound, And ev-ery tear be dry; We're
in a song of sweet ac-cord, And thus sur-round the throne.
chil-dren of the heav'n-ly King Should speak their joys a-broad.
les-tial fruits on earth-ly ground From faith and hope may grow.
fore we reach the heav'n-ly fields, Or walk the gold-en streets.
marching thro' Em-man-uel's ground To fair-er worlds on high. A-men.

52 With Happy Voices Singing

BERTHOLD 7. 6. 7. 6. D.

William G. Tarrant, 1888 — Berthold Tours, 1872

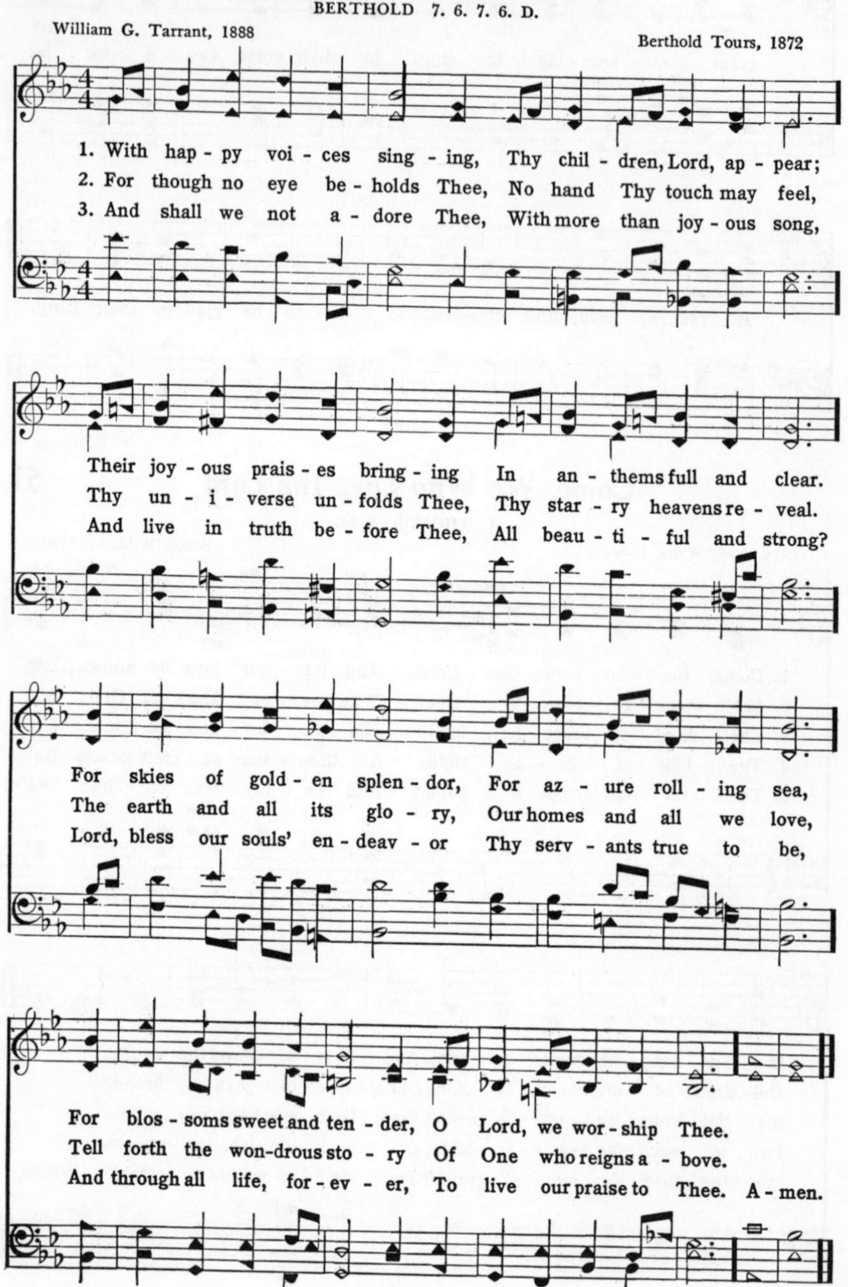
1. With hap - py voi - ces sing - ing, Thy chil - dren, Lord, ap - pear;
2. For though no eye be - holds Thee, No hand Thy touch may feel,
3. And shall we not a - dore Thee, With more than joy - ous song,
Their joy - ous prais - es bring - ing In an - thems full and clear.
Thy un - i - verse un - folds Thee, Thy star - ry heavens re - veal.
And live in truth be - fore Thee, All beau - ti - ful and strong?
For skies of gold - en splen - dor, For az - ure roll - ing sea,
The earth and all its glo - ry, Our homes and all we love,
Lord, bless our souls' en - deav - or Thy serv - ants true to be,
For blos - soms sweet and ten - der, O Lord, we wor - ship Thee.
Tell forth the won-drous sto - ry Of One who reigns a - bove.
And through all life, for - ev - er, To live our praise to Thee. A - men.

A Mighty Fortress 53

EIN' FESTE BURG P. M.

Martin Luther, 1529
Tr. Frederick H. Hedge, 1853

Martin Luther

1. A might-y for-tress is our God, A bul - wark nev-er fail - ing;
2. Did we in our own strength con-fide, Our striv - ing would be los - ing,
3. And tho' this world, with dev-ils filled, Should threat-en to un - do us,
4. That word a - bove all earth-ly pow'rs-No thanks to them—a - bid - eth;
Our help-er He, a - mid the flood Of mor-tal ills pre - vail - ing.
Were not the right Man on our side, The Man of God's own choos - ing.
We will not fear, for God hath willed His truth to tri - umph thro' us.
The Spir - it and the gifts are ours Thro' Him who with us sid - eth.
For still our an-cient foe Doth seek to work us woe; His craft and pow'r are
Dost ask who that may be? Christ Je - sus, it is He; Lord Sab-aoth is His
The prince of darkness grim-We trem-ble not for him; His rage we can en -
Let goods and kindred go, This mor-tal life al - so; The bod - y they may
great, And, armed with cru - el hate, On earth is not his e - qual.
name, From age to age the same, And He must win the bat - tle.
dure, For lo! his doom is sure; One lit - tle word shall fell him.
kill; God's truth a - bid-eth still, His king-dom is for - ev - er. A-men.

54 Come, Ye Thankful People, Come

ST. GEORGE'S (WINDSOR) 7. 7. 7. 7. D.

Henry Alford, 1844 — George J. Elvey, 1859

1. Come, ye thank-ful peo - ple, come, Raise the song of har - vest home:
2. All the world is God's own field, Fruit un - to His praise to yield;
3. For the Lord our God shall come, And shall take His har - vest home;
4. E - ven so, Lord, quick - ly come To Thy fi - nal har - vest home;
All is safe - ly gath - ered in, Ere the win - ter storms be - gin;
Wheat and tares to - geth - er sown, Un - to joy or sor - row grown;
From His field shall in that day All of - fens - es purge a - way;
Gath - er Thou Thy peo - ple in, Free from sor - row, free from sin;
God, our Mak - er, doth pro - vide For our wants to be sup - plied:
First the blade, and then the ear, Then the full corn shall ap - pear:
Give His an - gels charge at last In the fire the tares to cast,
There for - ev - er pu - ri - fied, In Thy pres - ence to a - bide:
Come to God's own tem - ple, come, Raise the song of har - vest home.
Lord of har - vest, grant that we Wholesome grain and pure may be.
But the fruit - ful ears to store In His gar - ner ev - er - more.
Come, with all Thine an - gels, come, Raise the glo - rious har - vest home.

The Dawn of God's Dear Sabbath

ENDSLEIGH 7. 6. 7. 6. D.

Ada Cross, 1844-

Salvatore Ferretti, 1817-1874
Arr. James Turle, 1802-1882

1. The dawn of God's dear Sab - bath Breaks o'er the earth a - gain,
2. And we would bring our bur - den Of sin - ful thought and deed,
3. And with that sor - row min - gling, A stead - fast faith and sure,
4. So be it, Lord, for - ev - er; O may we ev - er - more

As some sweet sum - mer morn - ing Af - ter a night of pain.
In Thy pure pres - ence kneel - ing From bond - age to be freed;
And love so deep and fer - vent That tries to make it pure:
In Je - sus' ho - ly pres - ence His bless - ed name a - dore,

It comes as cool - ing show - ers To some ex - haust - ed land,
Our hearts' most bit - ter sor - row For all Thy work un - done—
In His dear pres - ence find - ing The par - don that we need;
Up - on His peace - ful Sab - bath, With - in His tem - ple - walls—

As shade of clus - tered palm trees 'Mid wea - ry wastes of sand.
So man - y tal - ents wast - ed, So few bright lau - rels won!
And then the peace so last - ing, Ce - les - tial peace in - deed!
Type of the stain - less wor - ship In Zi - on's gold - en halls. A - men.

56 This Is the Day of Light

FRANCONIA S. M.

John Ellerton, 1867

König's Choralbuch, 1738

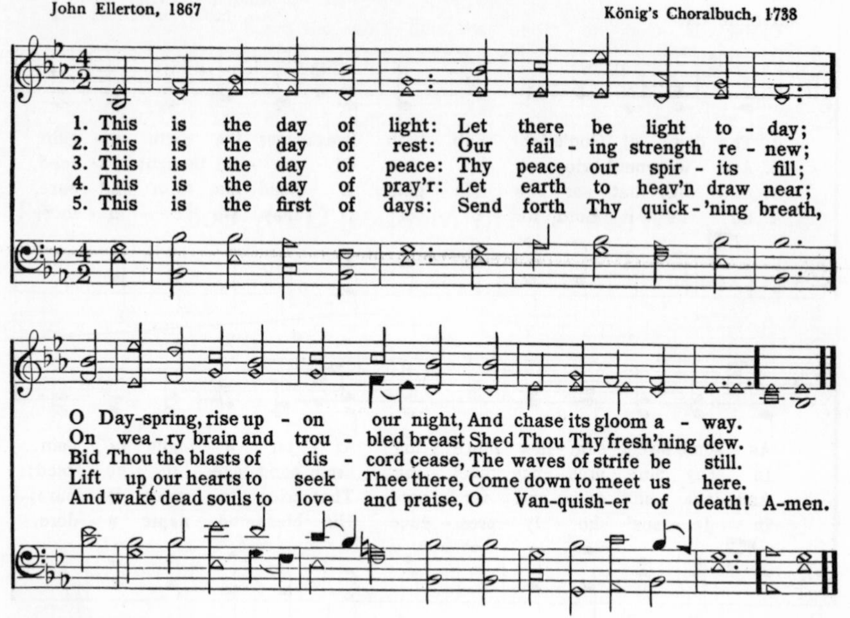
1. This is the day of light: Let there be light to - day;
2. This is the day of rest: Our fail - ing strength re - new;
3. This is the day of peace: Thy peace our spir - its fill;
4. This is the day of pray'r: Let earth to heav'n draw near;
5. This is the first of days: Send forth Thy quick - 'ning breath,
O Day-spring, rise up - on our night, And chase its gloom a - way.
On wea - ry brain and trou - bled breast Shed Thou Thy fresh'ning dew.
Bid Thou the blasts of dis - cord cease, The waves of strife be still.
Lift up our hearts to seek Thee there, Come down to meet us here.
And wake dead souls to love and praise, O Van - quish - er of death! A - men.

57 For the Beauty of the Earth

DIX 7. 7. 7. 7. 7. 7.

Folliott S. Pierpont

Conrad Kocher 1838

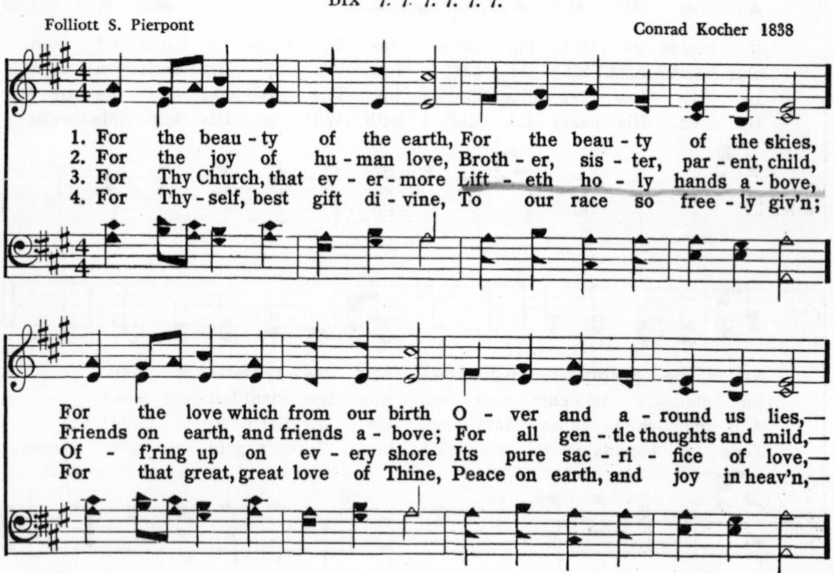
1. For the beau - ty of the earth, For the beau - ty of the skies,
2. For the joy of hu - man love, Broth - er, sis - ter, par - ent, child,
3. For Thy Church, that ev - er - more Lift - eth ho - ly hands a - bove,
4. For Thy - self, best gift di - vine, To our race so free - ly giv'n;
For the love which from our birth O - ver and a - round us lies,—
Friends on earth, and friends a - bove; For all gen - tle thoughts and mild,—
Of - f'ring up on ev - ery shore Its pure sac - ri - fice of love,—
For that great, great love of Thine, Peace on earth, and joy in heav'n,—

Christ our God, to Thee we raise This our hymn of grate - ful praise.

When All Thy Mercies, O My God

58

GENEVA C. M.

Joseph Addison

John Cole

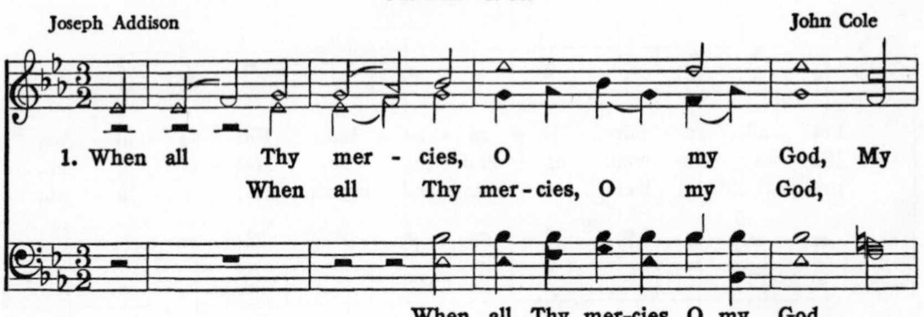
1. When all Thy mer - cies, O my God, My
When all Thy mer - cies, O my God,
When all Thy mer-cies, O my God,

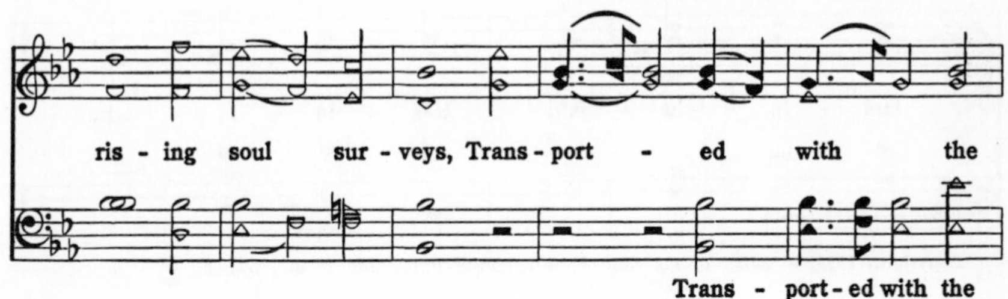
ris - ing soul sur - veys, Trans - port - ed with the
Trans - port - ed with the

view, I'm lost In won - - der, love, and praise.
view, I'm lost

2. Unnumber'd comforts on my soul
Thy tender care bestowed,
Before my infant heart conceived
From whom these comforts flowed.

3. Ten thousand thousand precious gifts
My daily thanks employ:
Nor is the least a cheerful heart
That tastes those gifts with joy.

59 A Child Is Born in Bethlehem

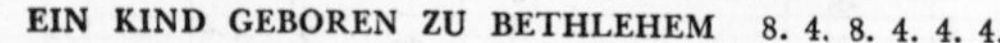
EIN KIND GEBOREN ZU BETHLEHEM 8. 4. 8. 4. 4. 4.

Tr. W. E. Yoder | Har. Walter E. Yoder

1. A child is born in Beth-le-hem, In Beth-le-hem,
Let all re-joice Je-ru-sa-lem, Hal-le-lu-jah,
Hal-le-lu-jah, Hal-le-lu-jah.

2. See here He lies in man-ger crib, In man-ger crib,
His king-dom shall un-end-ing be. Hal-le-lu-jah,
Hal-le-lu-jah, Hal-le-lu-jah.

3. The wise men came to greet their King, To greet their King,
Brought gold and frank-in-cense and myrrh. Hal-le-lu-jah,
Hal-le-lu-jah, Hal-le-lu-jah.

60 I Heard the Bells on Christmas Day

WALTHAM L. M.

Henry W. Longfellow, 1863 | J. Baptiste Calkin, 1872

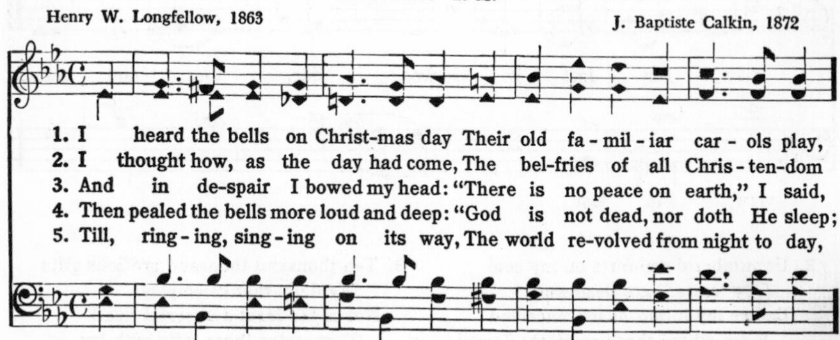
1. I heard the bells on Christ-mas day Their old fa-mil-iar car-ols play,
2. I thought how, as the day had come, The bel-fries of all Chris-ten-dom
3. And in de-spair I bowed my head: "There is no peace on earth," I said,
4. Then pealed the bells more loud and deep: "God is not dead, nor doth He sleep;
5. Till, ring-ing, sing-ing on its way, The world re-volved from night to day,

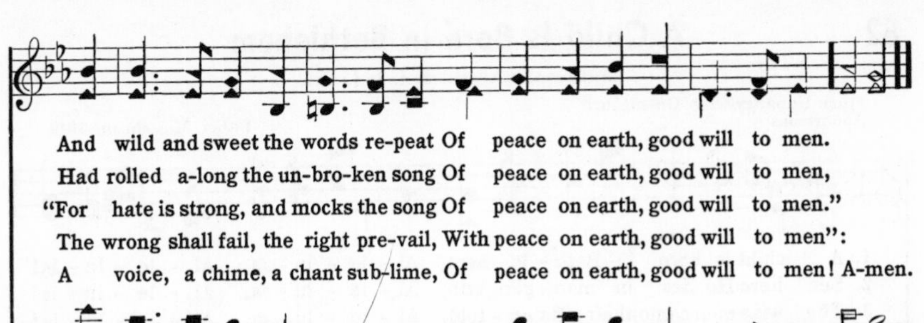
And wild and sweet the words re-peat Of peace on earth, good will to men.
Had rolled a-long the un-bro-ken song Of peace on earth, good will to men,
"For hate is strong, and mocks the song Of peace on earth, good will to men."
The wrong shall fail, the right pre-vail, With peace on earth, good will to men":
A voice, a chime, a chant sub-lime, Of peace on earth, good will to men! A-men.

All My Heart This Night Rejoices 61

FRÖLICH 8. 6. 6. 8. 6. 6.

Paul Gerhardt
Tr. Catherine Winkworth

Johann Ebeling

1. All my heart this night re - joic - es, As I hear, far and near,
2. Come, then, let us has - ten yon - der; Here let all great and small

Sweet-est an - gel voi - ces; "Christ is born," their choirs are sing - ing.
Kneel in awe and won - der, Love Him who with love is yearn - ing.

Till the air, ev - ery - where Now with joy is ring - ing.
Hail the star that from far Bright with hope is burn - ing.

62 A Child Is Born in Bethlehem

CHRISTMAS CAROL 8. 4. 8. 4. 4. 4.

From Unparteyisches Gesangbuch
Anonymous
Esther Musselman, 1949
1. A child is born in Beth - le - hem, Al - le - lu - ia, Al - le - lu - ia!
2. See here He lies in man - ger crib, Al - le - lu - ia, Al - le - lu - ia!
3. The wise men came, their gifts un - fold, Al - le - lu - ia, Al - le - lu - ia!
4. The Sav-iour came, rich grace He bore, Al - le - lu - ia, Al - le - lu - ia!
5. Ex - ult - ing in that glo-rious birth. Al - le - lu - ia, Al - le - lu - ia!
Joy is in Je - ru - sa - lem, Al - le - lu - ia, Al - le - lu - ia.
Whose kingdom is with - out end. Al - le - lu - ia, Al - le - lu - ia.
Brought myrrh and frank-in - cense and gold. Al - le - lu - ia, Al - le - lu - ia.
May God be praised for - ev - er - more. Al - le - lu - ia, Al - le - lu - ia.
Bless we the Lord of heaven and earth. Al - le - lu - ia, Al - le - lu - ia.
Al - le - lu - ia, Al - le - lu - ia, Al - le - lu - ia, Al - le - lu - ia,
Al - le - lu - ia Al - le - lu - ia Al - le - lu - ia Al - le-
Al - le - lu - ia, Al - le - lu - ia, Al - le - lu - ia, Al - le - lu - ia.
Last stanza
lu - ia, Al - le - lu - ia........

Come, All Ye Shepherds 63

KOMMET IHR HIRTEN 10. 10. 10. 10. 4.
Bohemian Folk Song
Tr. Mari Ruef Hofer, 1912
Bohemian Folk Tune
Arr. E. S. B.
1. Come, all ye shep - herds, ye chil - dren of earth,
2. Has - ten then, has - ten to Beth - le - hem's stall,
3. An - gels and shep - herds to - geth - er we go,
Come, come,
Haste to
So to -
Come ye, bring greet - ings to yon heaven-ly birth.
There to see heav - en de - scend to us all.
Seek - ing this Sav - iour from all earth - ly woe;
Come, greet
Heav'n de-
Saved from
For Christ the Lord un - to us is giv - en, Whom God for Sav-iour
With ho - ly feel - ing there hum-bly kneel-ing, We will a - dore Him,
While an - gels wing - ing, His prais - es sing-ing, Heaven's ech-oes ring - ing,
sent down from heav - en: Fear not ye Him!
bow down be - fore Him, Wor - ship the King.
peace on earth bring - ing, Good will to men. A - men.

From *New Church Hymnal,* Fleming H. Revell Co. Publisher. Used by permission.

64 Angels We Have Heard on High

WESTMINSTER CAROL 7. 7. 7. 7. Ref.

Bishop Chadwick
Old French Carol
1. An - gels we have heard on high, Sweet - ly sing - ing o'er the plains,
2. Shep-herds, why this ju - bi - lee? Why your joy - ous strains pro - long?
3. Come to Beth - le - hem and see Him whose birth the an - gels sing;
4. See Him in a man - ger laid, Whom the choirs of an - gels praise;
And the moun - tains in re - ply Ech - o back their joy - ous strains.
What the glad - some ti - dings be Which in - spire your heav'n-ly song?
Come, a - dore on bend - ed knee, Christ the Lord, the new born King.
Ma - ry, Jo - seph, lend your aid, While our hearts in love we raise.
Glo - - - - - - - - - - - - - - - - ri - a
in Ex - cel - sis De - o, Glo - - - - - - - - - -

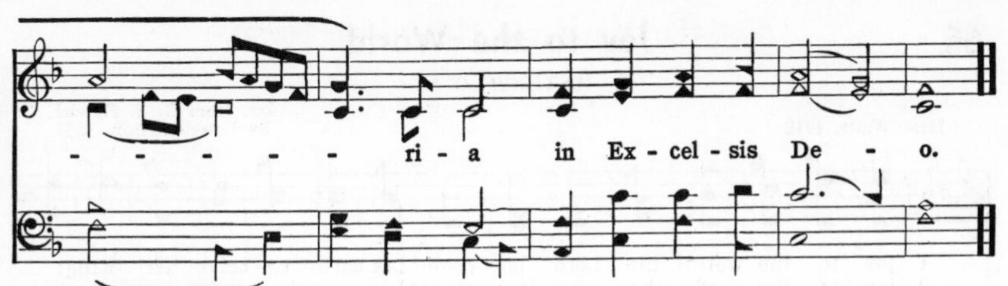

Hark! What Mean Those Holy Voices 65

SHIELDS 8. 7. 8. 7. 8. 7. 8. 7.

John Cawood, 1819

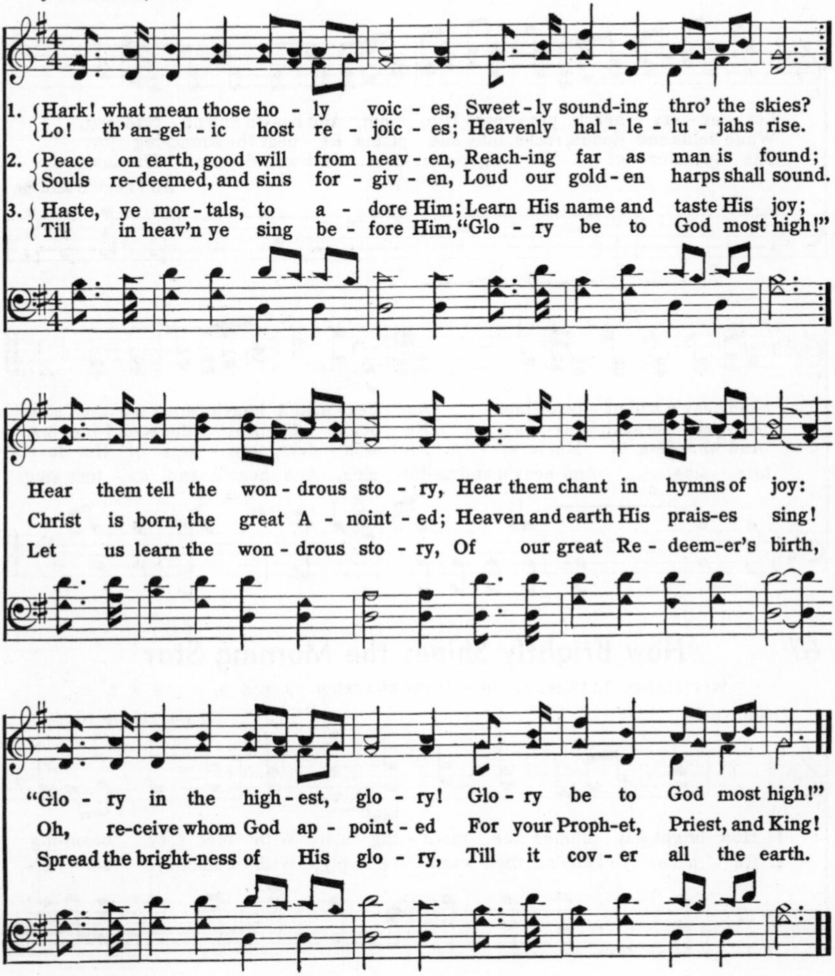

1. Hark! what mean those ho - ly voic - es, Sweet - ly sound - ing thro' the skies?
Lo! th' an - gel - ic host re - joic - es; Heavenly hal - le - lu - jahs rise.
Hear them tell the won - drous sto - ry, Hear them chant in hymns of joy:
"Glo - ry in the high - est, glo - ry! Glo - ry be to God most high!"

2. Peace on earth, good will from heav - en, Reach - ing far as man is found;
Souls re - deemed, and sins for - giv - en, Loud our gold - en harps shall sound.
Christ is born, the great A - noint - ed; Heaven and earth His prais - es sing!
Oh, re - ceive whom God ap - point - ed For your Proph - et, Priest, and King!

3. Haste, ye mor - tals, to a - dore Him; Learn His name and taste His joy;
Till in heav'n ye sing be - fore Him, "Glo - ry be to God most high!"
Let us learn the won - drous sto - ry, Of our great Re - deem - er's birth,
Spread the bright - ness of His glo - ry, Till it cov - er all the earth.

66 Joy to the World

ANTIOCH C. M.
Isaac Watts, 1719
Arr. from G. F. Handel
By Lowell Mason, 1830
1. Joy to the world! the Lord is come! Let earth re - ceive her King;
2. Joy to the earth! the Sav - iour reigns! Let men their songs em - ploy;
3. He rules the world with truth and grace; And makes the na - tions prove
Let ev - ery heart pre - pare Him room, And heav'n and na - ture sing,
While fields and floods, rocks, hills and plains, Re - peat the sound - ing joy,
The glo - ries of His right - eous - ness, And won - ders of His love,
And heav'n and na -
And heav'n and na - ture sing, And heav'n, and heav'n and na - ture sing.
Re - peat the sound - ing joy; Re - peat, re - peat the sound - ing joy.
And won - ders of His love, And won - ders, won - ders of His love.
ture sing, And heav'n and na - ture sing, And heav'n and na - ture sing.

67 How Brightly Shines the Morning Star

WIE SCHON LEUCHTET DER MORGENSTERN 8. 8. 6. 8. 8. 7. 8. 8. 8.

Philip Nicolai

Melody—Philip Nicolai

1. How bright - ly shines the morn - ing star, With mer - cy beam - ing
2. Re - joice ye heav'ns; thou earth re - ply; With praise, ye sin - ners,

from a - far, The host of heav'n re - joic - es; O right-eous branch, O
fill the sky, For this His in - car - na - tion. In - car - nate God, put
Jes - se's rod, Thou Son of Man and Son of God, We, too, will lift our
forth Thy power, Ride on, ride on, great con-quer - or, Till all know Thy sal -
voic - es. Je - sus, Je - sus, Ho - ly ho - ly, yet most low - ly,
va - tion. A - men, A - men, Hal - le - lu - jah, hal - le - lu - jah,
Draw Thou near us, Great Im - man - uel, come and hear us.
Praise be giv - en Ev - er - more by earth and heav - en.

68 Our Song of Praise

CAROL 8. 8. 8. 8. 4.

Zion's Harp

1. Our songs of praise to God as - cend, And there with
2. From heav - en, in the dark of night, He came and
3. He, who in glo - ry there doth reign, Did dwell on
an - gels' voic - es blend. The day of glad - ness now is here;
brought e - ter - nal light. Be - hold now how this light di - vine
earth as hum - ble man; That through His no - ble sac - ri - fice
Sing hal - le - lu - jah with good cheer, Hal - le - lu - jah.
Throughout this pil - grims' dale doth shine. Hal - le - lu - jah!
We find the path to par - a - dise. Hal - le - lu - jah!

69 Silent Night, Holy Night

STILLE NACHT 6. 6. 8. 8. 6. 6.

Joseph Mohr, 1818 — Franz Gruber

1. Si - lent night! Ho - ly night! All is calm, all is bright,
2. Si - lent night! Ho - ly night! Shep - herds quake at the sight!
3. Si - lent night! Ho - ly night! Son of God, love's pure light

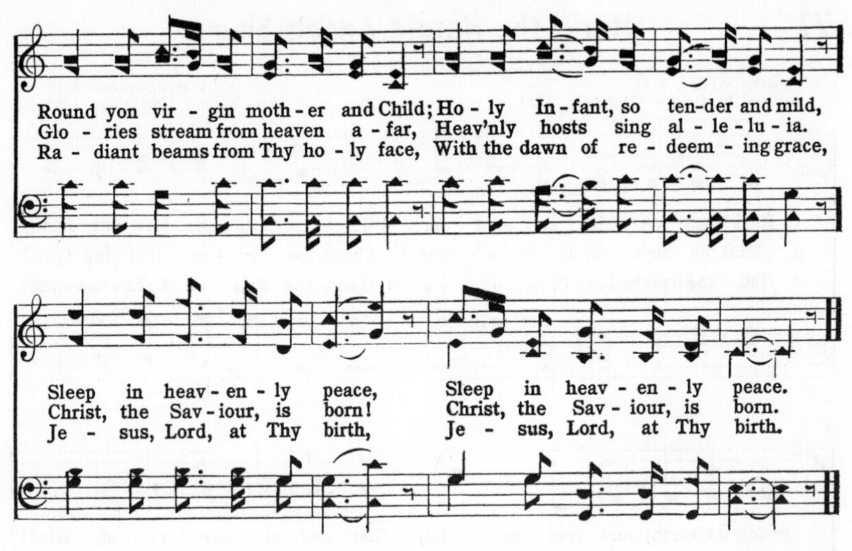

Round yon vir - gin moth - er and Child; Ho - ly In - fant, so ten - der and mild,
Glo - ries stream from heaven a - far, Heav'nly hosts sing al - le - lu - ia.
Ra - diant beams from Thy ho - ly face, With the dawn of re - deem - ing grace,
Sleep in heav - en - ly peace, Sleep in heav - en - ly peace.
Christ, the Sav - iour, is born! Christ, the Sav - iour, is born.
Je - sus, Lord, at Thy birth, Je - sus, Lord, at Thy birth.

While Shepherds Watched 70

CHRISTMAS C. M.

Nahum Tate, 1762

From George F. Handel

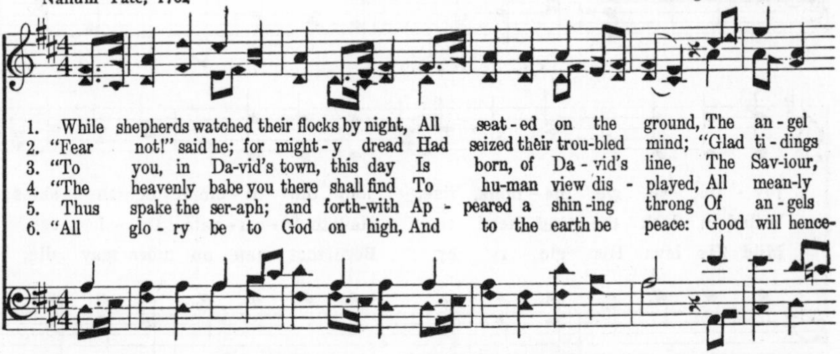

1. While shepherds watched their flocks by night, All seat - ed on the ground, The an - gel
2. "Fear not!" said he; for might - y dread Had seized their trou - bled mind; "Glad ti - dings
3. "To you, in Da - vid's town, this day Is born, of Da - vid's line, The Sav - iour,
4. "The heavenly babe you there shall find To hu - man view dis - played, All mean - ly
5. Thus spake the ser - aph; and forth - with Ap - peared a shin - ing throng Of an - gels
6. "All glo - ry be to God on high, And to the earth be peace: Good will hence -

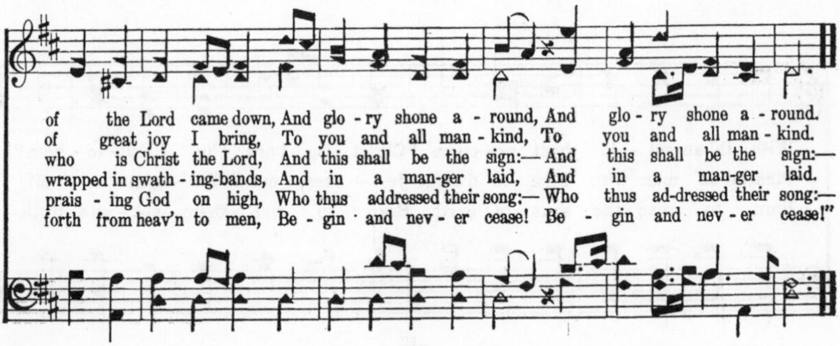

of the Lord came down, And glo - ry shone a - round, And glo - ry shone a - round.
of great joy I bring, To you and all man - kind, To you and all man - kind.
who is Christ the Lord, And this shall be the sign:— And this shall be the sign:—
wrapped in swath - ing - bands, And in a man - ger laid, And in a man - ger laid.
prais - ing God on high, Who thus addressed their song:— Who thus ad - dressed their song:—
forth from heav'n to men, Be - gin and nev - er cease! Be - gin and nev - er cease!"

71 Hark! the Herald Angels Sing

MENDELSSOHN 7. 7. 7. 7. D.
Charles Wesley, 1743
Altered by George Whitefield, 1753
Felix Mendelssohn, 1840
Arr. William Cummings, 1850
1. Hark! the her - ald an - gels sing, "Glo - ry to the new-born King;
2. Christ, by high - est heav'n a - dored, Christ, the ev - er - last - ing Lord!
3. Hail the heav'n-born Prince of Peace! Hail the Sun of Right-eous-ness!
Peace on earth, and mer - cy mild, God and sin - ners rec - on - ciled!"
Come, De - sire of Na - tions, come, Fix in us Thy hum - ble home.
Light and life to all He brings, Ris'n with heal - ing in His wings;
Joy - ful, all ye na - tions, rise, Join the tri - umph of the skies;
Veiled in flesh the God - head see; Hail th' In - car - nate De - i - ty!
Mild He lays His glo - ry by, Born that man no more may die,
With th' an-gel - ic host pro-claim, "Christ is born in Beth - le - hem!"
Pleased as man with men to dwell, Je - sus, our Em - man - u - el!
Born to raise the sons of earth, Born to give them sec - ond birth.

Hark! the her-ald an-gels sing, "Glo-ry to the new-born King!" A-men.

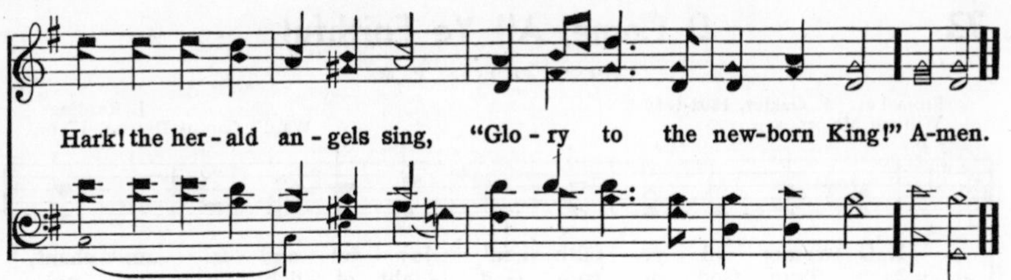

To Us a Child of Hope Is Born 72

ZERAH C. M.

Harmonia Sacra

Anonymous

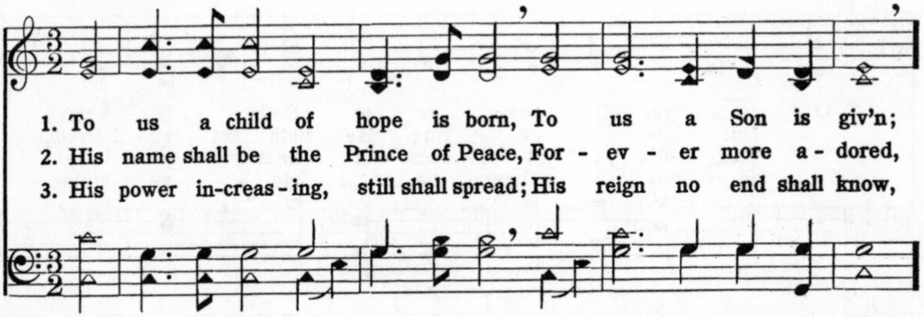

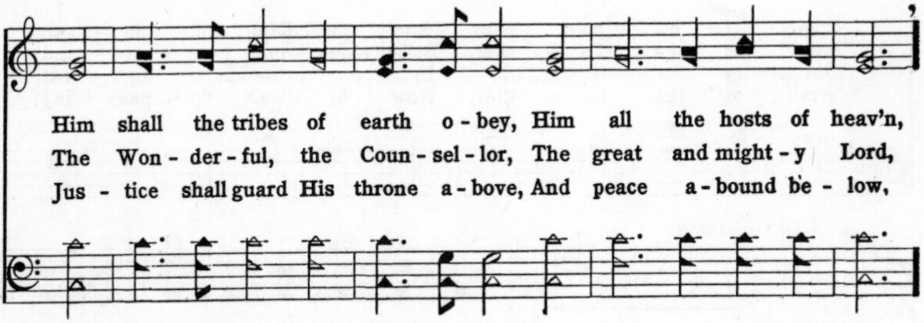

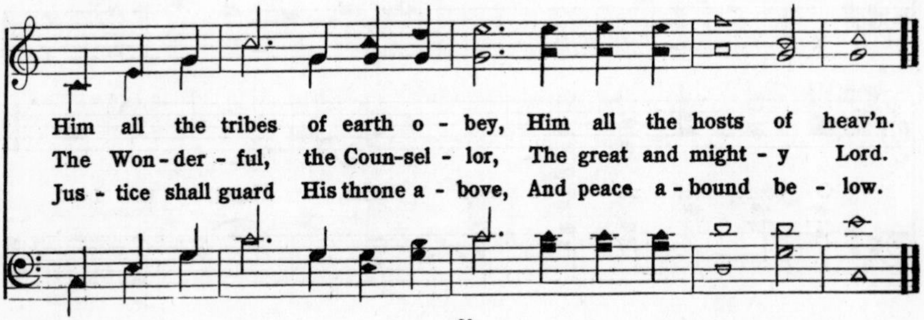

1. To us a child of hope is born, To us a Son is giv'n;
2. His name shall be the Prince of Peace, For - ev - er more a - dored,
3. His power in-creas-ing, still shall spread; His reign no end shall know,

Him shall the tribes of earth o-bey, Him all the hosts of heav'n,
The Won-der-ful, the Coun-sel-lor, The great and might-y Lord,
Jus-tice shall guard His throne a-bove, And peace a-bound be-low,

Him all the tribes of earth o-bey, Him all the hosts of heav'n.
The Won-der-ful, the Coun-sel-lor, The great and might-y Lord.
Jus-tice shall guard His throne a-bove, And peace a-bound be-low.

73 O Come, All Ye Faithful

ADESTE FIDELES P. M.

From Lat. F. Oakley, 1802-1880
William Mercer, v. 2

J. Reading
Ward's Cantus Diversa, 1751

1. O come, all ye faith - ful, Joy - ful and tri - um - phant,
2. True God of true God, Light of light e - ter - nal,
3. Sing, choirs of an - gels, Sing in ex - ul - ta - tion,
4. Yea, Lord, we greet Thee, Born this hap - py morn - ing,
O come ye, O come ye to Beth - le - hem;
Our low - ly na - ture He hath not ab - horred;
Sing, all ye cit - i - zens of heav'n a - bove:
Je - sus, to Thee be........... glo - ry giv'n;
Come and be - hold Him Born, the King of an - gels;
Son of the Fa - ther, Be-got - ten, not cre - a - ted;
Glo - ry to God........... In........... the......... high - est;
Word of the Fa - ther, Now in flesh ap - pear - ing;
After each verse
O come, let us a - dore Him, O come, let us a - dore Him,
O come, let us a - dore Him, Christ, the Lord.

Watchman, Tell Us of the Night

WATCHMAN 7. 7. 7. 7. D.

Sir John Bowring

Lowell Mason

1. Watch-man, tell us of the night, What its signs of prom-ise are.
2. Watch-man, tell us of the night, High-er yet that star as-cends,
3. Watch-man, tell us of the night, For the morn-ing seems to dawn.
Trav-'ler, o'er yon moun-tain's height, See the glo-ry beam-ing star.
Trav-'ler, bless-ed-ness and light, Peace and truth, its course por-tends.
Trav-'ler, dark-ness takes its flight; Doubt and ter-ror are with-drawn.
Watch-man, does its beau-teous ray Aught of hope or joy fore-tell?
Watch-man, will its beams, a-lone, Gild the spot that gave them birth?
Watch-man, let thy wan-dering cease, Hie thee to thy qui-et home.
Trav-'ler, yes, it brings the day— Prom-ised day of Is-ra-el.
Trav-'ler, a-ges are its own; See, it bursts o'er all the earth.
Trav-'ler, lo! the Prince of Peace, Lo! the Son of God is come.

75 Lift Up Your Heads, Rejoice

BLESSED HOME 6. 6. 6. 6. D.

Thomas T. Lynch, 1856

John Stainer, 1875

1. Lift up your heads, re - joice, Re - demp - tion draw - eth nigh:
2. Lift up your heads, re - joice, Re - demp - tion draw - eth nigh:
3. Lift up your heads, re - joice, Re - demp - tion draw - eth nigh:
4. He comes, the wide world's King; He comes, the true heart's Friend,
Now breathes a soft - er air, Now shines a mild - er sky;
Now mount the lad - en clouds, Now flames the darken - ing sky;
O note the vary - ing signs Of earth, and air, and sky!
New glad - ness to be - gin, And an - cient wrong to end;
The ear - ly trees put forth Their new and ten - der leaf;
The ear - ly scat - tered drops De - scend with heav - y fall,
The God of glo - ry comes In gen - tle - ness and might,
He comes, to fill with light The wea - ry, wait - ing eye:
Hushed is the moan - ing wind That told of win - ter's grief.
And to the wait - ing earth The hid - den thun - ders call.
To com - fort and a - larm, To suc - cor and to smite.
Lift up your heads, re - joice, Re - demp - tion draw - eth nigh. A - men.

Lo, How a Rose E'er Blooming 76

ES IST EIN ROS' 7. 6. 7. 6. 6. 7. 6.

St. Germanus
Har. M. Praetorius
Arr. W. E. Yoder
1. Lo, how a Rose e'er bloom - ing, From ten - der stem hath sprung. Of Jes - se's lin - eage com - ing, As men of old have sung. It came a flow - ret bright, A - mid the cold of win - ter, When half - spent was the night.
2. I - sa - iah 'twas fore - told it, The Rose I have in mind. With Ma - ry we be - hold it, The vir - gin moth - er kind. To show God's love a - right, She bore to men a Sav - iour When half - spent was the night.

77 O Come, O Come, Emmanuel

VENI EMMANUEL L. M. 6 l.

Anon. (Latin, c. 12th Cent.)
Tr. J. M. Neale

Ancient Plain Song

1. O come, O come, Em - man - u - el, And ran - som cap - tive
2. O come, Thou Rod of Jes - - se, free Thine own from Sa - tan's
3. O come, Thou Day-Spring, come and cheer Our spir - its by Thine
4. O come, Thou Key of Da - - vid, come, And o - pen wide our
Is - ra - el, That mourns in lone - ly ex - ile here Un -
tyr - an - ny, From depths of hell Thy peo - ple save, And
ad - vent here; Dis - perse the gloom - y clouds of night, And
heaven - ly home; Make safe the way that leads on high, And
til the Son of God ap - pear. Re - joice! Re - joice! Em -
give them vic - tory o'er the grave. Re - joice! Re - joice! Em -
death's dark shad - ows put to flight. Re - joice! Re - joice! Em -
close the path to mis - - - er - y. Re - joice! Re - joice! Em -
man - u - el Shall come to thee, O Is - ra - el. A - men.

Once in Royal David's City

IRBY 8. 7. 8. 7. 7. 7.

Cecil Frances Alexander, 1848

Henry J. Gauntlett, 1856

1. Once in roy - al Da - vid's cit - y Stood a low - ly
2. He came down to earth from heav - en Who is God and
3. And, through all His won - drous child - hood, He would hon - or
4. Not in that poor low - ly sta - ble, With the ox - en
cat - tle shed, Where a moth - er laid her ba - by,
Lord of all, And His shel - ter was a sta - ble,
and o - bey, Love and watch the low - ly maid - en
stand - ing by, We shall see Him; but in heav - en,
In a man - ger for His bed: Ma - ry was that moth - er
And His cra - dle was a stall; With the poor, and mean, and
In whose gen - tle arms He lay; Chris - tian chil - dren all must
Set at God's right hand on high: When like stars His chil - dren
mild, Je - sus Christ her lit - tle Child.
low - ly, Lived on earth our Sav - iour ho - ly.
be Mild, o - be - dient, good as He.
crowned, All in white shall wait a - round. A - men.

79 We Three Kings of Orient Are

KINGS OF ORIENT 8. 8. 8. 6. Ref.

John H. Hopkins, 1862, alt. — John H. Hopkins, 1862

1. We three kings of O - ri - ent are, Bear - ing gifts we trav-erse a - far
2. Born a King on Beth - le-hem's plain, Gold I bring to crown Him a - gain,
3. Frank - in-cense to of - fer have I, In - cense owns a De - i - ty nigh;
4. Myrrh is mine; its bit - ter per - fume Breathes a life of gath-er-ing gloom;
5. Glo - rious now be - hold Him a - rise, King and God and Sac - ri - fice;

Field and foun - tain, moor and mountain, Fol - low - ing yon - der star.
King for - ev - er, ceas - ing nev - er O - ver us all to reign.
Prayer and prais - ing, all men rais - ing, Wor - ship Him, God on high.
Sor - r'wing, sigh - ing, bleed - ing, dy - ing, Sealed in the stone - cold tomb.
Al - le - lu - ia, Al - le - lu - ia! Peals thro' the earth and skies.

REFRAIN *a tempo*

O star of won - der, star of night, Star with roy - al beau - ty bright,

West-ward lead - ing, still pro - ceed - ing, Guide us to thy per - fect light.

Veiled in Darkness Judah Lay 80

EBELING 7. 7. 7. 7. 7. 7. 7.
Douglas L. Rights, 1915
Johann G. Ebeling 1666
1. Veiled in dark - ness Ju - dah lay, Wait - ing for the
2. Still the earth in dark - ness lies. Up from death's dark
3. Light of light, we hum - bly pray, Shine up - on Thy
prom - ised day, While a - cross the shad - owy night
vale a - rise Voi - ces of a world in grief,
world to - day; Break the gloom of our dark night,
Streamed a flood of glo - rious light, Heav'n - ly voic - es
Prayers of men who seek re - lief: Now our dark - ness
Fill our souls with love and light, Send Thy bless - ed
chant - ing then, "Peace on earth, good will to men."
pierce a - gain, "Peace on earth, good will to men."
word a - gain, "Peace on earth, good will to men." A-men.

Used by permission of Douglas L. Rights and the Beacon Press.

81 Ride On, Ride On in Majesty

ST. DROSTANE L. M.

Henry H. Milman, 1827 John B. Dykes, 1862

1. Ride on, ride on in maj - es - ty! Hark! all the tribes Ho - san - na cry;
2. Ride on, ride on in maj - es - ty! In low - ly pomp ride on to die;
3. Ride on, ride on in maj - es - ty! The wing - ed squad - rons of the sky
4. Ride on, ride on in maj - es - ty! The last and fierc - est strife is nigh;
O Sav - iour meek, pur - sue Thy road, With palms and scattered garments strowed.
O Christ, Thy triumphs now be - gin O'er cap - tive death and conquered sin.
Look down with sad and wondering eyes To see th' approaching sac - ri - fice.
Bow Thy meek head to mor - tal pain, Then take, O Christ, Thy power and reign. A - men.

82 When I Survey the Wondrous Cross

HAMBURG L. M.

Isaac Watts, 1707 Arr. Lowell Mason

1. When I sur - vey the won - drous cross On which the Prince of glo - ry died,
2. For - bid it, Lord, that I should boast, Save in the death of Christ my Lord;
3. See, from His head, His hands, His feet, Sor - row and love flow min - gled down;
4. Were the whole realm of na - ture mine, That were a pres - ent far too small;
My rich - est gain I count but loss, And pour con - tempt on all my pride.
All the vain things that charm me most, I sac - ri - fice them to His blood.
Did e'er such love and sor - row meet, Or thorns compose so rich a crown?
Love so a - maz - ing, so di - vine, De - mands my soul, my life, my all.

Into the Woods My Master Went 83

LANIER P. M.

Sidney Lanier, (1842-1881) Peter C. Lutkin

1. In - to the woods my Mas - ter went, Clean for-spent, for - spent;
2. Out of the woods my Mas - ter went, And He was well con - tent;
In - to the woods my Mas-ter came, For spent with love and shame. But the
Out of the woods my Mas-ter came, Con - tent with death and shame. When
ol - ives they were not blind to Him, The lit - tle gray leaves were kind to Him,
death and shame would woo Him last, From un-der the trees they drew Him last,
The thorn-tree had a mind to Him, When in - to the woods He came.
'Twas on a tree they slew Him last, When out of the woods He came. A - men.

Music by permission of H. C. Lutkin.

84 Beneath the Cross of Jesus

ST. CHRISTOPHER 7. 6. 8. 6. 8. 6. 8. 6.

Elizabeth C. Clephane, 1868 — Frederick C. Maker, 1881

1. Be - neath the cross of Je - sus I fain would take my stand,
2. Up - on the cross of Je - sus Mine eye at times can see
3. I take, O cross, thy shad - ow For my a - bid - ing place;
The shad - ow of a might - y rock With - in a wea - ry land;
The ver - y dy - ing form of One Who suf - fered there for me.
I ask no oth - er sun-shine than The sun - shine of His face;
A home with - in the wil - der - ness, A rest up - on the way,
And from my smit-ten heart with tears, These won - ders I con - fess,
Con - tent to let the world go by, To know no gain nor loss,
From the burn-ing of the noon-tide heat, And the bur - den of the day.
The won - der of His glo-rious love, And my own worthlessness.
My sin - ful self my on - ly shame, My glo - ry all the cross. A-men.

Christ, We Do All Adore Thee

ADORAMUS TE 7. 8. 7. 8. 6. 6. 9. 7. 8. 7.

From Seven Last Words

Theodore Dubois

p

Christ, we do all a - dore Thee, And we do praise Thee for - ev - er, Christ we do all a - dore Thee, And we do praise Thee for - ev - er,

cres.

For on the ho - ly cross Thou hast the world from

mf

sin re - deem - ed.

pp

Christ, we do all a - dore Thee, And we do praise Thee for - ev - er.

ppp — *p* *ppp*

Christ, we do all a - dore Thee.

86 On a Hill Far Away

OLD RUGGED CROSS P. M.

Geo. Bennard — Rev. Geo. Bennard

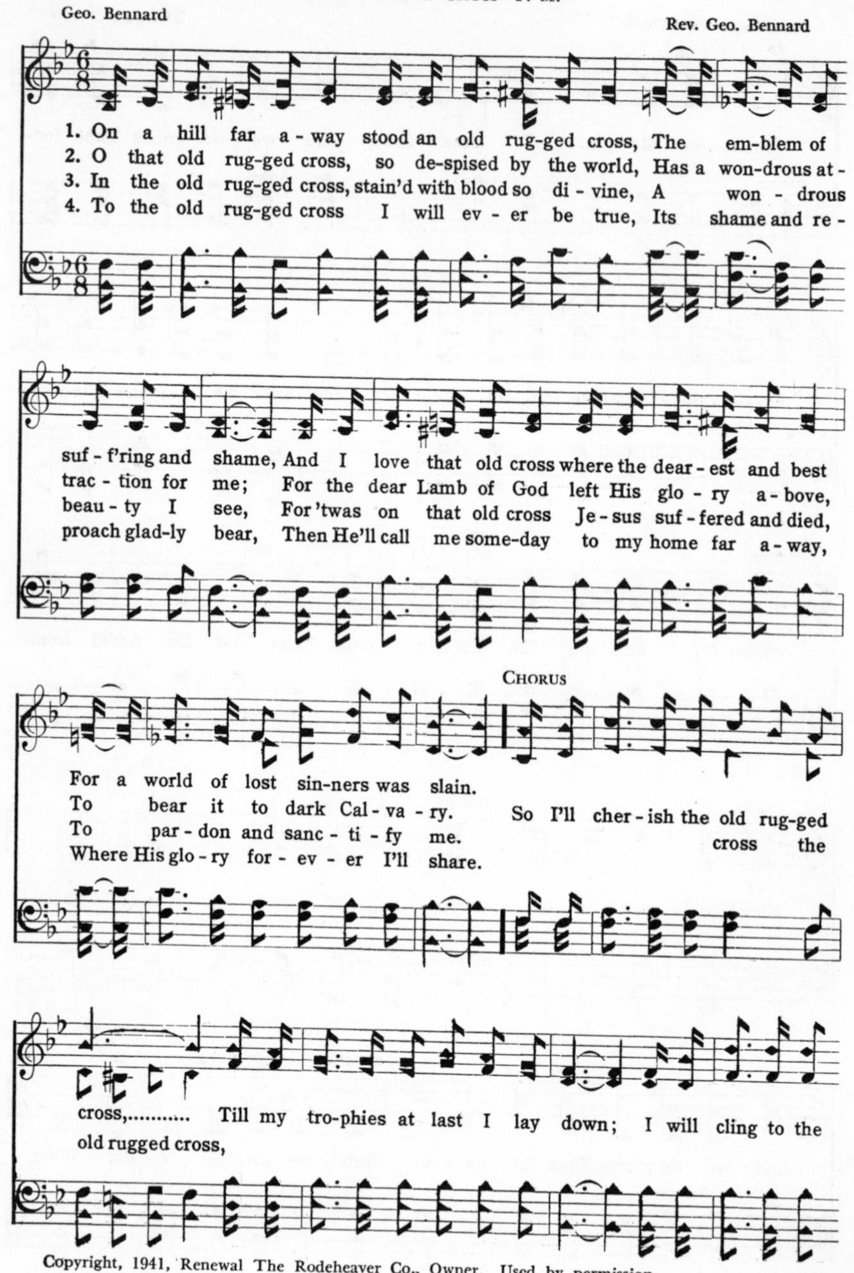

1. On a hill far a-way stood an old rug-ged cross, The em-blem of suf-f'ring and shame, And I love that old cross where the dear-est and best For a world of lost sin-ners was slain.
2. O that old rug-ged cross, so de-spised by the world, Has a won-drous at-trac-tion for me; For the dear Lamb of God left His glo-ry a-bove, To bear it to dark Cal-va-ry.
3. In the old rug-ged cross, stain'd with blood so di-vine, A won-drous beau-ty I see, For 'twas on that old cross Je-sus suf-fered and died, To par-don and sanc-ti-fy me.
4. To the old rug-ged cross I will ev-er be true, Its shame and re-proach glad-ly bear, Then He'll call me some-day to my home far a-way, Where His glo-ry for-ev-er I'll share.
CHORUS
So I'll cher-ish the old rug-ged cross, cross the cross,........... old rugged cross, Till my tro-phies at last I lay down; I will cling to the

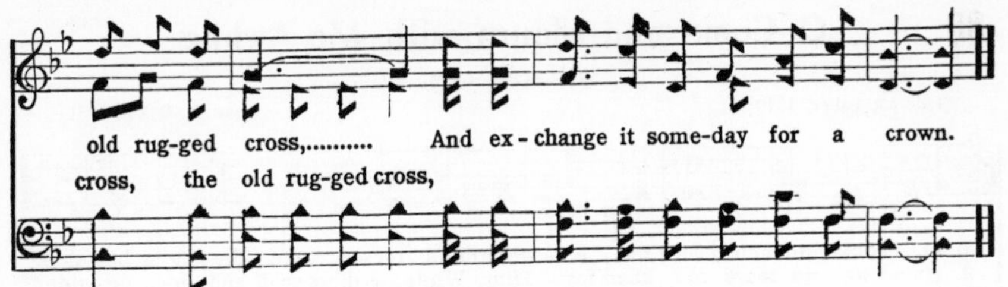
old rug-ged cross,.......... And ex - change it some-day for a crown.
cross, the old rug-ged cross,

Ask Ye What Great Thing I Know

87

CRUCIFIED AND GLORIFIED 7. 7. 7. 7. 7.

Zion's Harp

1. Ask ye what great thing I know That de - lights and
2. Who hath loosed the pris - on door, By His might - y
3. Who hath giv - en strength to me, By His life and
4. This is that great thing I know; This de - lights and

stirs me so? What the high re - ward I win? Whose the
word and power? Who to life hath wak - ened me, Ev - er
vic - to - ry? Rec - on - ciled me un - to God, Com - forts
stirs me so; Faith in Him who died to save, Him, who

name I glo - ry in? Je - sus Christ the cru - ci - fied.
there with Him to be? Je - sus Christ, our ris - en Lord.
by His staff and rod? Je - sus Christ, ex - alt - ed Lord.
tri - umphed o'er the grave, Je - sus, God of maj - es - ty.

88 O Come and Mourn with Me Awhile

ST. CROSS L. M.

Frederick Faber, 1849

John B. Dykes, 1861

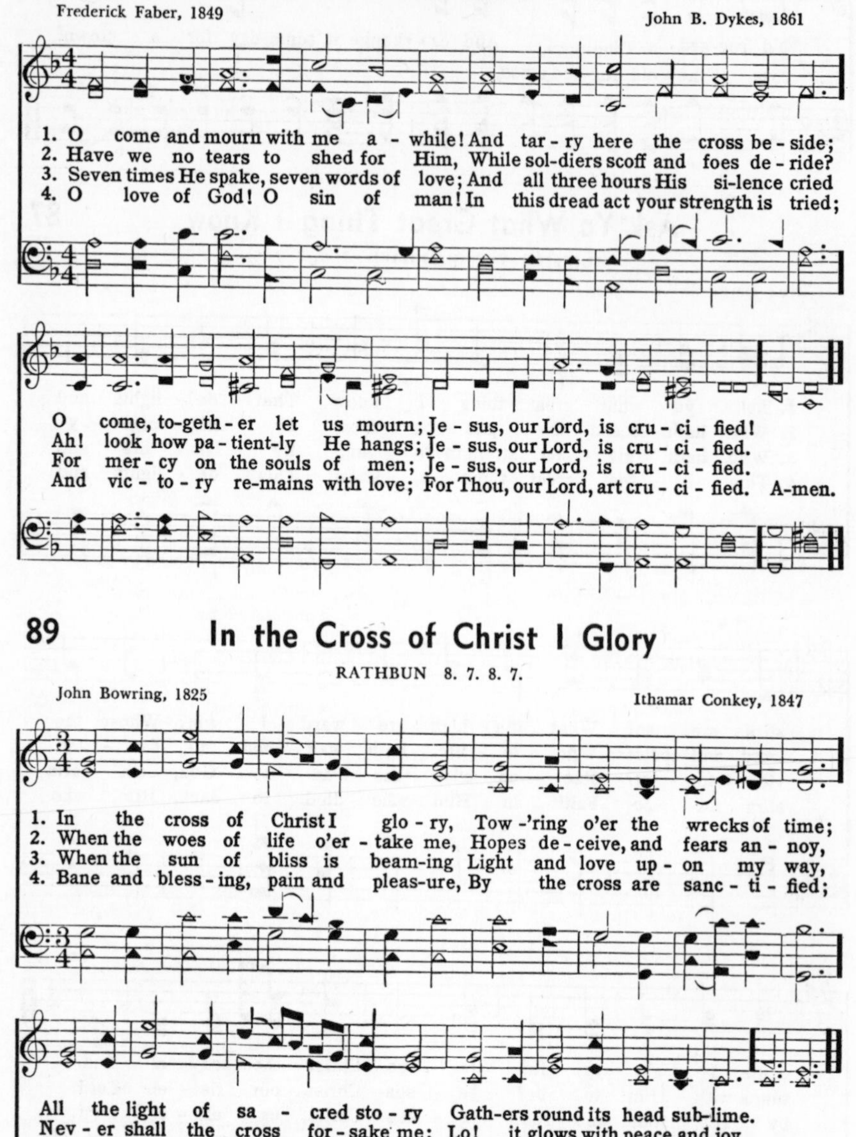
1. O come and mourn with me a - while! And tar - ry here the cross be - side;
2. Have we no tears to shed for Him, While sol-diers scoff and foes de - ride?
3. Seven times He spake, seven words of love; And all three hours His si-lence cried
4. O love of God! O sin of man! In this dread act your strength is tried;
O come, to-geth - er let us mourn; Je - sus, our Lord, is cru - ci - fied!
Ah! look how pa - tient-ly He hangs; Je - sus, our Lord, is cru - ci - fied.
For mer - cy on the souls of men; Je - sus, our Lord, is cru - ci - fied.
And vic - to - ry re-mains with love; For Thou, our Lord, art cru - ci - fied. A-men.

89 In the Cross of Christ I Glory

RATHBUN 8. 7. 8. 7.

John Bowring, 1825

Ithamar Conkey, 1847

1. In the cross of Christ I glo - ry, Tow -'ring o'er the wrecks of time;
2. When the woes of life o'er - take me, Hopes de - ceive, and fears an - noy,
3. When the sun of bliss is beam-ing Light and love up - on my way,
4. Bane and bless - ing, pain and pleas-ure, By the cross are sanc - ti - fied;

All the light of sa - cred sto - ry Gath-ers round its head sub-lime.
Nev - er shall the cross for - sake me; Lo! it glows with peace and joy.
From the cross the ra - diance stream-ing Adds new lus - ter to the day.
Peace is there that knows no meas - ure, Joys that thro' all time a - bide. A-men.

Out onto Calvary's Hill 90

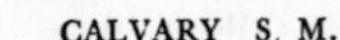

CALVARY S. M.

Zion's Harp

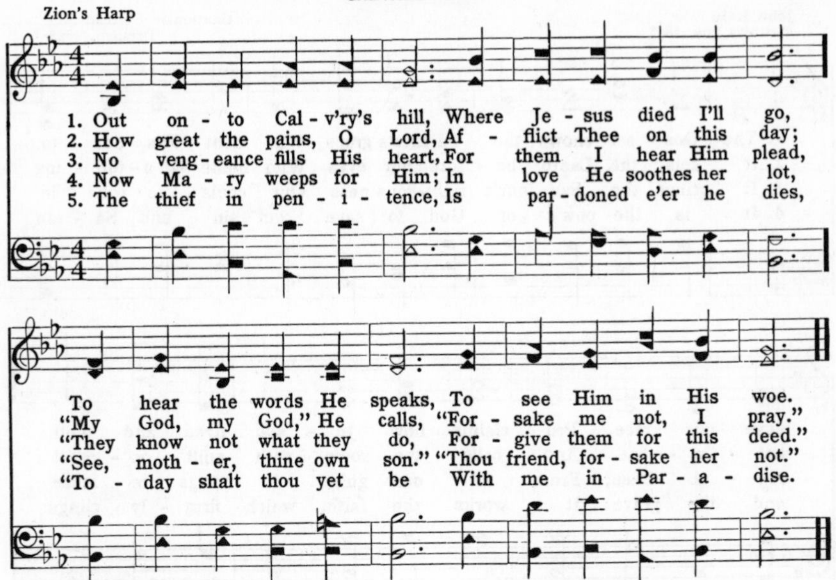
1. Out on - to Cal - v'ry's hill, Where Je - sus died I'll go,
2. How great the pains, O Lord, Af - flict Thee on this day;
3. No veng - eance fills His heart, For them I hear Him plead,
4. Now Ma - ry weeps for Him; In love He soothes her lot,
5. The thief in pen - i - tence, Is par - doned e'er he dies,
To hear the words He speaks, To see Him in His woe.
"My God, my God," He calls, "For - sake me not, I pray."
"They know not what they do, For - give them for this deed."
"See, moth - er, thine own son." "Thou friend, for - sake her not."
"To - day shalt thou yet be With me in Par - a - dise.

6. "I thirst," He cries in pain;
For there is no distress,
Which Christ, the Friend of Man,
Endured not at His death.

7. He bows His head and cries,
"'Tis finished, all is done,
O God, receive my soul,"
Life's victory is won.

Draw Nigh and Take the Body 91

MORECAMBE 10. 10. 10. 10.

Anonymous

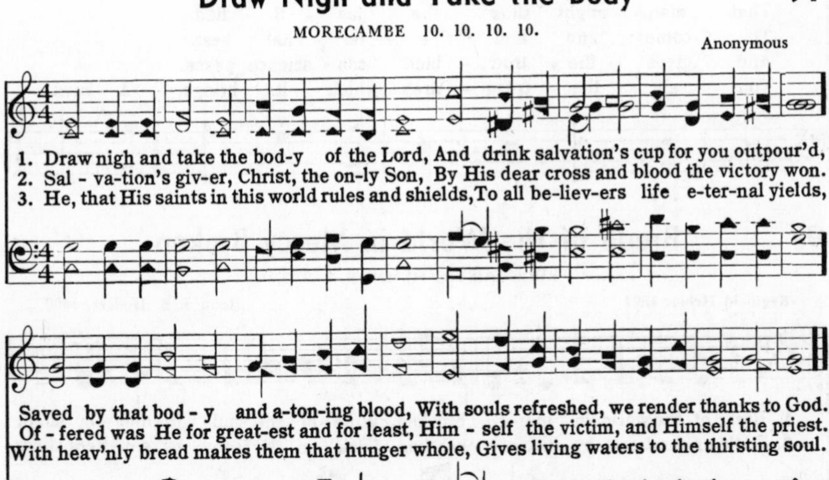
1. Draw nigh and take the bod-y of the Lord, And drink salvation's cup for you outpour'd,
2. Sal - va-tion's giv-er, Christ, the on-ly Son, By His dear cross and blood the victory won.
3. He, that His saints in this world rules and shields, To all be-liev-ers life e-ter-nal yields,
Saved by that bod - y and a-ton-ing blood, With souls refreshed, we render thanks to God.
Of - fered was He for great-est and for least, Him - self the victim, and Himself the priest.
With heav'nly bread makes them that hunger whole, Gives living waters to the thirsting soul.

92 The Gospel Shows the Father's Grace

HERR JESU CHRIST, DICH L. M.

John 3: 16
Matthias Loy, 1863

Cantionale Germanicum
Dresden, 1628

1. The Gos - pel shows the Fa-ther's grace, Who sent His Son to
2. It sets the Lamb be - fore our eyes, Who made th' a - ton - ing
3. It brings the Sav - iour's right-eous-ness Our souls to robe in
4. It is the pow'r of God to save From sin and Sa - tan
save our race, Pro - claims how Je - sus lived and died
sac - ri - fice, And calls the souls with guilt op - prest
roy - al dress; From all our guilt it brings re - lease
and the grave; It works the faith, which firm - ly clings
That man might thus be jus - ti - fied.
To come and find e - ter - nal rest.
And gives the trou - bled con - science peace.
To all the treas - ures which it brings. A - men.

93 Bread of the World in Mercy Broken

EUCHARISTIC HYMN 9. 8. 9. 8.

Reginald Heber, 1827

John S. B. Hodges, 1869

1. Bread of the world in mer-cy bro-ken, Wine of the soul in mer - cy shed,
2. Look on the heart by sor-row bro-ken, Look on the tears by sin - ners shed;

By whom the words of life were spo-ken, And in whose death our sins are dead;
And be Thy feast to us the to-ken That by Thy grace our souls are fed. A-men.

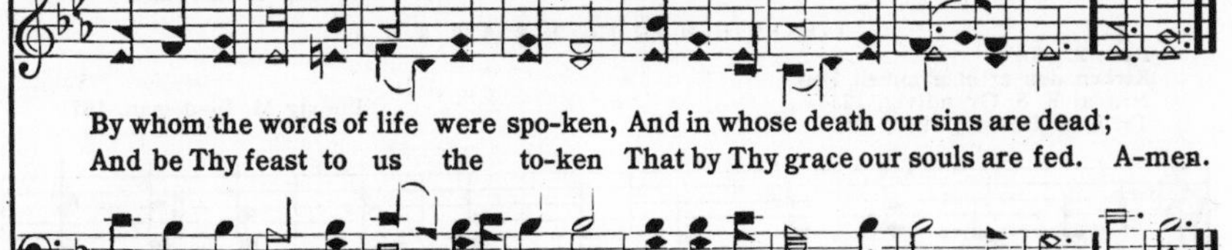

Come, Risen Lord, and Deign to Be Our Guest 94

BIRMINGHAM 10. 10. 10. 10.

G. W. Briggs, 1875-

From F. Cunningham's
A Selection of Psalm Tunes, 1834

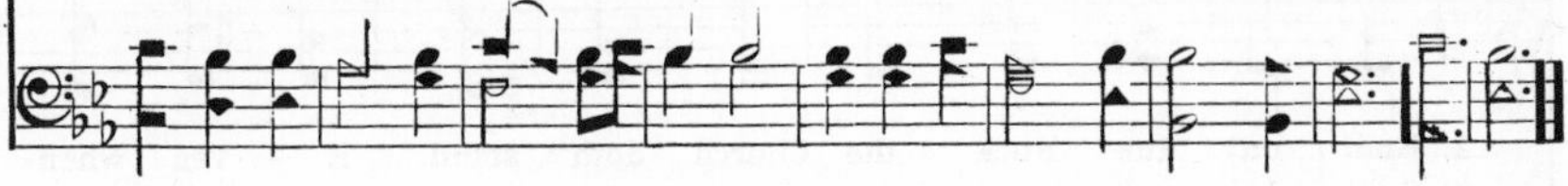

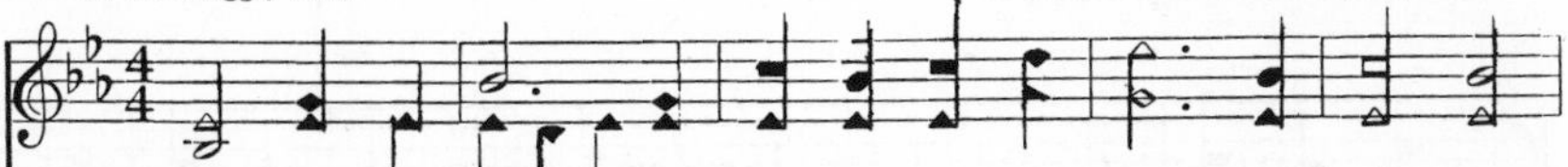

1. Come, ris - en Lord, and deign to be our guest; Nay, let us
2. We meet, as in that up - per room they met; Thou at the
3. One bod - y we, one bod - y who par - take, One Church u -
4. One with each oth - er, Lord, for one in Thee, Who art our

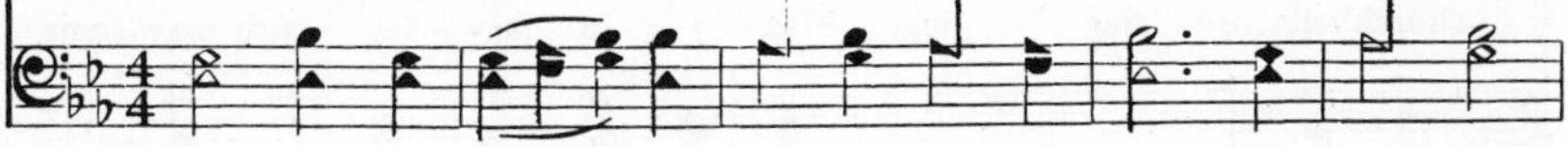

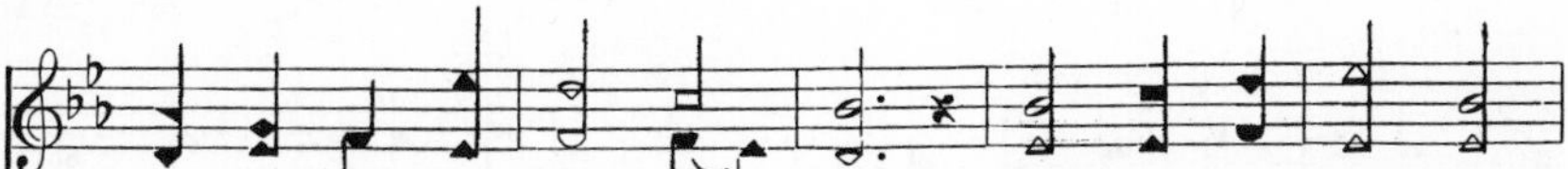

be Thy guests; the feast is Thine; Thy - self at Thine own
ta - ble, bless - ing, yet dost stand: "This is my bod - y":
nit - ed in com - mun - ion blest; One name we bear, one
Sav - iour and our liv - ing Head; Then o - pen Thou our

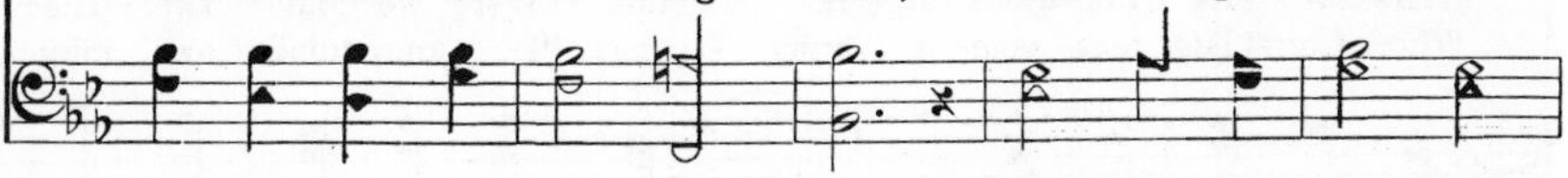

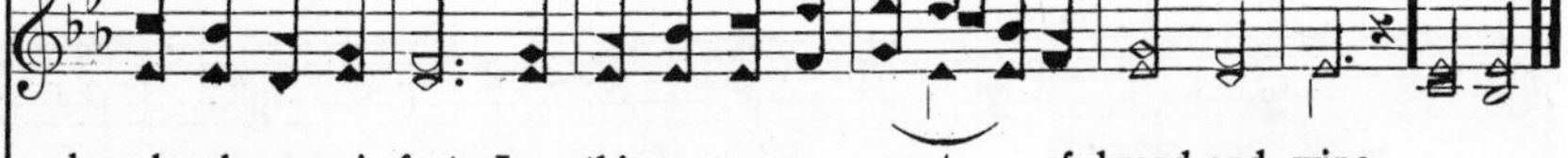

board make man-i - fest, In this our sac-ra - ment of bread and wine.
so Thou giv-est yet; Faith still receives the cup as from Thy hand.
bread of life we break, With all Thy saints on earth and saints at rest.
eyes, that we may see; Be known to us in break - ing of the bread. A-men.

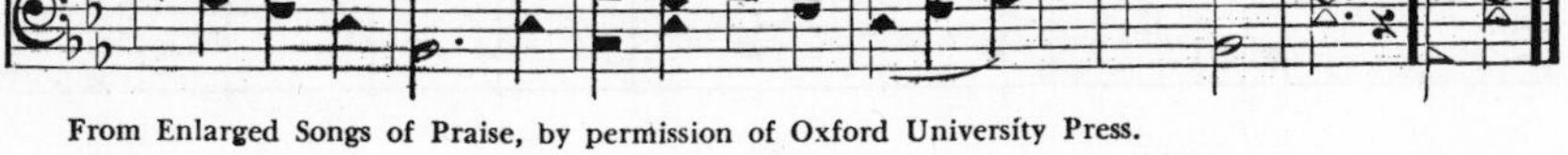

95 Built on the Rock the Church Doth Stand

KIRKEN DEN ER ET 8. 8. 8. 8. 8. 8. 8. 8.

Eph. 2: 19-22
Kirken den er et gammelt Hus
Nicolai F. S. Grundtvig, 1837
Tr. Carl Döving, 1909, alt.

Ludvig M. Lindeman, 1871

1. Built on the Rock the Church doth stand, E - ven when
2. Sure - ly in tem - ples made with hands, God, the Most
3. We are God's house of liv - ing stones, Build - ed for
4. Grant, then, O God, wher - e'er men roam, That, when the

stee - ples are fall - ing; Crum - bled have spires in ev - ery land,
High, is not dwell - ing; High a - bove earth His tem - ple stands,
His hab - i - ta - tion; He through bap - tis - mal grace us owns
churchbells are ring - ing, Man - y in sav - ing faith may come

Bells still are chim - ing and call - ing, Call - ing the young and
All earth - ly tem - ples ex - cel - ling. Yet He whom heav'ns can -
Heirs of His won - drous sal - va - tion. Were we but two His
Where Christ His mes - sage is bring - ing: "I know mine own, mine

old to rest, But a - bove all the soul dis - tressed,
not con - tain Chose to a - bide on earth with men,
name to tell, Yet He would deign with us to dwell,
own know me; Ye, not the world, my face shall see.

Long - ing for rest ev - er - last - - ing.
Built in our bod - ies His tem - - ple.
With all His grace and His fa - - vor.
My peace I leave with you." A - - men.

Blessed Saviour, Thee I Love 96

SPANISH HYMN 7. 7. 7. 7. 7. 7.

Rev. George Duffield, 1851 | Arr. Benjamin Carr, 1824

1. Bless - ed Sav - iour, Thee I love, All my oth - er joys a - bove;
2. Once a - gain be - side the cross, All my gain I count but loss;
3. Bless - ed Sav - iour, Thine am I, Thine to live, and Thine to die;

All my hopes in Thee a - bide, Thou my hope, and naught be - side;
Earth - ly pleas - ures fade a - way— Clouds they are that hide my day;
Height or depth, or crea - ture pow'r, Ne'er shall hide my Sav - iour more;

Ev - er let my glo - ry be, On - ly, on - ly, on - ly Thee.
Hence, vain shad - ows! let me see Je - sus cru - ci - fied for me.
Ev - er shall my glo - ry be, On - ly, on - ly, on - ly Thee. A - men.

97 A Parting Hymn We Sing

OLMUTZ S. M.

Aaron R. Wolfe, 1858

From Gregorian Chant
Arr. Lowell Mason, 1824

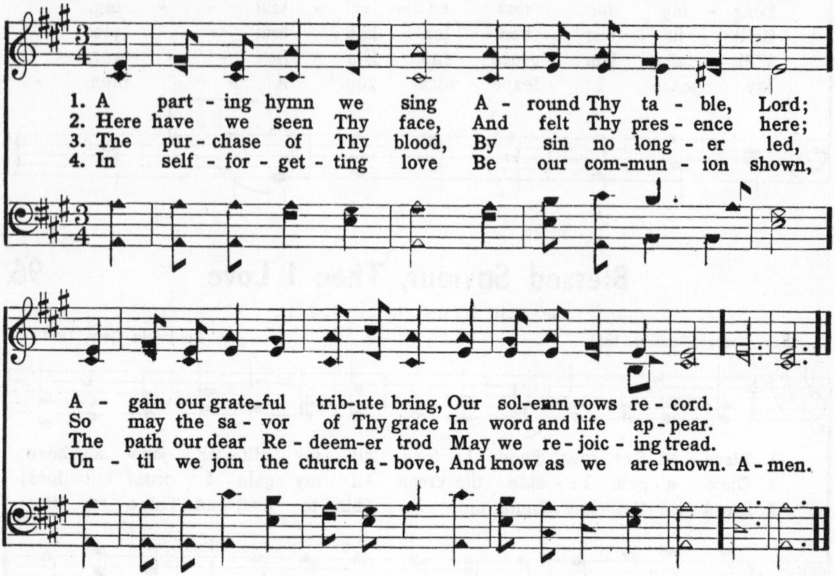

1. A part - ing hymn we sing A - round Thy ta - ble, Lord;
A - gain our grate-ful trib-ute bring, Our sol-emn vows re - cord.

2. Here have we seen Thy face, And felt Thy pres - ence here;
So may the sa - vor of Thy grace In word and life ap - pear.

3. The pur - chase of Thy blood, By sin no long - er led,
The path our dear Re - deem-er trod May we re - joic - ing tread.

4. In self - for - get - ting love Be our com-mun - ion shown,
Un - til we join the church a - bove, And know as we are known. A - men.

98 Christ, the Lord, Is Risen Today

RESURREXIT 7. 7. 7. 7.

Charles Wesley

Rev. J. A. Freylinghausen

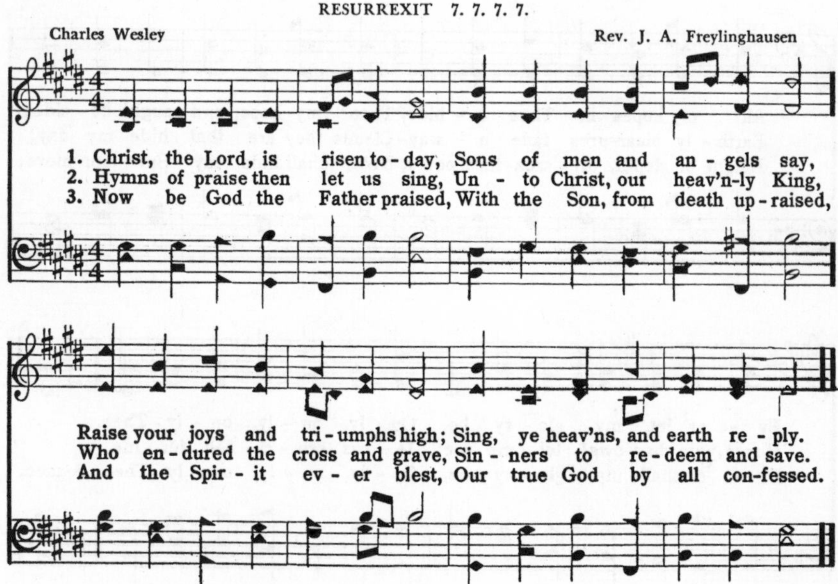
1. Christ, the Lord, is risen to - day, Sons of men and an - gels say,
2. Hymns of praise then let us sing, Un - to Christ, our heav'n-ly King,
3. Now be God the Father praised, With the Son, from death up - raised,
Raise your joys and tri - umphs high; Sing, ye heav'ns, and earth re - ply.
Who en - dured the cross and grave, Sin - ners to re - deem and save.
And the Spir - it ev - er blest, Our true God by all con-fessed.

Here, O My Lord, I See Thee Face to Face 99

PENITENTIA 10. 10. 10. 10.

Rev. Horatius Bonar, 1855
Edward Dearle, 1874
1. Here, O my Lord, I see Thee face to face;
2. Here would I feed up - on the bread of God,
3. I have no help but Thine, nor do I need
4. Mine is the sin, but Thine the right - eous - ness;
Here would I touch and han - dle things un - seen;
Here drink with Thee the roy - al wine of heav'n;
An - oth - er arm save Thine to lean up - on;
Mine is the guilt, but Thine the cleans - ing blood;
Here grasp with firm - er hand e - ter - nal grace,
Here would I lay a - side each earth - ly load,
It is e - nough, my Lord, e - nough in - deed;
Here is my robe, my ref - uge, and my peace,
And all my wea - ri - ness up - on Thee lean.
Here taste a - fresh the calm of sin for - giv'n.
My strength is in Thy might, Thy might a - lone.
Thy blood, Thy right - eous - ness, O Lord, my God. A - men.

100 Christ, the Lord, Is Risen Again

MACHE DICH, MEIN GEIST, BEREIT 7. 7. 7. 7. With Alleluia

Michael Weisse, 1531
Tr. Catherine Winkworth, 1858

From Gesangbuch mit Noten

1. Christ, the Lord, is ris'n a - gain; Christ hath bro - ken ev - ery chain;
2. He who gave for us His life, Who for us en-dured the strife,
3. He who bore all pain and loss Com - fort-less up - on the cross,
4. He who slum-bered in the grave, Is ex - alt - ed now to save;
Hark, an - gel - ic voic - es cry, Sing - ing ev - er - more on high:
Is our Pas - chal Lamb to - day; We too sing for joy, and say:
Lives in glo - ry now on high, Pleads for us, and hears our cry:
Now through Christen - dom it rings That the Lamb is King of kings:
Refrain
Christ the Lord, Christ the Lord, Christ the Lord is
ris - en! Al - le - lu - ia! A - men.

5. Now He bids us tell abroad,
How the lost may be restored,
How the penitent forgiven,
How we, too, may enter heaven.

6. Thou our Paschal Lamb indeed,
Christ, Thy ransomed people feed;
Take our sins and guilt away,
That we all may sing for aye:

Christ Who Left His Home in Glory

CHRIST IS RISEN 8. 7. 8. 7. Ref.

A. B. Kolb, 1896 — A. B. Kolb

Joyfully

1. Christ who left His home in glory, And upon the cross was slain, Now is ris'n! Oh, tell the story That the Saviour lives again.
2. While the world in peace was sleeping, Early on that Easter day, Came the faithful women, weeping, But the stone was rolled away.
3. Christ, our loving Mediator, Now with God for you and me Intercedes, and our Creator Hears and answers every plea.

REFRAIN

Hail Him! Hail Him! Tell the story;
Hail to the King, the mighty Redeemer! Hail Him who robbed the grave of its pow'r!
Hail! all hail!........... Jesus lives forevermore.
Tell ev'ry nation, all is well,

102 Thine Is the Glory, Risen, Conquering Son

HANDEL 10. 11. 11. 11. Ref.

Edmond L. Budry (Richard B. Hoyle, Tr.) George F. Handel

1. Thine is the glo - ry, ris - en, con-qu'ring Son, End - less is the vic - t'ry
2. Lo! Je - sus meets us, ris - en from the tomb; Lov - ing- ly He greets us,
3. No more we doubt Thee, glo - rious Prince of life; Life is nought with-out Thee:
Thou o'er death hast won; An - gels in bright rai-ment rolled the stone a - way,
scat - ters fear and gloom; Let the Church with gladness, hymns of tri-umph sing,
aid us in our strife; Make us more than conqu'rors, thro' Thy deathless love.
Refrain
Kept the fold - ed grave-clothes, where Thy bod - y lay.
For her Lord now liv - eth, death hath lost its sting. Thine is the glo - ry,
Bring us safe thro' Jor - dan to Thy home a - bove.
ris - en, conqu'ring Son, End - less is the vic - t'ry Thou o'er death hast won.

Alleluia! Sing to Jesus

103

ALLELUIA 8. 7. 8. 7. D.

William C. Dix, 1837-1898

Traditional Melody
From St. Basil's Hymnal

1. Al - le - lu - ia! sing to Je - sus! His the scep - ter, His the throne; Al - le -
2. Al - le - lu - ia! not as or-phans Are we left in sor - row now; Al - le -
3. Al - le - lu - ia! sing to Je - sus! His the scep - ter, His the throne; Al - le -
lu - ia! His the tri - umph, His the vic - to - ry a - lone. Hark! the
lu - ia! He is near us, Faith be - lieves, nor ques - tions how. Though the
lu - ia! His the tri - umph, His the vic - to - ry a - lone. Hark! the
songs of peace-ful Zi - on Thun-der like a might - y flood: "Je - sus,
cloud from sight re-ceived Him When the for - ty days were o'er, Shall our
songs of peace-ful Zi - on Thun-der like a might - y flood: "Je - sus,
out of ev - ery na - tion, Hath re - deemed us by His blood."
hearts for - get His prom - ise, "I am with you ev - er - more"?
out of ev - ery na - tion, Hath re - deemed us by His blood." A - men.

104
Ye Sons and Daughters of the King
GELOBT SEI GOTT 8. 8. 8. With Alleluias
John 20
Author unknown, c. 1600
Tr. John M. Neale, 1851
Melchior Vulpius, 1609
1. Ye sons and daugh-ters of the King, Whom heav'nly hosts in glo-ry sing, To-day the grave hath lost its sting:
2. On that first morn-ing of the week, Be-fore the day be-gan to break, The Ma-rys went their Lord to seek:
3. An an-gel bade their sor-row flee, For thus he spake un-to the three: "Your Lord is gone to Gal-i-lee:"
Al-le-lu-ia! . . . Al-le-lu-ia! . . . Al-le-lu-ia!
Al-le-lu-ia! . . . Al-le-lu-ia! . . . Al-le-lu-ia!
Al-le-lu-ia! . . . Al-le-lu-ia! . . . Al-le-lu-ia! A-men.
105
Jesus, O'er the Grave Victorious
TALMAR 8. 7. 8. 7.
E. E. Higbee
Isaac B. Woodbury
1. Je-sus, o'er the grave vic-to-rious, Conqu'ring death and conqu'ring hell,
2. Down to earth in all its dark-ness, From the Fa-ther Thou didst come;
3. By a life of love and la-bor Do-ing all the Fa-ther's will;
4. Pa-tient ev-er in well-do-ing, Mov-ing on in steps of blood,

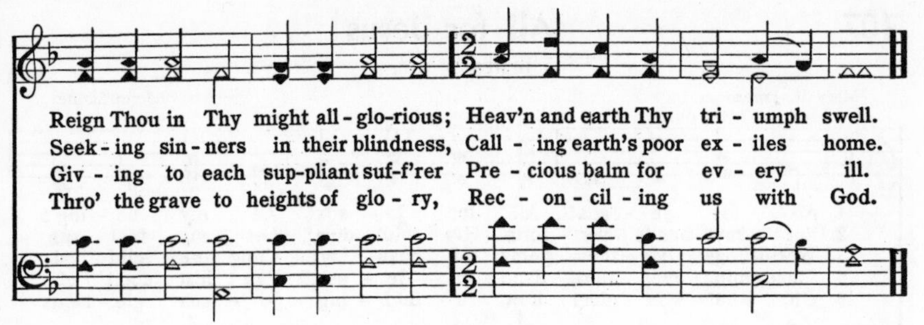
Reign Thou in Thy might all-glo-rious; Heav'n and earth Thy tri - umph swell.
Seek-ing sin-ners in their blindness, Call - ing earth's poor ex - iles home.
Giv - ing to each sup-pliant suf-f'rer Pre - cious balm for ev - ery ill.
Thro' the grave to heights of glo - ry, Rec - on - cil - ing us with God.

I Am the Lord, O Hear My Voice 106

CHRIST'S VOICE 8. 7. 8. 7. 8. 8.

Johann Scheffler, 1624-1677
Tr. Joanna Sudermann Andres, 1940

Hermann Rhein

1. I am the Lord, O hear my voice, A - rise ye Chris-tians, fol - low!
2. I am the Light, I light the way Un - to a life vic - to - rious.
3. Fear not, I am your con-stant Stay Though strong the foe as - sail - eth;
4. Dear Lord, we rise to fol - low Thee, In Thee is grace suf - fi - cient;

De - ny your - self, for - sake the world, My name a - lone to hal - low.
He that will come and fol - low me Shall find his path-way glo - rious.
I am your Vic - tor in the fight, No foe o'er me pre - vail - eth.
In Thee is strength, is vic - to - ry, In Thee is love om - nis - cient.

Take up your cross, your burdens bear And fol - low me, my life to share.
I am the Way, the heav'nly Light By which the soul may walk a - right.
Woe un - to him that standeth still And fol - lows not to do my will.
Help us to tri-umph in the strife And grant to us the crown of Life. A-men.

107 All for Jesus

JAMES 8. 7. 8. 7.

Mary D. James | John Stainer

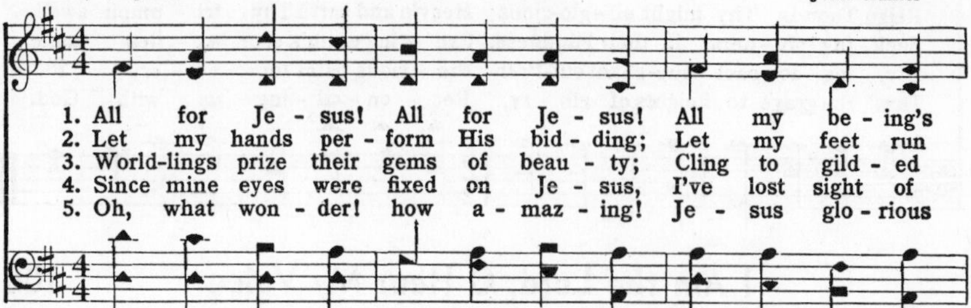

1. All for Je - sus! All for Je - sus! All my be - ing's
2. Let my hands per - form His bid - ding; Let my feet run
3. World-lings prize their gems of beau - ty; Cling to gild - ed
4. Since mine eyes were fixed on Je - sus, I've lost sight of
5. Oh, what won - der! how a - maz - ing! Je - sus glo - rious

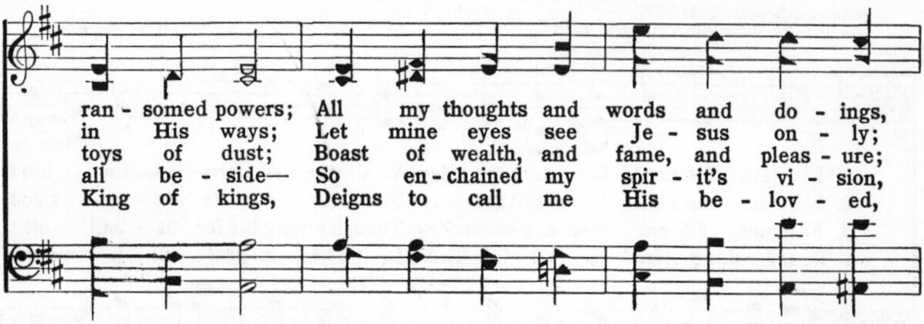

ran - somed powers; All my thoughts and words and do - ings,
in His ways; Let mine eyes see Je - sus on - ly;
toys of dust; Boast of wealth, and fame, and pleas - ure;
all be - side— So en - chained my spir - it's vi - sion,
King of kings, Deigns to call me His be - lov - ed,

All my days and all my hours.
Let my lips speak forth His praise.
On - ly Je - sus will I trust.
Look - ing at the Cru - ci - fied.
Lets me rest be - neath His wings. A - men.

108 Abide with Us, Our Saviour

ACH, BLEIB MIT DEINER GNADE 7. 6. 7. 6.

Josua Stegmann, 1628
Tr. unknown, 1848 | Melchior Vulpius, 1609

1. A - bide with us, our Sav - iour, Nor let Thy mer - cy cease;
2. A - bide with us, our Sav - iour, Sus - tain us by Thy Word;
3. A - bide with us, our Sav - iour, Thou Light of end-less Light,

From Sa-tan's might de-fend us, And grant our souls re-lease.
That we with all Thy peo-ple To life may be re-stored.
In-crease to us Thy bless-ings, And save us by Thy might. A-men.

By Cool Siloam's Shady Rill **109**

SILOAM C. M.

Reginald Heber, 1827 — Isaac Woodbury, 1842

1. By cool Siloam's shady rill
How sweet the lily grows!
How sweet the breath beneath the hill
Of Sharon's dewy rose!

2. Lo, such the child whose early feet
The paths of peace have trod;
Whose secret heart, with influence sweet,
Is upward drawn to God.

3. O Thou, whose infant feet were found
Within Thy Father's shrine,
Whose years, with changeless virtue crowned,
Were all alike divine;

4. Dependent on Thy bounteous breath,
We seek Thy grace alone
In childhood, manhood, age, and death,
To keep us still Thine own. Amen.

110 A Charge to Keep I Have

ST. THOMAS S. M.

Charles Wesley, 1762 | Aaron Williams, 1763

1. A charge to keep I have, A God to glo - ri - fy, A
2. To serve the pres - ent age, My call - ing to ful - fill; O
3. Arm me with jeal - ous care, As in Thy sight to live, And
4. Help me to watch and pray, And on Thy - self re - ly, As -
nev - er - dy - ing soul to save, And fit it for the sky.
may it all my pow'rs en - gage, To do my Mas - ter's will.
O, Thy ser - vant, Lord, pre - pare, A strict ac - count to give.
sured, if I my trust be - tray, I shall for - ev - er die. A-men.

111 Eternal God, We Look to Thee

WINCHESTER OLD C. M.

James Merrick, 1763 | Este's Psalter, 1592

1. E - ter - nal God, we look to Thee, To Thee for help we fly;
2. Lord, let Thy fear with - in us dwell, Thy love our foot - steps guide:
3. Not what we wish, but what we want, O let Thy grace sup - ply:

Thine eye a - lone our wants can see, Thy hand a - lone sup - ply.
That love will all vain love ex - pel; That fear, all fear be - side.
The good un-asked in mer - cy grant; The ill, though asked, de - ny. A-men.

Deck Thyself, My Soul, with Gladness 112

CRÜGER 8. 8. 8. 8. D.

J. Franck, 1650
Tr. Catherine Winkworth, Ab.

J. Crüger, 1649

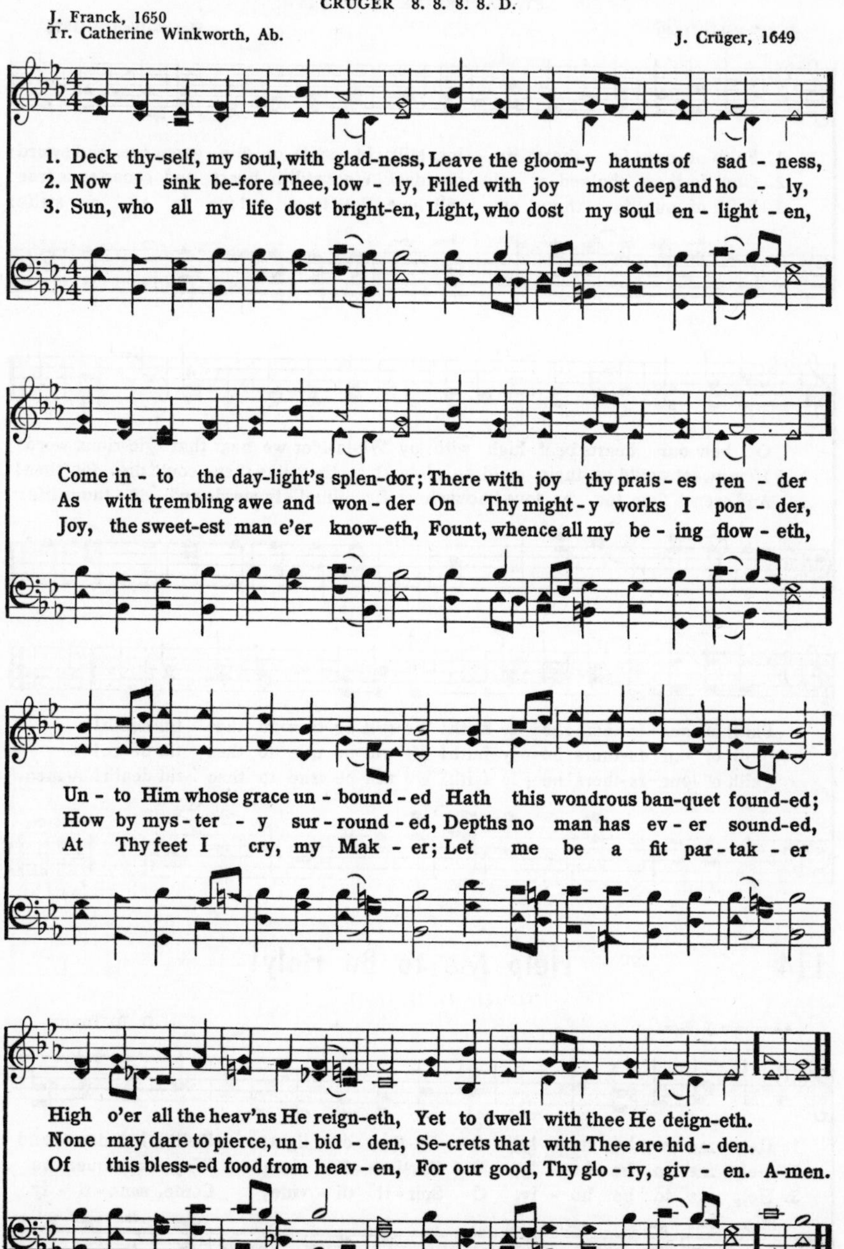
1. Deck thy-self, my soul, with glad-ness, Leave the gloom-y haunts of sad - ness,
2. Now I sink be-fore Thee, low - ly, Filled with joy most deep and ho - ly,
3. Sun, who all my life dost bright-en, Light, who dost my soul en - light - en,
Come in - to the day-light's splen-dor; There with joy thy prais - es ren - der
As with trembling awe and won - der On Thy might - y works I pon - der,
Joy, the sweet-est man e'er know-eth, Fount, whence all my be - ing flow - eth,
Un - to Him whose grace un - bound - ed Hath this wondrous ban-quet found-ed;
How by mys - ter - y sur - round - ed, Depths no man has ev - er sound-ed,
At Thy feet I cry, my Mak - er; Let me be a fit par-tak - er
High o'er all the heav'ns He reign-eth, Yet to dwell with thee He deign-eth.
None may dare to pierce, un - bid - den, Se-crets that with Thee are hid - den.
Of this bless-ed food from heav - en, For our good, Thy glo - ry, giv - en. A-men.

113 Faith of Our Fathers

ST. CATHERINE L. M. 6 L.

F. W. Faber, 1849 — Hemy—Walton, 1874

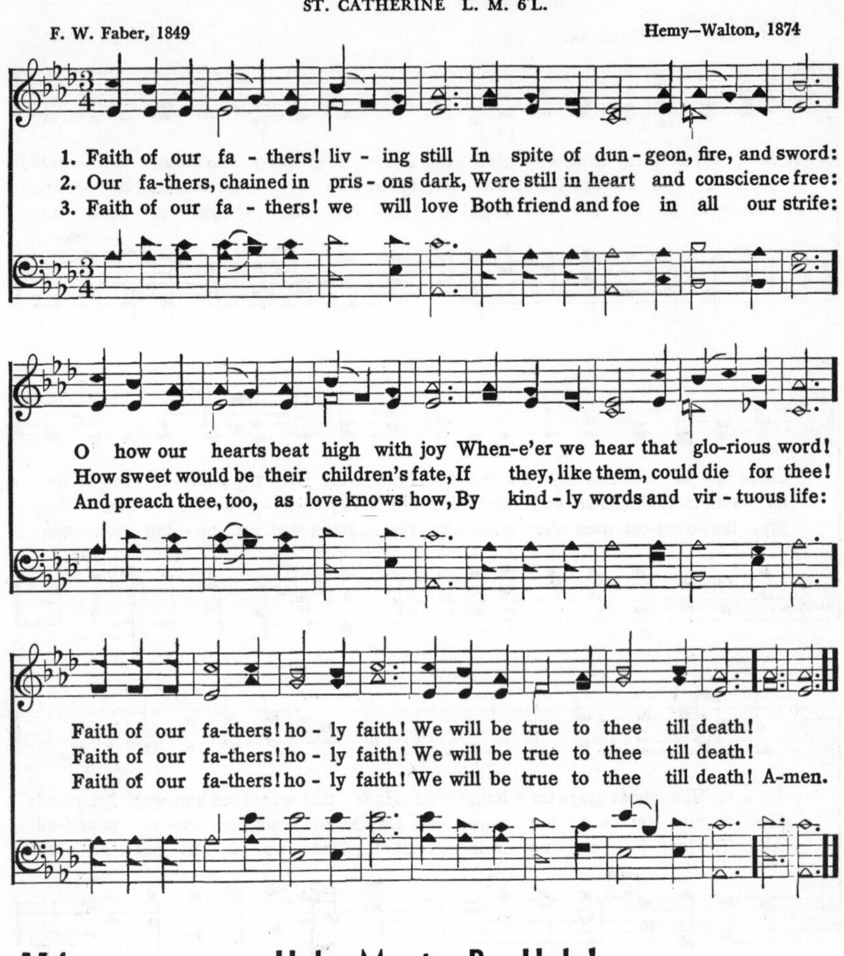
1. Faith of our fa - thers! liv - ing still In spite of dun - geon, fire, and sword:
2. Our fa-thers, chained in pris - ons dark, Were still in heart and conscience free:
3. Faith of our fa - thers! we will love Both friend and foe in all our strife:
O how our hearts beat high with joy When-e'er we hear that glo-rious word!
How sweet would be their children's fate, If they, like them, could die for thee!
And preach thee, too, as love knows how, By kind - ly words and vir - tuous life:
Faith of our fa-thers! ho - ly faith! We will be true to thee till death!
Faith of our fa-thers! ho - ly faith! We will be true to thee till death!
Faith of our fa-thers! ho - ly faith! We will be true to thee till death! A-men.

114 Help Me to Be Holy!

DANIEL 11. 11. 11. 11.

Adoniram J. Gordon — D. B. Towner

1. Help me to be ho - ly, O Fa-ther of light; Guilt - bur-dened and
2. Help me to be ho - ly, O Sav-iour di - vine; Why con-quer so
3. Help me to be ho - ly, O Spir - it di - vine; Come, sanc - ti - fy

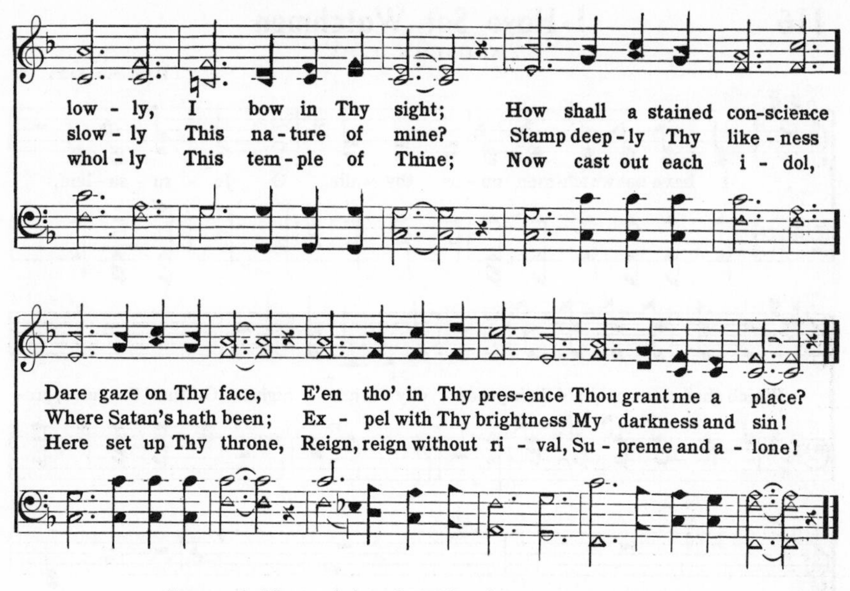

low - ly, I bow in Thy sight; How shall a stained con-science
slow - ly This na - ture of mine? Stamp deep - ly Thy like - ness
whol - ly This tem - ple of Thine; Now cast out each i - dol,
Dare gaze on Thy face, E'en tho' in Thy pres-ence Thou grant me a place?
Where Satan's hath been; Ex - pel with Thy brightness My darkness and sin!
Here set up Thy throne, Reign, reign without ri - val, Su - preme and a - lone!

Jesus! How Much Thy Name Unfolds 115

THY NAME 8. 6. 8. 6.

Mary Bowley Peters

William Arnold

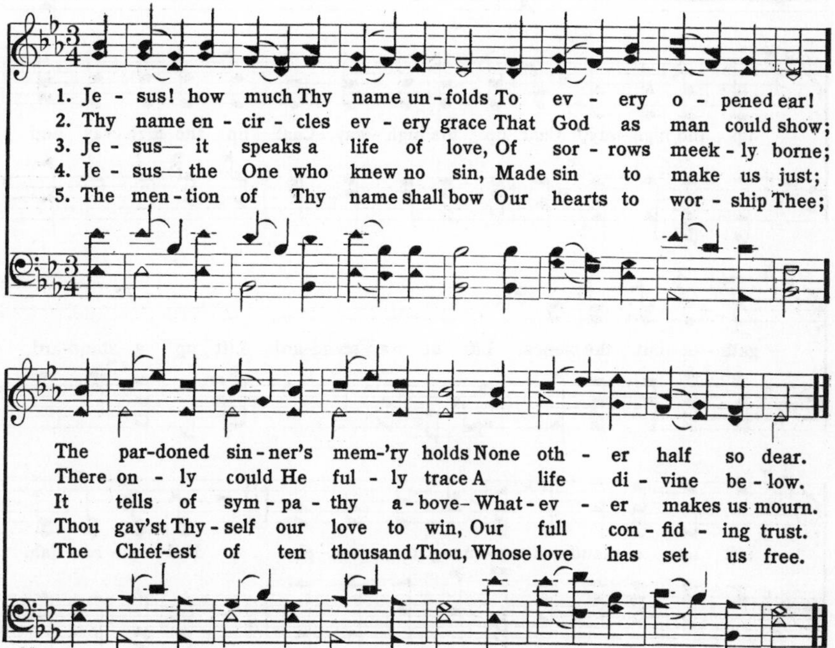

1. Je - sus! how much Thy name un - folds To ev - ery o - pened ear!
2. Thy name en - cir - cles ev - ery grace That God as man could show;
3. Je - sus— it speaks a life of love, Of sor - rows meek - ly borne;
4. Je - sus— the One who knew no sin, Made sin to make us just;
5. The men - tion of Thy name shall bow Our hearts to wor - ship Thee;

The par-doned sin - ner's mem-'ry holds None oth - er half so dear.
There on - ly could He ful - ly trace A life di - vine be - low.
It tells of sym - pa - thy a - bove— What - ev - er makes us mourn.
Thou gav'st Thy - self our love to win, Our full con - fid - ing trust.
The Chief-est of ten thousand Thou, Whose love has set us free.

116 I Have Set Watchmen

WATCHMEN P. M.
Harmonia Sacra
I have set watch-men up-on thy walls, O Je-ru-sa-lem,
Which shall nev-er hold their peace day nor night. Go thro' the gates, pre-
pare ye the way, pre-pare ye the way of the peo-ple. Cast
up the high-way, Cast up the high-way, Cast up the high-way and
gath-er out the stones. Lift up a stand-ard, Lift up a stand-ard,
Lift up a stand-ard a-mong the peo-ple. Hal-le-lu-jah,

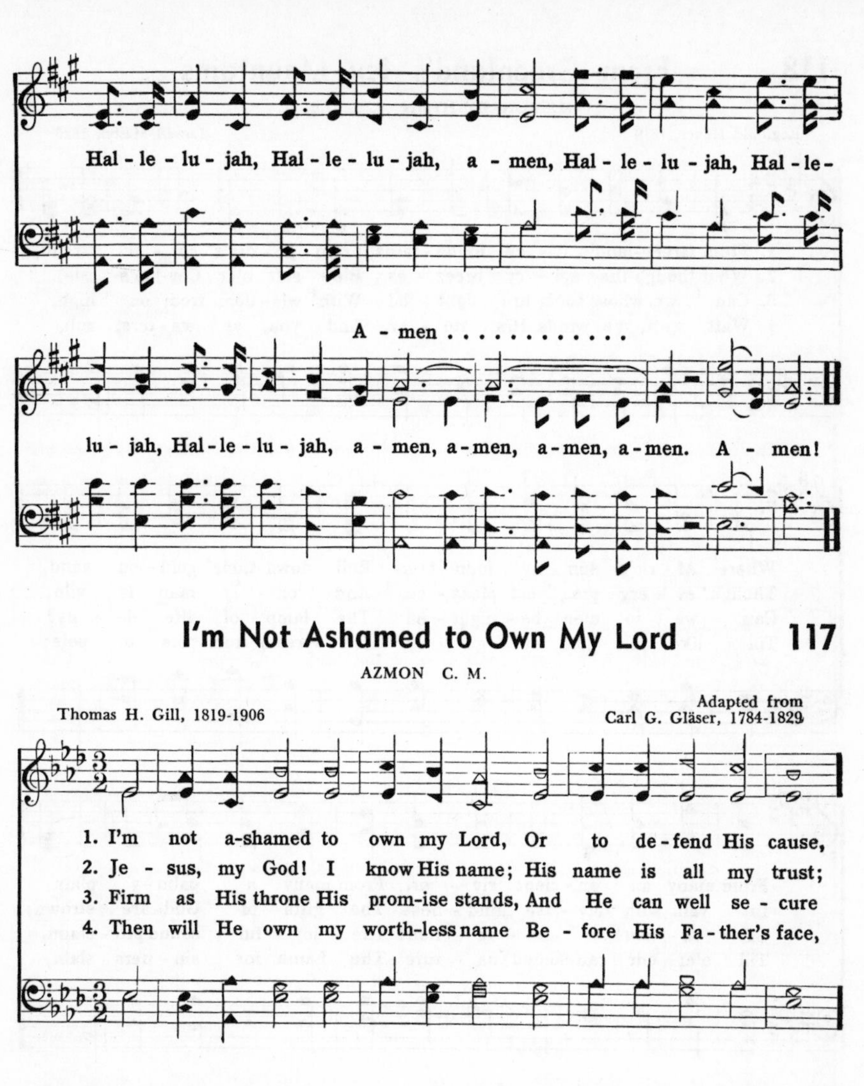

I'm Not Ashamed to Own My Lord 117

AZMON C. M.

Thomas H. Gill, 1819-1906

Adapted from Carl G. Gläser, 1784-1829

1. I'm not a-shamed to own my Lord, Or to de-fend His cause, Main-tain the hon - or of His Word, The glo - ry of His cross.

2. Je - sus, my God! I know His name; His name is all my trust; Nor will He put my soul to shame, Nor let my hope be lost.

3. Firm as His throne His prom-ise stands, And He can well se - cure What I've com-mit - ted to His hands Till the de - ci - sive hour.

4. Then will He own my worth-less name Be - fore His Fa - ther's face, And in the New Je - ru - sa - lem Ap - point my soul a place. A-men.

118 From Greenland's Icy Mountains

MISSIONARY HYMN 7. 6. 7. 6. D.

Reginald Heber, 1819
Lowell Mason, 1823
1. From Green-land's i - cy moun - tains, From In - dia's cor - al strand,
2. What though the spi - cy breez - es Blow soft o'er Cey-lon's isle,
3. Can we, whose souls are light - ed With wis - dom from on high,
4. Waft, waft, ye winds, His sto - ry, And you, ye wa - ters, roll,
Where Af - ric's sun - ny foun - tains Roll down their gold - en sand,
Though ev - ery pros - pect pleas - es, And on - ly man is vile;
Can we to men be - night - ed The lamp of life de - ny?
Till like a sea of glo - ry It spreads from pole to pole;
From many an an - cient riv - er, From many a palm - y plain,
In vain with lav - ish kind - ness The gifts of God are strown;
Sal - va - tion! O sal - va - tion! The joy - ful sound pro - claim,
Till o'er our ran-somed na - ture The Lamb for sin - ners slain,
They call us to de - liv - er Their land from er - ror's chain.
The hea - then in his blind-ness Bows down to wood and stone.
Till each re - mot - est na - tion Has learned Mes - si - ah's name.
Re - deem - er, King, Cre - a - tor, In bliss re - turns to reign. A-men.

Immortal Love, Within Whose Righteous Will 119

SANDON 10. 4. 10. 4. 10. 10.

Stopford A. Brooke, 1881 — Charles H. Purday, 1860

1. Im - mor - tal love, with - in whose right-eous will Is al - ways peace,
2. The days are gone, when far and wide my will Drove me a - stray;
3. What - e'er of pain Thy lov - ing hand al - lot I glad - ly bear;
4. So may I, far a - way, when eve - ning falls On life and love,
O pit - y me, storm-tossed on waves of ill; Let pas - sion cease;
And now I fain would climb the ar-duous hill, That nar - row way,
On - ly, O Lord, let peace be not for - got, Nor yet Thy care,
Ar - rive at last the ho - ly, hap - py halls, With Thee a - bove;
Come down in power with - in my heart to reign,
Which leads through mists and rocks to Thine a - bode,
Free - dom from storms, and wild de - sires with - in,
Wound - ed yet healed, sin - lad - en yet for - given,
For I am weak, and striv - ing has been vain.
Toil - ing for man, and Thee, Al - might - y God.
Peace from the fierce op - pres - sion of my sin.
And sure that good - ness is my on - ly heaven. A - men.

120 Join All the Glorious Names

CULLODEN 6. 6. 6. 6. 8. 8.

Isaac Watts — Walter E. Yoder

1. Join all the glo - rious names Of wis - dom, love, and power,
That mor - tals ev - er knew, Or an - gels ev - er bore:
All are too mean to speak His worth, Too mean to set the Sav - iour forth.

2. Great Proph - et of our God, Our tongues shall bless Thy name,
By Thee the joy - ful news Of our sal - va - tion came,
The joy - ful news of sins for - given, Of hell subdued, and peace with heaven.

3. Je - sus, our great High Priest, Has shed His blood and died;
Our guilt - y con - science needs No sac - ri - fice be - side:
His precious blood did once a - tone, And now it pleads be - fore the throne.

121 Lord of Might and Lord of Glory

ILIFF 8. 8. 8. 2. 7.

John S. Blackie, 1876 — Lindsay B. Longacre, 1912

1. Lord of might and Lord of glo - ry, On my
2. Grop - ing dim, and bend - ing low - ly, Mor - tal
3. In the deed that no man know - eth, Where no
4. In the work that no gold pay - eth, Where he
5. In His name, who meek and low - ly, Died to

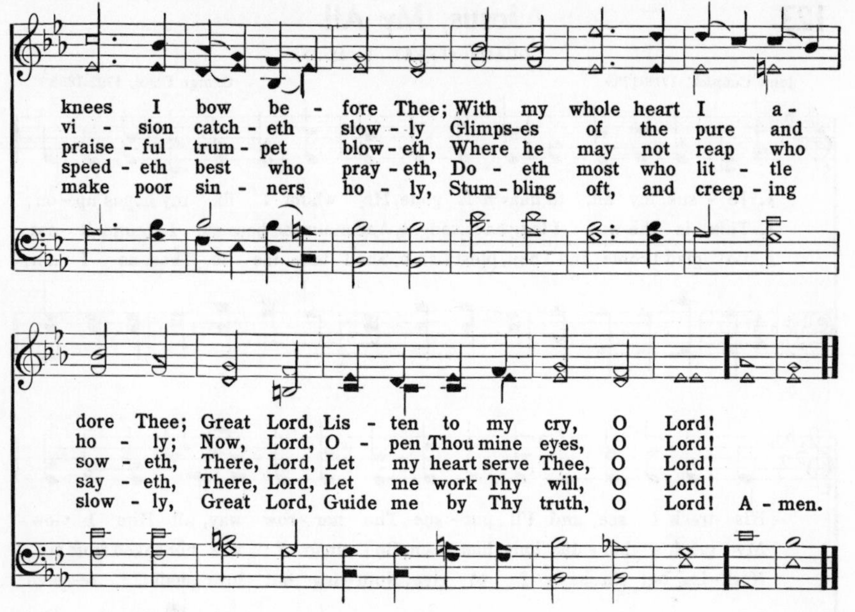

knees I bow be - fore Thee; With my whole heart I a -
vi - sion catch - eth slow - ly Glimps-es of the pure and
praise - ful trum - pet blow - eth, Where he may not reap who
speed - eth best who pray - eth, Do - eth most who lit - tle
make poor sin - ners ho - ly, Stum - bling oft, and creep - ing
dore Thee; Great Lord, Lis - ten to my cry, O Lord!
ho - ly; Now, Lord, O - pen Thou mine eyes, O Lord!
sow - eth, There, Lord, Let my heart serve Thee, O Lord!
say - eth, There, Lord, Let me work Thy will, O Lord!
slow - ly, Great Lord, Guide me by Thy truth, O Lord! A - men.

Lord, in the Fullness of My Might 122

ES IST EIN BORN 8. 6. 8. 6.

Thomas H. Gill — C. E. Miller

1. Lord, in the full - ness of my might, I would for Thee be strong;
2. I would not give the world my heart, And then pro - fess Thy love;
3. I would not with swift wing - ed zeal On the world's er - rands go:
4. O not for Thee my weak de - sires, My poor - er bas - er part!
5. O choose me in my gold - en time, In my dear joys have part!

While runneth o'er each dear de - light, To Thee should soar my song.
I would not feel my strength de - part, And then Thy serv - ice prove.
And la - bor up the heav'n - ly hill With wea - ry feet and slow.
O not for Thee my fad - ing fires, The ash - es of my heart.
For Thee the glo - ry of my prime, The full - ness of my heart. A - men.

123 Jesus, My All

DUANE STREET L. M. D.

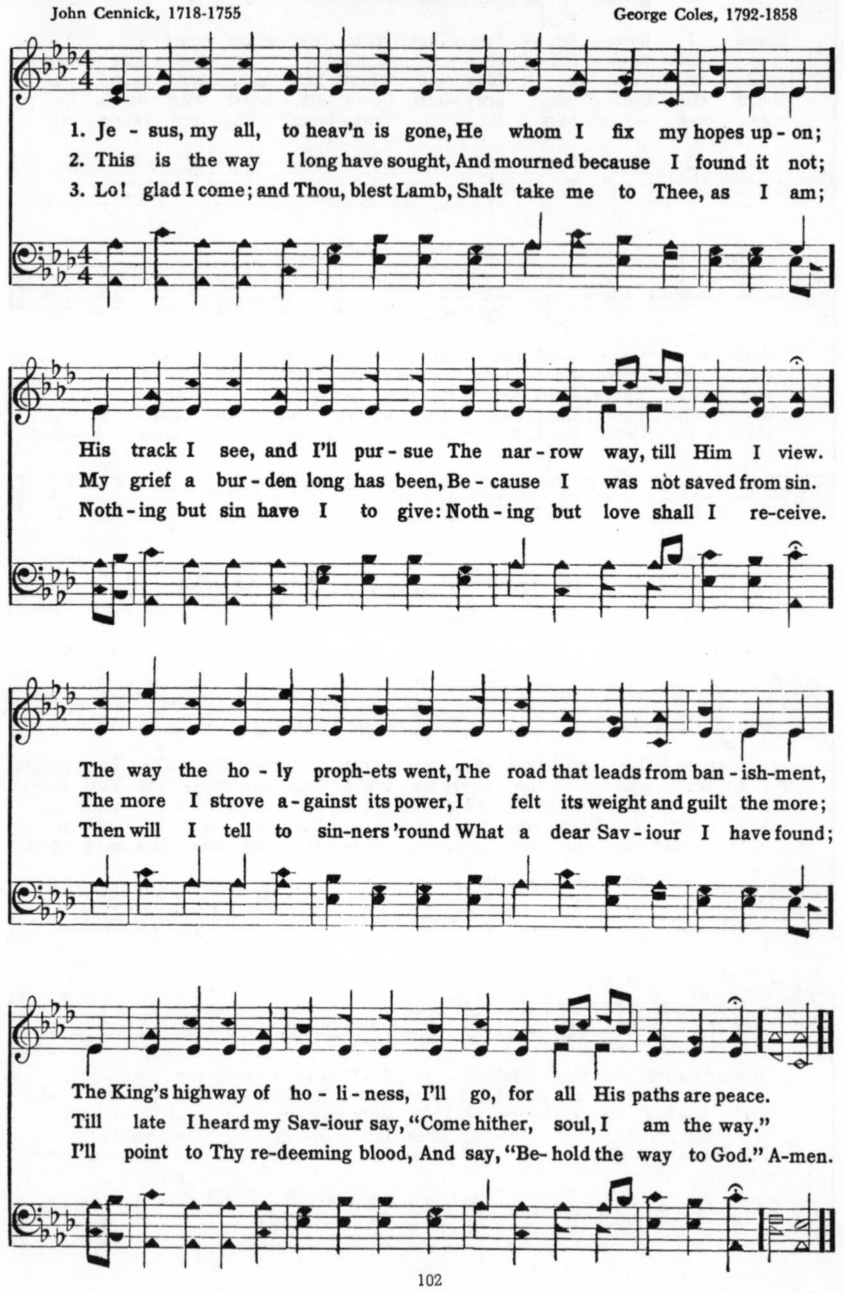

John Cennick, 1718-1755
George Coles, 1792-1858
1. Je - sus, my all, to heav'n is gone, He whom I fix my hopes up - on;
2. This is the way I long have sought, And mourned because I found it not;
3. Lo! glad I come; and Thou, blest Lamb, Shalt take me to Thee, as I am;
His track I see, and I'll pur - sue The nar - row way, till Him I view.
My grief a bur - den long has been, Be - cause I was not saved from sin.
Noth - ing but sin have I to give: Noth - ing but love shall I re-ceive.
The way the ho - ly proph-ets went, The road that leads from ban - ish-ment,
The more I strove a - gainst its power, I felt its weight and guilt the more;
Then will I tell to sin-ners 'round What a dear Sav - iour I have found;
The King's highway of ho - li - ness, I'll go, for all His paths are peace.
Till late I heard my Sav-iour say, "Come hither, soul, I am the way."
I'll point to Thy re-deeming blood, And say, "Be- hold the way to God." A-men.

Lamb of God! Our Souls Adore Thee 124

BEHOLD THE LAMB OF GOD 8. 7. 8. 7. D.

James G. Deck James Langran

1. Lamb of God! our souls a - dore Thee, While up - on Thy face we gaze;
2. Lamb of God! Thy Fa-ther's bo - som Ev - er was Thy dwell-ing place;
3. Lamb of God! When we be - hold Thee Low - ly in the man-ger laid,
4. When we see Thee, as the vic - tim, Bound to the ac - curs - ed tree,
5. Lamb of God, Thou soon in glo - ry Wilt to this sad earth re - turn;
There the Fa-ther's love and glo - ry Shine in all their bright-est rays;
His de-light, in Him re - joic - ing, One with Him in pow'r and grace;
Wan-d'ring as a home-less stran - ger In the world Thy hands had made;
For our guilt and fol - ly strick - en, All our judg-ment borne by Thee,
All Thy foes shall quake be - fore Thee, All that now de - spise Thee mourn;
Thine Al-might - y pow'r and wis - dom All cre - a - tion's works pro-claim;
Oh, what won-drous love and mer - cy! Thou didst lay Thy glo - ry by;
When we see Thee in the gar - den In Thine ag - o - ny of blood,
Lord, we own, with hearts a - dor - ing, Thou hast loved us un - to blood;
Then Thy saints all gath-ered to Thee, With Thee in Thy king-dom reign;
Heav'n and earth a - like con - fess Thee As the ev - er great "I AM."
And for us didst come from heav - en As the Lamb of God to die.
At Thy grace we are con-found - ed, Ho - ly, spot - less Lamb of God!
Glo - ry, glo - ry ev - er - last - ing Be to Thee, Thou Lamb of God.
Thine the praise and Thine the glo - ry, Lamb of God, for sin - ners slain!

125 Draw Us to Thee

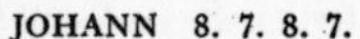
JOHANN 8. 7. 8. 7.

F. Fabricius, 1668
Tr. Catherine Winkworth
Har. J. S. Bach
1. Draw us to Thee, For then shall we Walk in Thy steps for - ev - er,
2. Draw us to Thee, Lord, lov - ing - ly; Let us de - part with glad - ness,
3. Draw us to Thee Un - ceas - ing - ly, In - to Thy king - dom take us;
And has - ten on where Thou art gone, To be with Thee, dear Sav - iour.
That we may be for - ev - er free From sor - row, grief and sad - ness.
Let us for - e'er Thy glo - ry share, Thy saints and joint-heirs make us.

126 Lord Jesus Christ, with Us Abide

SELNECKER L. M.

Tr. Anonymous
N. Selnecker

Melody—Dresden Hymn Book
Har. J. S. Bach

1. Lord Je - sus Christ, with us a - bide, For round us falls
2. In these last days of sore dis - tress Grant us, dear Lord,
3. And since the cause and glo - ry, Lord, Are Thine, not ours,

the e - ven - tide; Let not Thy Word, that heav'n - ly light,
true stead - fast - ness, That pure we keep, till life is spent,
do Thou af - ford Us help and strength and con - stan - cy;

For us be ev - - - er veiled in night.
Thy ho - ly Word and sac - ra - ment.
With all our hearts we trust in Thee.

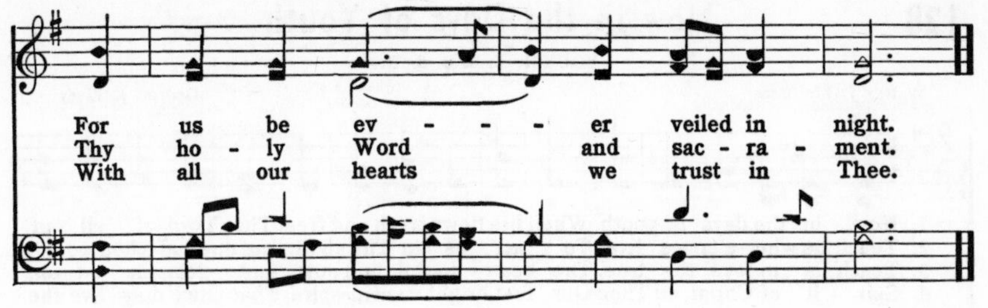

'Midst the Darkness, Storm, and Sorrow 127

TERSTEEGEN 8. 5. 8. 5. D.

Gerhard Tersteegen

Clara H. Scott

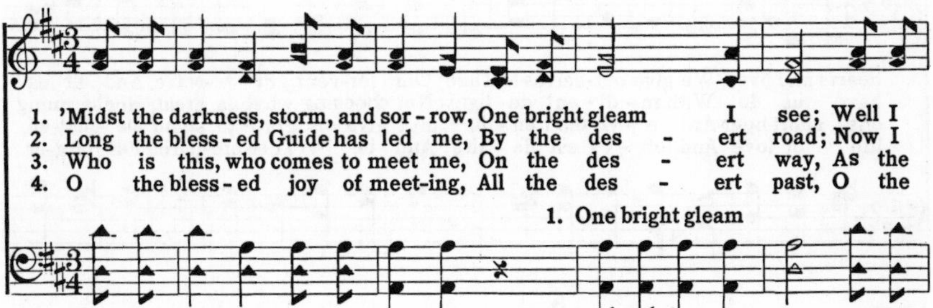

1. 'Midst the darkness, storm, and sor - row, One bright gleam I see; Well I
2. Long the bless - ed Guide has led me, By the des - ert road; Now I
3. Who is this, who comes to meet me, On the des - ert way, As the
4. O the bless - ed joy of meet - ing, All the des - ert past, O the
1. One bright gleam

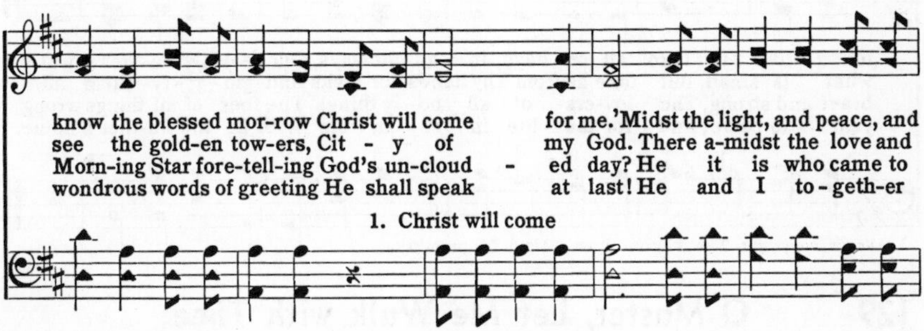

know the blessed mor - row Christ will come for me. 'Midst the light, and peace, and
see the gold - en tow - ers, Cit - y of my God. There a - midst the love and
Morn - ing Star fore - tell - ing God's un - cloud - ed day? He it is who came to
wondrous words of greeting He shall speak at last! He and I to - geth - er
1. Christ will come

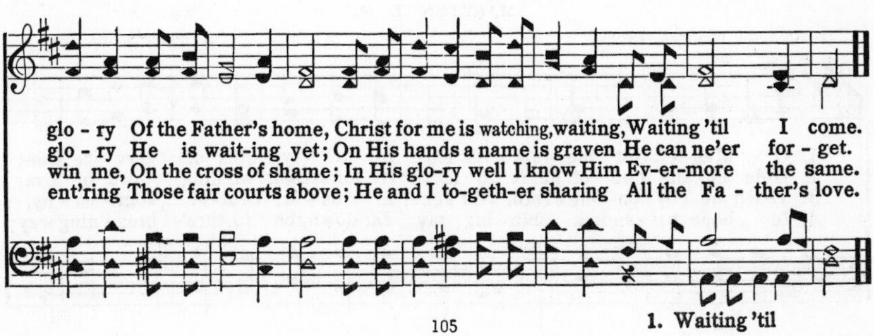

glo - ry Of the Father's home, Christ for me is watching, waiting, Waiting 'til I come.
glo - ry He is wait - ing yet; On His hands a name is graven He can ne'er for - get.
win me, On the cross of shame; In His glo - ry well I know Him Ev - er - more the same.
ent'ring Those fair courts above; He and I to - geth - er sharing All the Fa - ther's love.
1. Waiting 'til

128 Now in the Days of Youth

YOUTH 6. 6. 8. 6. D.

Walter J. Mathams — George J. Elvey

1. Now in the days of youth, When life flows fresh and free, Thou Lord of all our
2. Teach us wher-e'er we live, To act as in Thy sight, And do what Thou wouldst
3. Teach us to love the true, The beau - ti - ful and pure, And let us not for
4. Spir - it of Christ, do Thou Our first bright days in-spire, That we may live the

hearts and lives, We give our-selves to Thee; Our fer-vent gift re-ceive, And fit us
have us do With ra - di - ant de - light; Not choosing what is great, Nor spurning
one short hour An e - vil tho't en - dure. But give us grace to stand De - cid-ed,
life of love And loft - i - est de - sire; And be by Thee pre-pared For larg-er

to ful - fill, Thro' all our days, in all our ways, Our heav'nly Fa-ther's will.
what is small, But take as from Thy hands our tasks And glo - ri - fy them all.
brave and strong, The lov-ers of all ho - ly things, The foes of all things wrong.
years to come; And for the life in - ef - fa - ble With-in the Fa-ther's home.

129 O Master, Let Me Walk with Thee

MARYTON L. M.

Washington Gladden, 1879 — H. Percy Smith, 1874

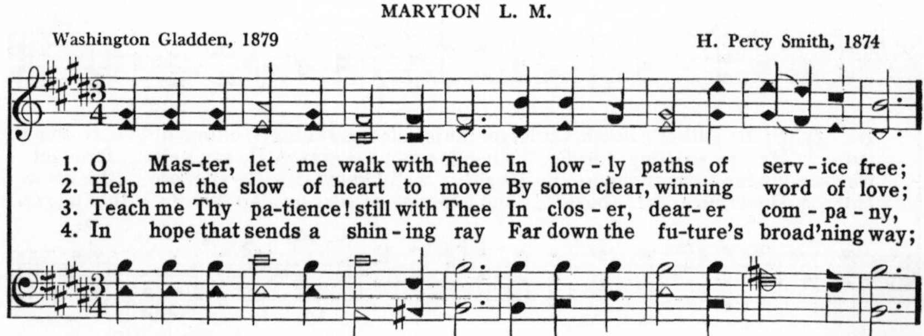
1. O Mas-ter, let me walk with Thee In low - ly paths of serv - ice free;
2. Help me the slow of heart to move By some clear, winning word of love;
3. Teach me Thy pa-tience! still with Thee In clos - er, dear- er com - pa - ny,
4. In hope that sends a shin - ing ray Far down the fu-ture's broad'ning way;

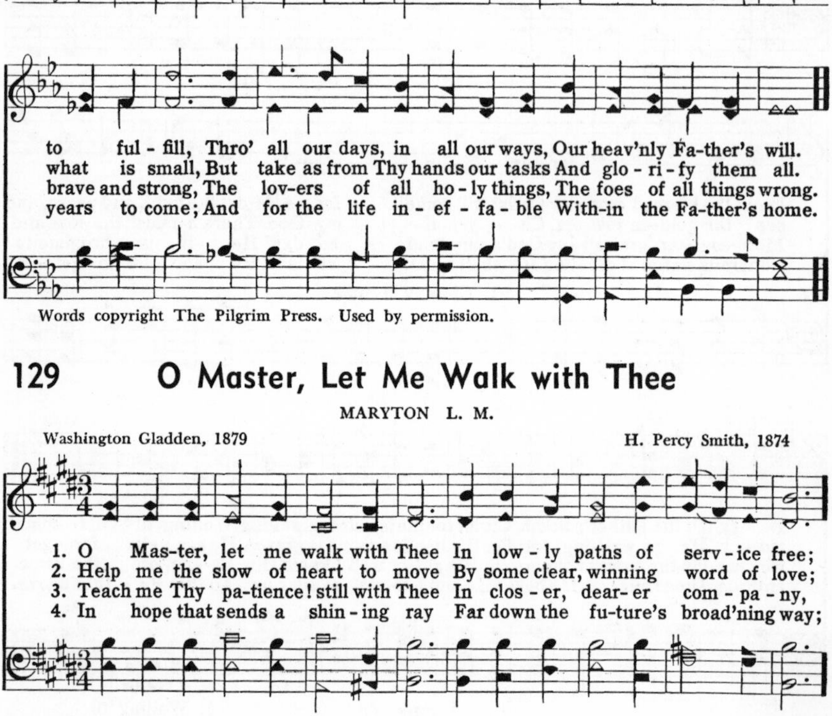

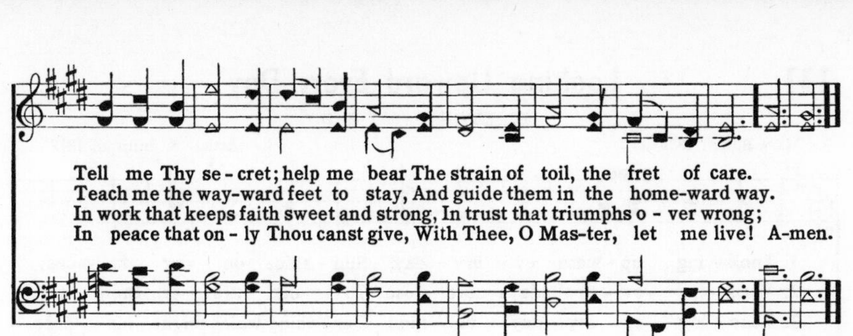
Tell me Thy se - cret; help me bear The strain of toil, the fret of care.
Teach me the way-ward feet to stay, And guide them in the home-ward way.
In work that keeps faith sweet and strong, In trust that triumphs o - ver wrong;
In peace that on - ly Thou canst give, With Thee, O Mas-ter, let me live! A-men.

O Thou God of My Salvation 130

REGENT SQUARE 8. 7. 8. 7. 8. 7.

Thomas Olivers

Henry Smart

1. O Thou God of my sal - va - tion, My Re - deem - er from all sin;
2. Though un - seen, I love the Sav-iour; He hath bro't sal - va - tion near;
3. While the an - gel choirs are cry - ing, "Glo - ry to the great I AM,"
4. An - gels now are hov - 'ring 'round us, Un - per - ceived a - mid the throng;

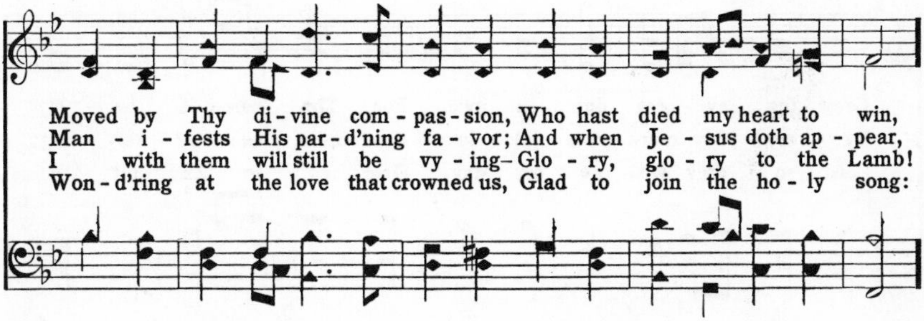

Moved by Thy di - vine com - pas - sion, Who hast died my heart to win,
Man - i - fests His par - d'ning fa - vor; And when Je - sus doth ap - pear,
I with them will still be vy - ing- Glo - ry, glo - ry to the Lamb!
Won - d'ring at the love that crowned us, Glad to join the ho - ly song:

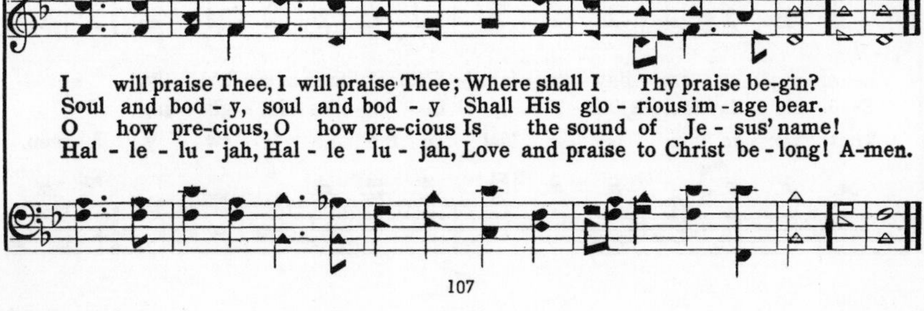

I will praise Thee, I will praise Thee; Where shall I Thy praise be-gin?
Soul and bod - y, soul and bod - y Shall His glo - rious im - age bear.
O how pre-cious, O how pre-cious Is the sound of Je - sus' name!
Hal - le - lu - jah, Hal - le - lu - jah, Love and praise to Christ be - long! A-men.

131 Looking Upward Every Day

ST. KEVIN 7. 6. 7. 6. D.

Mary Butler, 1881
Arthur S. Sullivan, 1872
1. Look - ing up - ward ev - ery day, Sun - shine on our fa - ces;
2. Walk - ing ev - ery day more close To our Eld - er Broth - er;
3. Leav - ing ev - ery day be - hind Some-thing which might hin - der;
Press - ing on - ward ev - ery day Toward the heaven - ly pla - ces;
Grow - ing ev - ery day more true Un - to one an - oth - er;
Run - ning swift - er ev - ery day, Grow - ing pur - er, kind - er,—
Grow - ing every day in awe, For Thy name is ho - ly;
Ev - ery day more grate - ful - ly Kind - ness - es re - ceiv - ing;
Lord, so pray we ev - ery day, Hear us in Thy pit - y,
Learn - ing ev - ery day to love With a love more low - ly;
Ev - ery day more read - i - ly In - ju - ries for - giv - ing;
That we en - ter in at last To the ho - ly cit - y. A - men.

O Jesus, Prince of Life

SEND ME 8. 6. 8. 6. D.

Anonymous

Roy E. Nolte

1. O Je - sus, Prince of life and truth, Be - neath Thy ban - ner bright,
2. In ser - ried ranks, with fear - less tread, O Cap - tain of us all,
3. O Je - sus, once a Naz-'reth boy, And tempt - ed like as we,
We ded - i - cate our strength and youth To the bat - tle for the right;
Thy glo - ry on our ban - ners shed, As we an - swer to Thy call;
All in - ward foes help us de - stroy, Ev - er spot - less all to be.
We give our lives with glad in - tent To serve the world and Thee,
And where the fierc - est bat - tles press A - gainst the hosts of sin,
We trust Thee for the grace to win The high, vic - to - rious goal,
To die, to suf - fer and be spent To set our broth - ers free.
To res - cue those in dire dis - tress We glad - ly en - ter in.
Where pu - ri - ty shall con - quer sin In Christ-like self - con - trol.

133 Rise, My Soul, and Stretch Thy Wings

AMSTERDAM 7. 6. 7. 6. 7. 7. 7. 6.

Robert Seagrave, 1742, altered

James Nares, 1715-1783

1. Rise, my soul, and stretch thy wings, Thy bet - ter por - tion trace;
2. Cease, my soul, O cease to mourn! Press on - ward to the prize;
Rise from tran - si - to - ry things, Toward heaven, thy des - tined place.
Soon the Sav - iour will re - turn, To take thee to the skies.
Sun and moon and stars de - cay, Time shall soon this earth re - move;
There is ev - er - last - ing peace, Rest, en - dur - ing rest, in heaven;
Rise, my soul, and haste a - way To seats pre-pared a - bove.
There will sor - row ev - er cease, And crowns of joy be given. A - men.

Rise Up, O Men of God 134

WALTER 6. 6. 8. 6.

William P. Merrill — William H. Walter

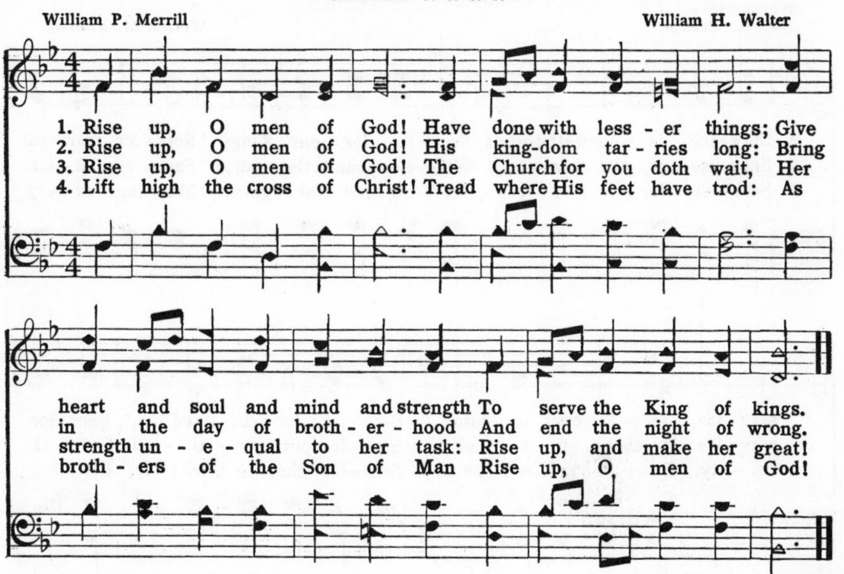
1. Rise up, O men of God! Have done with less - er things; Give
2. Rise up, O men of God! His king-dom tar - ries long: Bring
3. Rise up, O men of God! The Church for you doth wait, Her
4. Lift high the cross of Christ! Tread where His feet have trod: As
heart and soul and mind and strength To serve the King of kings.
in the day of broth - er - hood And end the night of wrong.
strength un - e - qual to her task: Rise up, and make her great!
broth - ers of the Son of Man Rise up, O men of God!

Praise the Saviour, Ye Who Know Him! 135

FELLOWSHIP 8. 8. 8. 8.

Thomas Kelly — Traditional German Melody

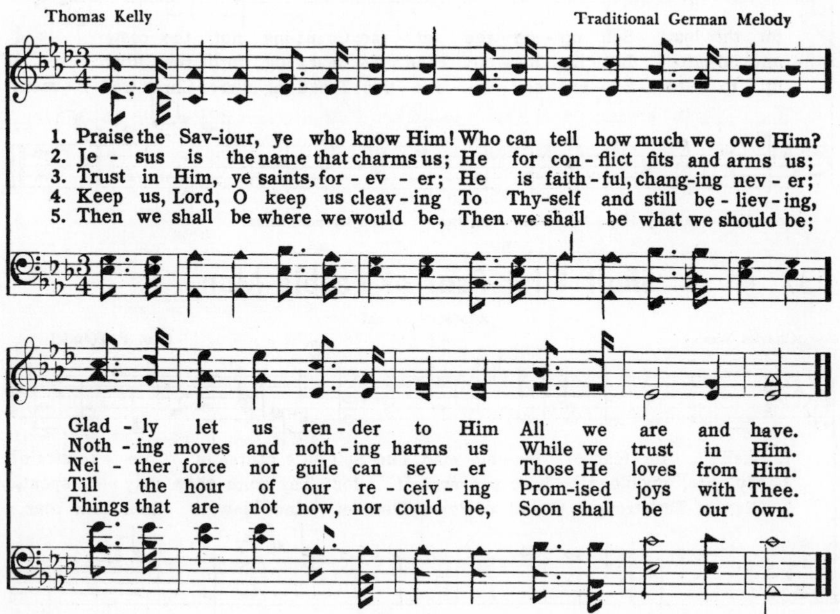
1. Praise the Sav-iour, ye who know Him! Who can tell how much we owe Him?
2. Je - sus is the name that charms us; He for con - flict fits and arms us;
3. Trust in Him, ye saints, for - ev - er; He is faith - ful, chang-ing nev - er;
4. Keep us, Lord, O keep us cleav - ing To Thy-self and still be - liev - ing,
5. Then we shall be where we would be, Then we shall be what we should be;
Glad - ly let us ren - der to Him All we are and have.
Noth - ing moves and noth - ing harms us While we trust in Him.
Nei - ther force nor guile can sev - er Those He loves from Him.
Till the hour of our re - ceiv - ing Prom-ised joys with Thee.
Things that are not now, nor could be, Soon shall be our own.

136 Service Is Our Watchword

SERVICE 6. 5. 6. 5. 6. 5.

William Shaw
John R. Clements

William M. Runyan

1. Serv-ice is our watch-word, Serv-ice for our King;
2. Serv-ice in the home-land Wher-e'er sounds the call;
3. Serv-ice o'er the o-cean, Serv-ing not for gain;

Serv-ice, fruit-ful serv-ice, Dai-ly ours to bring. Serv-ice for the need-y, Serv-ice for the lost;
Sac-ri-fi-cial serv-ice Reaching un-to all; Serv-ice pure, ex-alt-ed; Loy-al and un-priced;
Meet-ing ev-ery du-ty, Be it toil or pain; Serv-ice that is Christ-ly, Giv-ing up to God

Self up-on the al-tar; Count-ing not the cost.
Liv-ing, lov-ing chan-nels, Bear-ing forth the Christ.
Ev-ery self-ish mo-tive; Tread-ing where Christ trod. A-men.

137 Shall I for Fear of Feeble Man

SAMSON L. M.

Charles Wesley

Geo. F. Handel

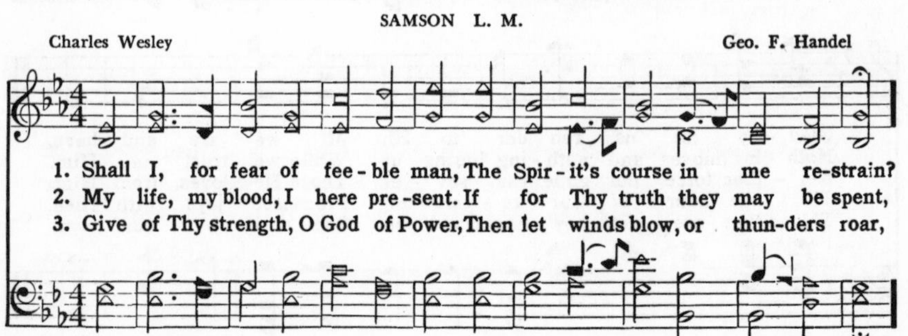
1. Shall I, for fear of fee-ble man, The Spir-it's course in me re-strain?
2. My life, my blood, I here pre-sent. If for Thy truth they may be spent,
3. Give of Thy strength, O God of Power, Then let winds blow, or thun-ders roar,

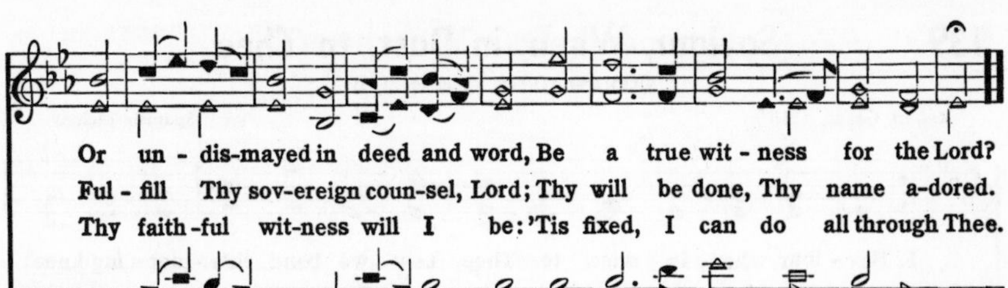

Or un - dis-mayed in deed and word, Be a true wit - ness for the Lord?
Ful - fill Thy sov-ereign coun-sel, Lord; Thy will be done, Thy name a-dored.
Thy faith-ful wit-ness will I be: 'Tis fixed, I can do all through Thee.

Soldiers of Christ, Arise 138

ELMSWOOD S. M. D.

Charles Wesley Isaac B. Woodbury

1. Sol - diers of Christ, a - rise, And put your ar-mor on, Strong in the strength which
2. Stand, then, in His great might, With all His strength endued; But take, to arm you
3. Leave no unguard-ed place, No weak-ness of the soul; Take ev - ery vir - tue

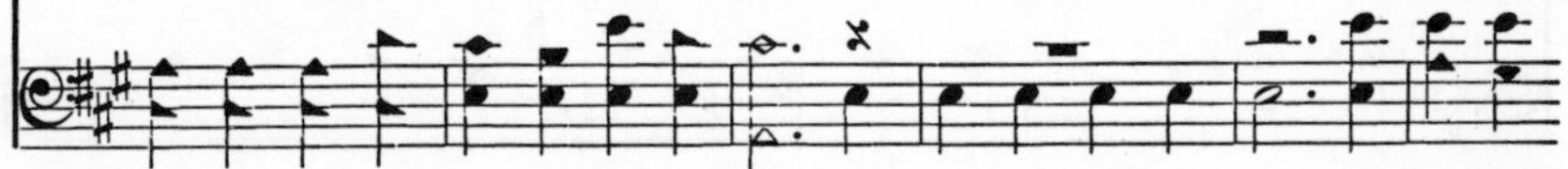

God sup-plies Thro' His e - ter-nal Son; Strong in the Lord of hosts, And in His
for the fight, The pan - o - ply of God; That, hav-ing all things done, And all your
ev - ery grace, And for - ti - fy the whole: In - dis - sol - u - bly joined, To bat-tle

might - y pow'r, Who in the strength of Je-sus trusts Is more than con-quer-or.
con-flicts passed, Ye may o'er-come thro' Christ a-lone, And stand en-tire at last.
all pro - ceed; But arm yourselves with all the mind That was in Christ your Head.

139 Saviour, When, in Dust, to Thee

SPANISH HYMN 7. 7. 7. 7. D.

Robert Grant, 1815
Spanish Melody
1. Sav - iour, when, in dust, to Thee, Low we bend th'a - dor - ing knee;
2. By Thy birth and ear - ly years, By Thy hu - man griefs and fears,
3. By Thine hour of dark de - spair, By Thine ag - o - ny of prayer,
When, re - pent - ant, to the skies, Scarce we lift our stream - ing eyes;
By Thy fast - ing and dis - tress In the lone - ly wil - der - ness:
By Thy pur - ple robe of scorn, By Thy wounds–Thy crown of thorn,
O by all Thy pains and woe Suf - fer'd once for man be - low,
By Thy vic - t'ry in the hour Of the sub - tle temp - ter's pow'r;
By Thy cross–Thy pangs and cries, By Thy per - fect sac - ri - fice;
Bend - ing from Thy throne on high, Hear Thy peo - ple when they cry.
Je - sus, look with pity - ing eye; Hear Thy peo - ple while they cry.
Je - sus, look with pity - ing eye; Hear Thy peo - ple while they cry. A-men.

Strive Aright When God Doth Call Thee 140

RINGE RECHT 8. 7. 8. 7.

Johann J. Winkler
Tr. Catherine Winkworth

From Gnadauer Choralbuch

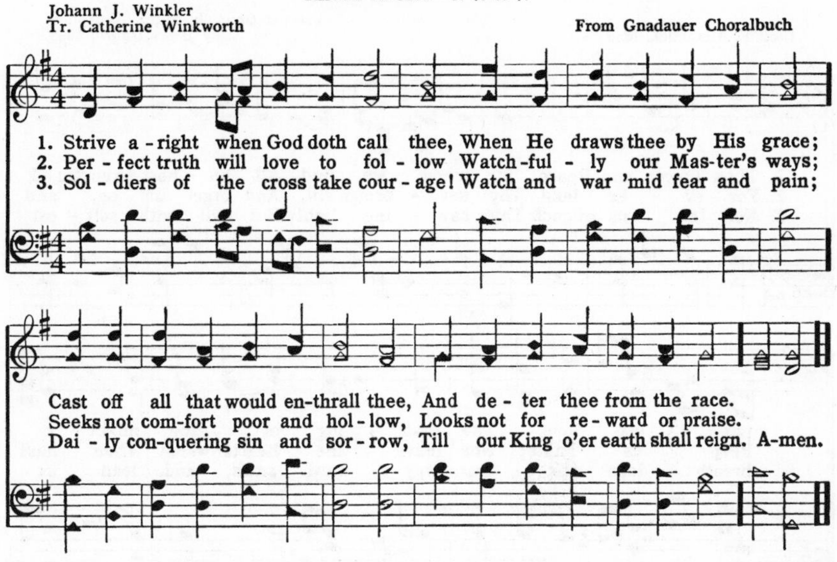

1. Strive a-right when God doth call thee, When He draws thee by His grace;
2. Per-fect truth will love to fol-low Watch-ful-ly our Mas-ter's ways;
3. Sol-diers of the cross take cour-age! Watch and war 'mid fear and pain;
Cast off all that would en-thrall thee, And de-ter thee from the race.
Seeks not com-fort poor and hol-low, Looks not for re-ward or praise.
Dai-ly con-quering sin and sor-row, Till our King o'er earth shall reign. A-men.

When I Can Read My Title Clear 141

NINETY-FIFTH C. M.

Isaac Watts

Arr. by J. H. H.

1. When I can read my ti-tle clear To mansions in the skies, I bid farewell to
2. Should earth against my soul engage, And fi-ery darts be hurled, Then I can smile at
3. Let cares like a wild deluge come, And storms of sor-row fall! May I but safe-ly
4. There shall I bathe my wea-ry soul In seas of heav'n-ly rest, And not a wave of
ev-ery fear, I bid fare-well to ev-ery fear, And wipe my weep-ing eyes.
Sa-tan's rage, Then I can smile at Sa-tan's rage, And face a frown-ing world.
reach my home, May I but safe-ly reach my home, My God, my heav'n, my all.
trou-ble roll, And not a wave of trou-ble roll A-cross my peace-ful breast.

142 Thou Power and Peace

ST. VINCENT L. M.

Cecil F. Alexander, 1858

Adapted from Sigismund Neukomm
By James Uglow, 1868

1. Thou Power and Peace, in whom we find All ho - liest strength, all pur - est love, The rush - ing of the might - y wind, The brood - ing of the gen - tle dove!
2. For - ev - er lend Thy sov - ereign aid, And urge us on, and keep us Thine; Nor leave the hearts which Thou hast made Fit tem - ples of Thy grace di - vine.
3. Nor let us quench Thy sav - ing light; But still with soft - est breath - ings stir Our way - ward souls, and lead us right, O Ho - ly Spir - it, Com - fort - er. A - men.

143 Where Cross the Crowded Ways of Life

GERMANY L. M.

Frank Mason North

Ludwig van Beethoven

1. Where cross the crowd-ed ways of life, Where sound the cries of race and clan,
2. In haunts of wretch-ed - ness and need, On shadowed thresh-olds dark with fears,
3. The cup of wa - ter given for Thee Still holds the freshness of Thy grace;
4. O Mas-ter, from the mountain side, Make haste to heal these hearts of pain,
5. Till sons of men shall learn Thy love And fol - low where Thy feet have trod:

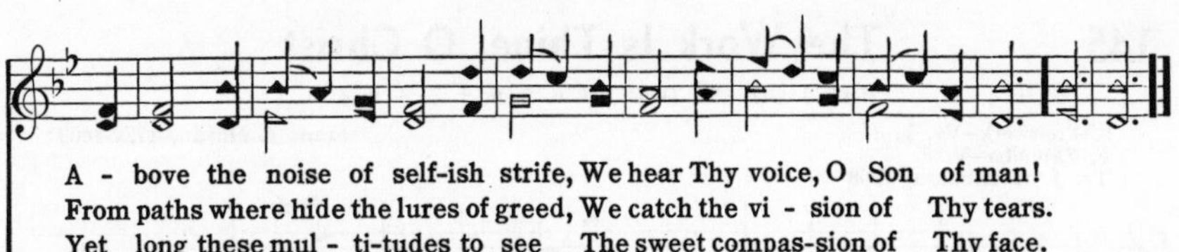

A - bove the noise of self-ish strife, We hear Thy voice, O Son of man!
From paths where hide the lures of greed, We catch the vi - sion of Thy tears.
Yet long these mul - ti-tudes to see The sweet compas-sion of Thy face.
A - mong these restless throngs a-bide, O tread the cit - y's street a-gain;
Till glo-rious from Thy heaven a-bove Shall come the cit - y of our God. A-men.

Ye Christian Heralds, Go Proclaim 144

MISSIONARY CHANT L. M.

Bourne H. Draper, 1803 — Charles Zeuner, 1832

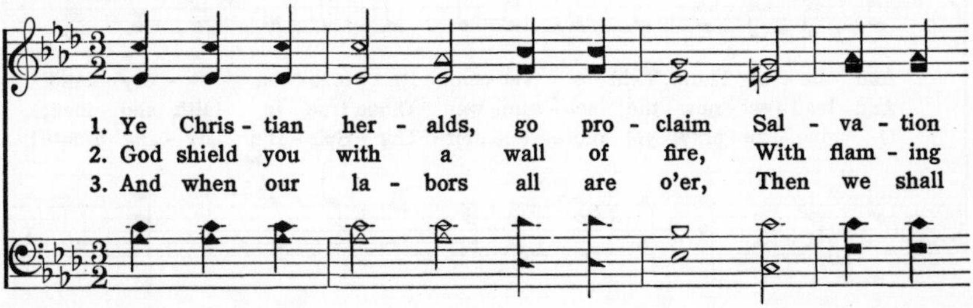

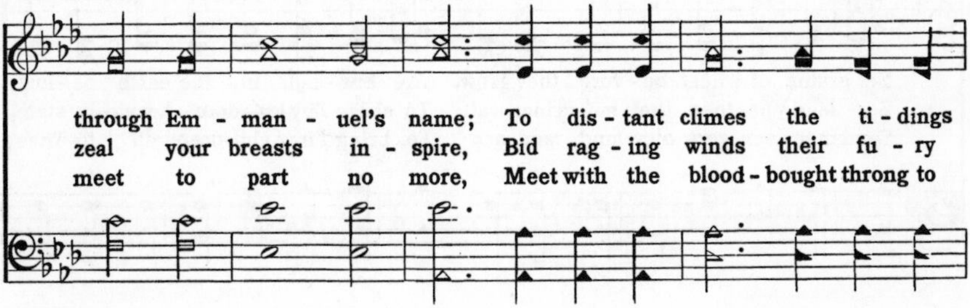

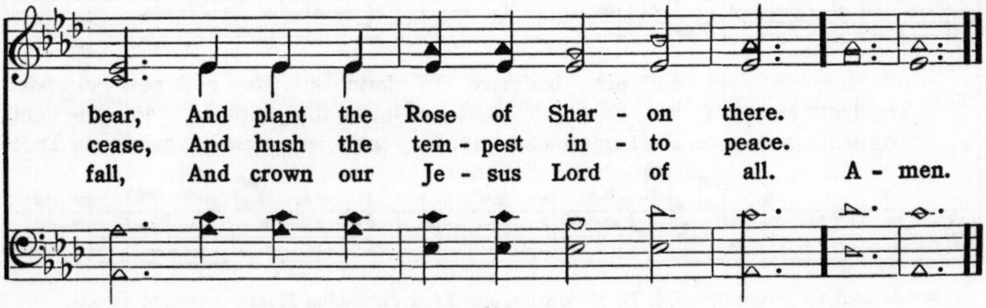

1. Ye Chris - tian her - alds, go pro - claim Sal - va - tion through Em - man - uel's name; To dis - tant climes the ti - dings bear, And plant the Rose of Shar - on there.

2. God shield you with a wall of fire, With flam - ing zeal your breasts in - spire, Bid rag - ing winds their fu - ry cease, And hush the tem - pest in - to peace.

3. And when our la - bors all are o'er, Then we shall meet to part no more, Meet with the blood - bought throng to fall, And crown our Je - sus Lord of all. A - men.

145 The Work Is Thine, O Christ

DIE SACH' IST DEIN 8. 6. 8. 6. 8. 8. 8. 8. 4. 6.

S. Preiswerk—Vv. 1, 2
F. Zaremba—V. 3
Tr. J. Horstmann, 1908
Franz J. Haydn, 1732-1809
1. The work is Thine, O Christ our Lord, The cause for which we stand;
2. Thro' suf-f'ring Thou, O Christ, didst go Un - to Thy throne a - bove,
3. Thou hast, O Sav-iour, led the way Thro' ag - o - ny and death;
And be - ing Thine, 'twill o - ver-come Its foes on ev - ery hand.
And lead - est now the self - same way Those true in faith and love;
O give, we pray, yet more and more Thy Spir - it's liv - ing breath!
Yet grains of wheat be - fore they grow, Are bur - ied in the earth be - low;
So lead us, then, tho' suf-f'rings wait, To share Thy kingdom's heav'n-ly state,
Send mes - sen-gers o'er land and sea To bring Thy chil-dren all to Thee;
All that is old doth per - ish there To form a life both new and fair:
Thy death has bro - ken Sa - tan's might, And leads the faith-ful to the light;
Thy name can save, Thy name makes free; We con - se - crate our-selves to Thee

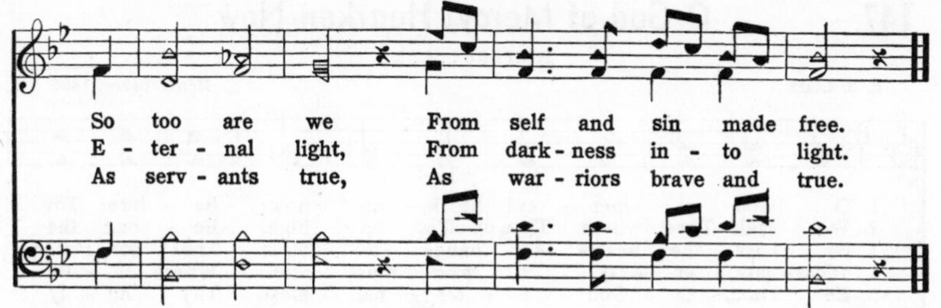
So too are we From self and sin made free.
E - ter - nal light, From dark - ness in - to light.
As serv - ants true, As war - riors brave and true.

O Spirit of the Living God 146

MELCOMBE L. M.

Acts 2: 3
James Montgomery, 1823

Samuel Webbe, 1782

1. O Spir - it of the liv - ing God, In
2. Give tongues of fire and hearts of love To
3. Be dark - ness, at Thy com - ing, light; Con -
4. O Spir - it of the Lord, pre - pare A

all Thy plen - i - tude of grace, Wher - e'er the foot of
preach the rec - on - cil - ing Word; Give pow'r and unc - tion
fu - sion, or - der, in Thy path; Souls with - out strength in -
sin - ful world their God to meet; Breathe Thou a - broad like

man hath trod, De - scend on our a - pos - tate race.
from a - bove Wher - e'er the joy - ful sound is heard.
spire with might; Bid mer - cy tri - umph o - ver wrath.
morn - ing air Till hearts of stone be - gin to beat. A-men.

147 O God of Mercy! Hearken Now

HESPERUS L. M.

E. S. Clark | Henry Baker, 1866

1. O God of mer - cy! heark - en now; Be - fore Thy
2. We seek Thee where Thou dwell'st on high, Be - yond the
3. Be ours the hearts and hands to bless The sor - r'wing
4. Where pov - er - ty in pain must lie, Where lit - tle
5. Be Thou, O God e - ter - nal, blest, Thy ho - ly
throne we hum - bly bow; With heart and voice to Thee we
glit - t'ring, star - ry sky: We find Thee where Thou dwell'st be -
sons of wretch - ed - ness; Send Thou the help we can - not
suf - f'ring chil - dren cry, Bid us haste forth as called by
name on earth con - fessed! Ech - o Thy praise from ev - ery
cry, For all on earth who suf - f'ring lie.
low Be - side the beds of want and woe.
give; Bid dy - ing souls a - rise and live.
Thee, And in Thy poor, Thy - self to see.
shore For - ev - er and for - ev - er - more. A - men.

148 Ye Servants of the Lord

OLD 134th S. M.

Phillip Doddridge | Geneva Psalter, 1551

1. Ye serv - ants of the Lord, Each in his of - fice wait,
2. O let your lamps be bright, And trim the gold - en flame;
3. Watch: 'tis your Lord's com - mand And while we speak He's near;
4. Christ shall the ban - quet spread With His own Roy - al hand,

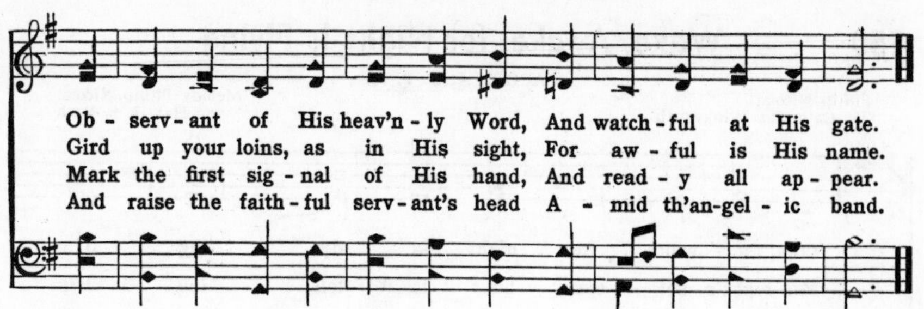
Ob - serv - ant of His heav'n - ly Word, And watch - ful at His gate.
Gird up your loins, as in His sight, For aw - ful is His name.
Mark the first sig - nal of His hand, And read - y all ap - pear.
And raise the faith - ful serv - ant's head A - mid th'an - gel - ic band.

Thou, Whose Almighty Word 149

PERKINS 6. 6. 4. 6. 6. 6. 4.

John Marriott E. A. Perkins

1. Thou, whose al - might - y word Cha - os and dark - ness heard,
2. Thou who didst come to bring On Thy re - deem - ing wing,
3. Spir - it of truth and love, Life - giv - ing, ho - ly Dove,
4. Ho - ly and bless - ed Three, Glo - ri - ous Trin - i - ty,

And took their flight; Hear us, we hum - bly pray, And where the
Heal - ing and sight, Health to the sick in mind, Sight to the
Speed forth Thy flight; Move o'er the wa - ters' face Bear - ing the
Wis - dom, Love, Might; Bound - less as o - cean's tide Roll - ing in

Gos - pel day Sheds not its glo - rious ray, Let there be light!
in - ly blind; O now, to all man-kind, Let there be light!
lamp of grace; And in earth's dark - est place, Let there be light!
full - est pride, Through the world far and wide, Let there be light!

150 Wake, Awake, for Night Is Flying

WACHET AUF P. M.

Philip Nicolai
Tr. Catherine Winkworth

Melody Philip Nicolai
Har. J. S. Bach

1. Wake, a - wake, for night is fly - ing: The
Mid-night's sol - emn hour is toll - ing, His
watch - men on the heights are cry - ing A -
char - iot wheels are near - er roll - ing, He
wake, Je - ru - sa - lem, a - rise.
comes! pre - pare, ye vir - gins wise.
Rise up with
will - ing feet, Go forth the Bride - groom meet: Al -

le - lu - ia. Bear through the night your well - trimm'd
light Speed forth to join the mar - riage rite.

Fierce Raged the Tempest 151

ST. AELRED 8. 8. 8. 3.

Godfrey Thring, 1861

John B. Dykes, 1823-1876

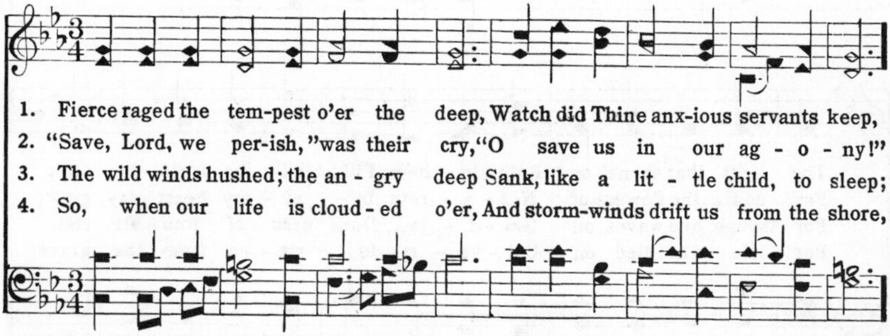

1. Fierce raged the tem-pest o'er the deep, Watch did Thine anx-ious servants keep,
2. "Save, Lord, we per-ish," was their cry, "O save us in our ag - o - ny!"
3. The wild winds hushed; the an - gry deep Sank, like a lit - tle child, to sleep;
4. So, when our life is cloud - ed o'er, And storm-winds drift us from the shore,

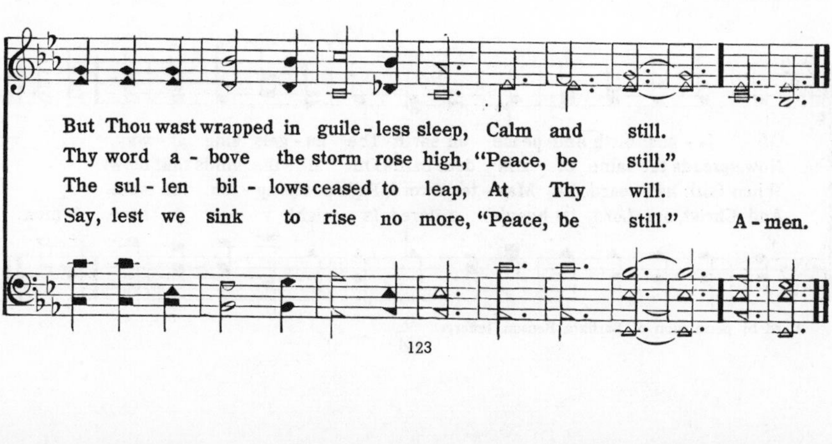

But Thou wast wrapped in guile - less sleep, Calm and still.
Thy word a - bove the storm rose high, "Peace, be still."
The sul - len bil - lows ceased to leap, At Thy will.
Say, lest we sink to rise no more, "Peace, be still." A - men.

152 O Sing a Song of Bethlehem

BETHLEHEM C. M. D.
Louis F. Benson, 1855-1930
Gottfried W. Fink, 1842
1. O sing a song of Beth-le-hem, Of shep-herds watch-ing there,
2. O sing a song of Naz-a-reth, Of sun-ny days of joy,
3. O sing a song of Gal-i-lee, Of lake and woods and hill,
4. O sing a song of Cal-va-ry, Its glo-ry and dis-may;
And of the news that came to them From an-gels in the air:
O sing of fra-grant flow-ers' breath, And of the sin-less Boy:
Of Him who walked up-on the sea And bade its waves be still:
Of Him who hung up-on the tree And took our sins a-way:
The light that shone on Beth-le-hem Fills all the world to-day;
For now the flowers of Naz-a-reth In ev-ery heart may grow;
For though, like waves on Gal-i-lee, Dark seas of trou-ble roll,
For He who died on Cal-va-ry Is ris-en from the grave,
Of Je-sus' birth and peace on earth The an-gels sing al-way.
Now spreads the fame of His dear name On all the winds that blow.
When faith has heard the Mas-ter's word, Falls peace up-on the soul.
And Christ, our Lord, by heav'n a-dored, Is might-y now to save. A-men.

The King Shall Come When Morning Dawns 153

JERUSALEM, JERUSALEM C. M. D.

From the Greek: Tr. John Brownlie, 1907 Thomas Hastings, 1784-1872

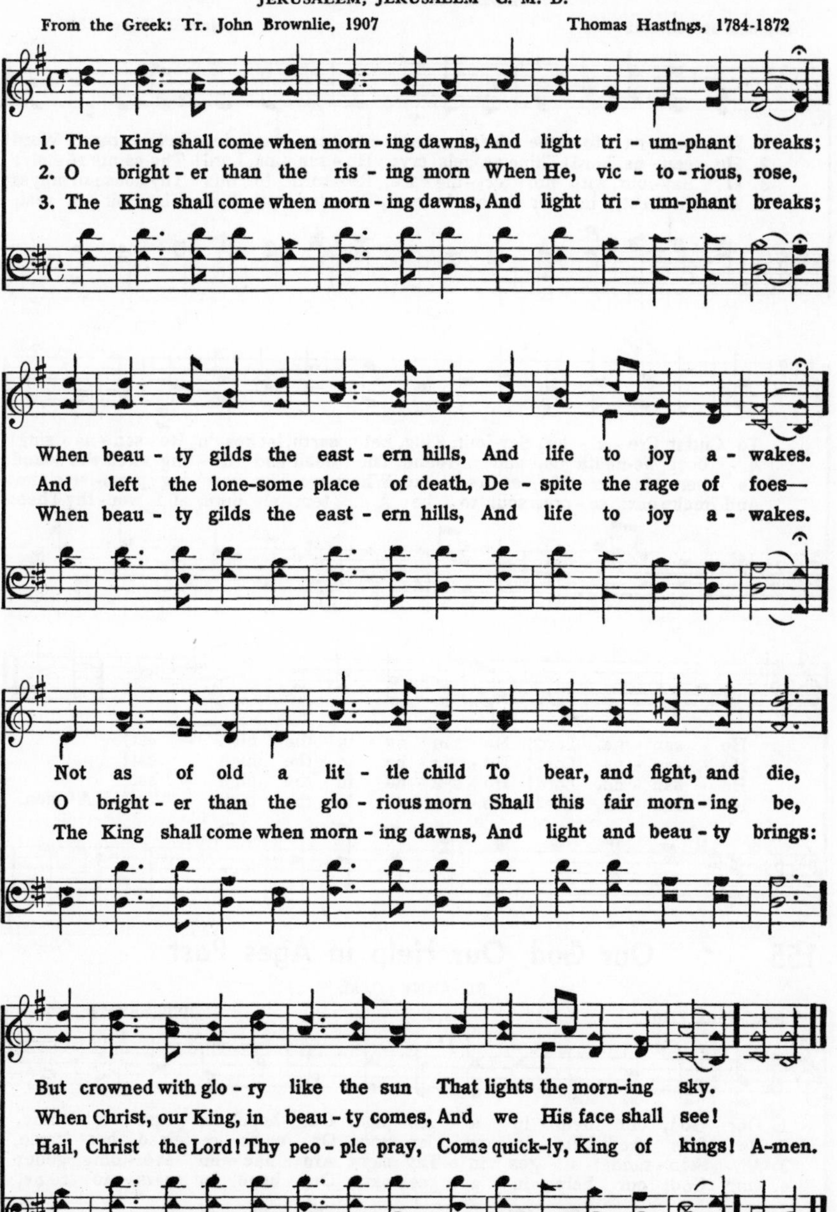

1. The King shall come when morn - ing dawns, And light tri - um-phant breaks;
2. O bright - er than the ris - ing morn When He, vic - to - rious, rose,
3. The King shall come when morn - ing dawns, And light tri - um-phant breaks;
When beau - ty gilds the east - ern hills, And life to joy a - wakes.
And left the lone-some place of death, De - spite the rage of foes—
When beau - ty gilds the east - ern hills, And life to joy a - wakes.
Not as of old a lit - tle child To bear, and fight, and die,
O bright - er than the glo - rious morn Shall this fair morn - ing be,
The King shall come when morn - ing dawns, And light and beau - ty brings:
But crowned with glo - ry like the sun That lights the morn-ing sky.
When Christ, our King, in beau - ty comes, And we His face shall see!
Hail, Christ the Lord! Thy peo - ple pray, Come quick-ly, King of kings! A-men.

From *Hymns of the Russian Church* by permission of the Oxford University Press.

154 Hosanna to the Living Lord

HOSANNA L. M. Ref.

Reginald Heber, 1812 | John B. Dykes, 1865

1. Ho - san - na to the liv - ing Lord! Ho - san - na to th'in-car-nate Word!
2. Ho - san - na, Lord! Thine an-gels cry; Ho - san - na, Lord! Thy saints re - ply;
3. O Sav-iour, with pro - tect - ing care, Re - turn to this Thy house of prayer;
4. But, chief-est, in our cleansed breast, E - ter - nal, bid Thy Spir - it rest,
To Christ, Cre - a - tor, Sav-iour, King, Let earth, let heav'n, Ho - san - na sing!
A - bove, be-neath us, and a-round, The dead and liv - ing swell the sound:
As - sem-bled in Thy sa-cred name, Where we Thy part - ing prom-ise claim:
And make our se - cret soul to be A tem - ple pure, and wor - thy Thee:
Ho - san - na, Lord! Ho - san - na in the high - est!
Ho - san - na, Lord! Ho - san - na in the high - est!
Ho - san - na, Lord! Ho - san - na in the high - est!
Ho - san - na, Lord! Ho - san - na in the high - est! A - men.

155 Our God, Our Help in Ages Past

ST. ANNE C. M.

Isaac Watts, 1719 | William Croft, 1708

1. Our God, our help in a - ges past, Our hope for years to come,
2. Be - fore the hills in or - der stood, Or earth re-ceived her frame,
3. A thou - sand a - ges in Thy sight Are like an eve - ning gone;
4. Our God, our help in a - ges past, Our hope for years to come,

Our shel - ter from the storm - y blast, And our e - ter - nal home!
From ev - er - last - ing Thou art God, To end - less years the same.
Short as the watch that ends the night, Be - fore the ris - ing sun.
Be Thou our guard while life shall last, And our e - ter - nal home. A-men.

Christ Is Coming! Let Creation 156

NEANDER 8. 7. 8. 7. 8. 7.

John R. Macduff, 1818-1895

Joachim Neander, 1650-1680

1. Christ is com - ing! let cre - a - tion From her groans and trav - ail cease;
2. Earth can now but tell the sto - ry Of Thy bit - ter cross and pain;
3. Long Thine ex - iles have been pin - ing, Far from rest, and home, and Thee:
4. With that bless - ed hope be - fore us, Let no harp re - main un - strung;
Let the glo - rious proc - la - ma - tion Hope re - store and faith in - crease:
She shall yet be - hold Thy glo - ry, When Thou com - est back to reign:
But, in heaven - ly ves - tures shin - ing, They their lov - ing Lord shall see:
Let the might - y ad - vent cho - rus On - ward roll from tongue to tongue:
Christ is com-ing! Christ is com-ing! Come, Thou bless-ed Prince of Peace.
Christ is com-ing! Christ is com-ing! Let each heart re - peat the strain.
Christ is com-ing! Christ is com-ing! Haste the joy - ous ju - bi - lee.
"Christ is com-ing! Christ is com-ing! Come, Lord Je - sus, quick-ly come!" A-men.

157 Glorious Things of Thee Are Spoken

AUSTRIAN HYMN 8. 7. 8. 7. D.

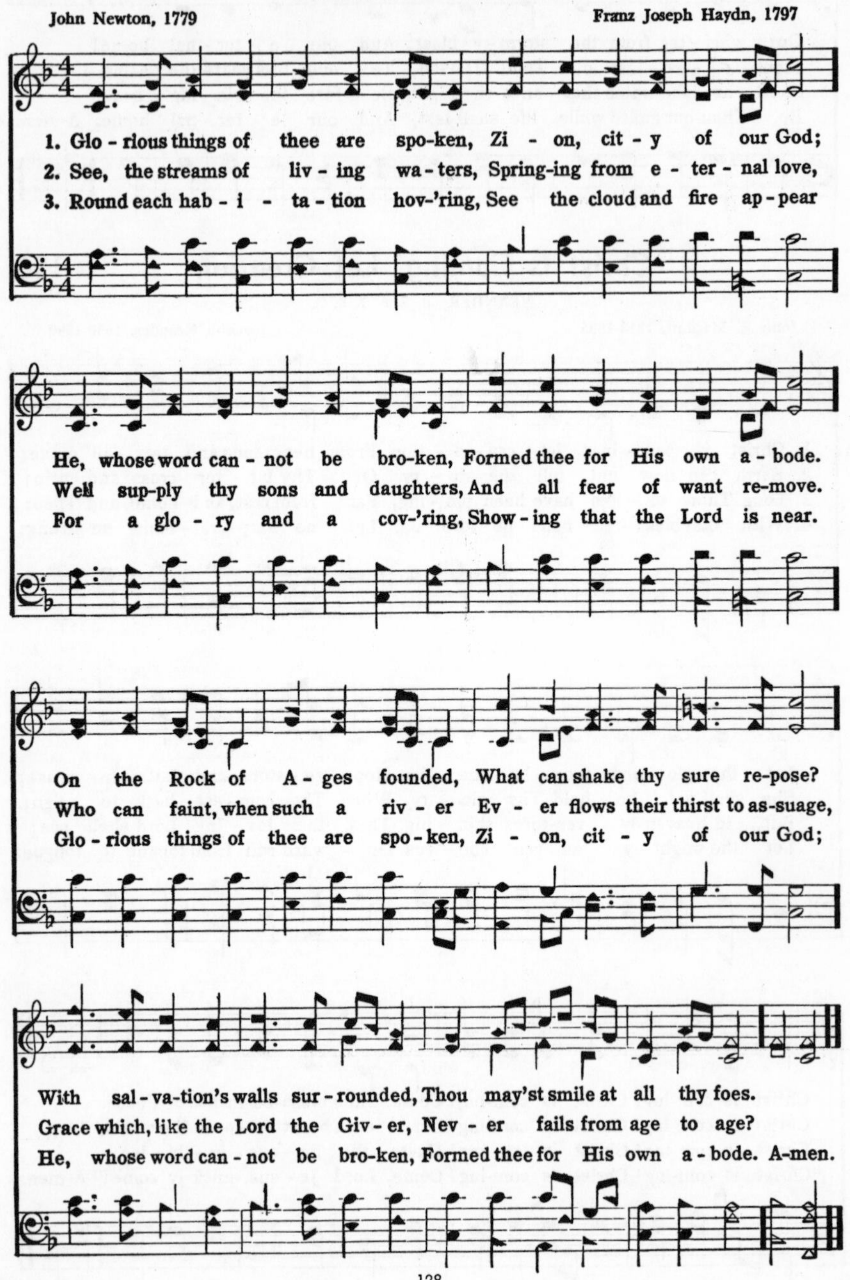
John Newton, 1779
Franz Joseph Haydn, 1797
1. Glo - rious things of thee are spo-ken, Zi - on, cit - y of our God;
2. See, the streams of liv - ing wa - ters, Spring-ing from e - ter - nal love,
3. Round each hab - i - ta - tion hov-'ring, See the cloud and fire ap - pear
He, whose word can - not be bro-ken, Formed thee for His own a - bode.
Well sup-ply thy sons and daughters, And all fear of want re-move.
For a glo - ry and a cov-'ring, Show - ing that the Lord is near.
On the Rock of A - ges founded, What can shake thy sure re-pose?
Who can faint, when such a riv - er Ev - er flows their thirst to as-suage,
Glo - rious things of thee are spo - ken, Zi - on, cit - y of our God;
With sal - va - tion's walls sur - rounded, Thou may'st smile at all thy foes.
Grace which, like the Lord the Giv - er, Nev - er fails from age to age?
He, whose word can - not be bro - ken, Formed thee for His own a - bode. A-men.

God of the Living Church

158

ACKLEY C. M. D.
A. H. Ackley
B. D. Ackley
1. God of the liv - ing church, em - pow'r, Thine an - cient might re - veal;
2. God of the liv - ing church, pro - vide, Not gar-nished words, but grain,
3. God of the liv - ing church, for - give, Re - new, per - fect, trans - late,
Give wis - dom for this cru - cial hour, And in Thy mer - cy, heal.
The char - i - ty Thou hast sup - plied, May we sup-ply a - gain.
In Thee to be, and move, and live, Im - man - u - el, we wait.
God of the liv - ing church, re - new, Fresh vi - sion now im - part, And
God of the liv - ing church, de - ny The reb - el cav - al - cade, That
God of the liv - ing church, we plead, Be - stow Thy might - y pow'r, Thy
tho' the rem-nant be but few, Sus - tain each faith-ful heart.
thun-ders forth its hate - de - fy 'Gainst all that Thou hast made.
lov - ing pres-ence, Lord, we need, To save us in this hour. A - men.

159 Jesus, from Whom All Blessings Flow

DUANE STREET L. M. D.

Rev. Geo. Cole

1. Je - sus, from whom all bless-ings flow, Great build-er of Thy church be - low;
2. O let them all Thy mind ex-press, Stand forth Thy cho-sen wit-ness - es;
3. Call them in - to Thy wondrous light, Wor - thy to walk with Thee in white;
If now Thy Spir - it move my breast, Hear, and ful - fill Thine own re - quest.
Thy power un - to sal - va - tion show, And per-fect ho - li - ness be - low.
Make up Thy jew - els, Lord, and show Thy glo-rious spot-less church be - low.
The few that tru - ly call Thee Lord, And wait Thy sanc - ti - fy - ing word,
In them let all man-kind be - hold How Chris-tians lived in days of old;
From ev - ery sin - ful wrin - kle free, Re-deemed from all in - iq - ui - ty,
And Thee their ut-most Sav-iour own—U - nite and per - fect them in one.
Might-y their en-vious foes to move– A prov-erb of re - proach and love.
The fel - low-ship of saints make known, And oh, my God, may I be one.

Unto Thy Temple, Lord, We Come 160

MENDON L. M.
Robert Collyer, 1873
German Melody arr. by Samuel Dyer, 1828
1. Un - to Thy tem - ple, Lord, we come With thank-ful hearts to wor - ship Thee;
2. The com-mon home of rich and poor, Of bond and free, and great and small;
3. And dwell Thou with us in this place, Thou and Thy Christ, to guide and bless.
4. May Thy whole truth be spo - ken here; Thy Gos - pel light for - ev - er shine;
And pray that this may be our home Un - til we touch e - ter - ni - ty;
Large as Thy love for - ev - er-more, And warm and bright and good to all.
Here make the well-springs of Thy grace Like fountains in the wil - der-ness.
Thy per - fect love cast out all fear, And hu-man life be - come di-vine. A-men.
Within Thy Tabernacle, Lord 161
TALLIS' ORDINAL C. M.
Psalm 15
Scottish Psalter, 1650
Thomas Tallis, c. 1520-1585
1. With - in Thy tab - er - na - cle, Lord, Who shall a - bide with Thee?
2. The man that walk - eth up - right - ly, And work - eth right-eous - ness,
3. Who doth not slan - der with his tongue, Nor to his friend doth hurt;
4. In whose eyes vile men are de - spised; But those that God do fear
5. His coin puts not to u - su - ry, Nor take re - ward will he
And in Thy high and ho - ly hill Who shall a dwell - er be?
And as he think-eth in his heart, So doth he truth ex - press:
Nor yet a-gainst his neigh-bor doth Take up an ill re - port:
He hon - or - eth; and chang-eth not, Though to his hurt he swear:
A - gainst the guilt-less. Who doth thus Shall nev - er mov - ed be. A-men.

162 Eternal Father

WAREHAM L. M.

Hervey D. Ganse, 1872 — William Knapp, 1738

1. E - ter - nal Fa - ther, when to Thee, Be - yond all
2. But, Sav - iour, Thou art by my side; Thy voice I
3. And Thou, great Spir - it, in my heart Dost make Thy
4. Blest Trin - i - ty, in whom a - lone All things cre -

worlds, by faith I soar, Be - fore Thy bound - less
hear, Thy face I see: Thou art my Friend, my
tem - ple day by day; The Ho - ly Ghost of
a - ted move or rest, High in the heav'ns Thou

maj - es - ty I stand in si - lence, and a - dore.
dai - ly Guide; God o - ver all, yet God with me.
God Thou art, Yet dwell - est in this house of clay.
hast Thy throne; Thou hast Thy throne with - in my breast.

163 Breathe on Me, Breath of God

TRENTHAM S. M.

Edwin Hatch, 1886 — Robert Jackson, 1894

1. Breathe on me, Breath of God, Fill me with life a - new, That I may
2. Breathe on me, Breath of God, Un - til my heart is pure, Un - til with
3. Breathe on me, Breath of God, Till I am whol - ly Thine, Till all this
4. Breathe on me, Breath of God, So shall I nev - er die, But live with

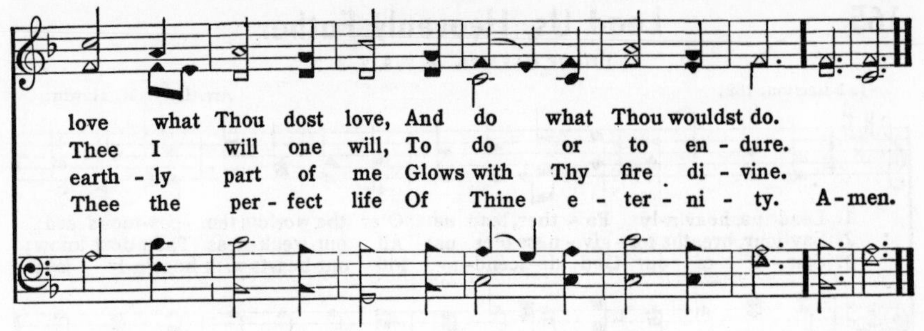
love what Thou dost love, And do what Thou wouldst do.
Thee I will one will, To do or to en - dure.
earth - ly part of me Glows with Thy fire di - vine.
Thee the per - fect life Of Thine e - ter - ni - ty. A - men.

Hover O'er Me, Holy Spirit 164

FILL ME NOW 8. 7. 8. 7. 6. 7. Ref.

Rev. E. H. Stokes, D. D. — John R. Sweney

1. Hov - er o'er me, Ho - ly Spir - it, Bathe my trembling heart and brow;
2. Thou canst fill me, gra - cious Spir - it, Tho' I can - not tell Thee how;
3. I am weak - ness, full of weak - ness; At Thy sa - cred feet I bow;
4. Cleanse and com - fort, bless and save me; Bathe, oh, bathe my heart and brow;

FINE

Fill me with Thy hal - lowed pres - ence, Come, oh, come and fill me now.
But I need Thee, great - ly need Thee, Come, oh, come and fill me now.
Blest, di - vine, e - ter - nal Spir - it, Fill with power, and fill me now.
Thou art com - fort - ing and sav - ing, Thou art sweet - ly fill - ing now.

D.S. *Fill me with Thy hal - lowed pres - ence—Come, oh, come and fill me now.*

REFRAIN

D. S.

Fill me now, fill me now, Je - sus, come and fill me now;

165 Lead Us, Heavenly Father

DULCE CARMEN 8. 7. 8. 7. 8. 7.
J. Edmeston, 1821
Arr. fr. J. M. Haydn
1. Lead us, heav'n-ly Fa - ther, lead us O'er the world's tem - pes-tuous sea;
2. Sav-iour, breathe for - giv - ness o'er us; All our weak-ness Thou dost know;
3. Spir - it of our God de-scend-ing, Fill our hearts with heav'n-ly joy;
Guard us, guide us, keep us, feed us, For we have no help but Thee:
Thou didst tread this earth be - fore us; Thou didst feel its keen - est woe;
Love with ev - ery pas - sion blend-ing, Pleas-ure that can nev - er cloy;
Yet pos-sess-ing ev - ery bless-ing, If our God our Fa - ther be.
Lone and drear - y, faint and wea - ry, Through the desert Thou didst go.
Thus pro - vid - ed, pardoned, guid-ed, Noth-ing can our peace de - stroy. A-men.
166 Holy Spirit, Hear Us
1 Cor. 12: 7-9
WEM IN LEIDENSTAGEN 6. 5. 6. 5.
From the German by
Joseph Mohr, 1816
Tr. Claudia F. Hernaman, *1898
Friedrich Filitz, 1847
1. Ho - ly Spir - it, hear us On this sa - cred day;
2. Come as once Thou cam - est To the faith - ful few
3. Up to heav'n as - cend - ing, Our dear Lord has gone;
4. Spir - it of A - dop - tion, Make us o - ver - flow

Come to us with bless - ing, Come with us to stay.
Pa - tient - ly a - wait - ing Je - sus' prom - ise true.
Yet His faith - ful chil - dren Leaves He not a - lone.
With Thy seven - fold bless - ing And in grace to grow. A - men.

We All Believe in One True God 167

THE APOSTLES' CREED 8. 7. 7. 7. 7. 7. 7.

Tobias Clausnitzer, 1668
Tr., Catherine Winkworth, 1863, alt.

Kirchengesangbuch
Darmstadt, 1699

1. We all be - lieve in one true God, Fa - ther, Son, and Ho - ly Ghost,
2. We all be - lieve in Je - sus Christ, Son of God and Ma - ry's Son,
3. We all con - fess the Ho - ly Ghost, Who from both for - e'er pro - ceeds;

Ev - er - pres - ent Help in need, Praised by all the heav'n - ly host,
Who de - scend - ed from His throne And for us sal - va - tion won;
Who up - holds and com - forts us In all tri - als, fears, and needs,

But whose might - y pow'r a - lone All is made and wrought and done.
By whose cross and death are we Res - cued from all mis - er - y.
Blest and Ho - ly Trin - i - ty, Praise for - ev - er be to Thee! A - men.

168 Cast Thy Burden upon the Lord

BIRMINGHAM P. M.

Psalm 55: 22; 25: 3 — Felix Mendelssohn, 1846

Cast thy bur - den up - on the Lord, And He shall sus -
tain thee: He nev - er will suf - fer the
right - eous to fall; He is at thy right hand. Thy
mer - cy, Lord, is great, and far a - bove the heav'ns; Let
none be made a - sham - ed, that wait up - on Thee.

Father, to Thee We Look

ST. BARNABAS 11. 10. 11. 10.

Frederick Hosmer, 1881

John B. Dykes, 1875

1. Fa - ther, to Thee we look in all our sor - row,
2. When fond hopes fail and skies are dark be - fore us,
3. Nought shall af - fright us on Thy good - ness lean - ing,
4. Pa - tient, O heart, though heav - y be thy sor - rows!
Thou art the foun - tain whence our heal - ing flows;
When the vain cares that vex our life in - crease—
Low in the heart faith sing - eth still her song;
Be not cast down, dis - qui - et - ed in vain;
Dark though the night, joy com - eth with the mor - row;
Comes with its calm the thought that Thou art o'er us,
Chas - tened by pain we learn life's deep - er mean - ing,
Yet shalt thou praise Him when these dark - ened fur - rows,
Safe - ly they rest who on Thy love re - pose.
And we grow qui - et, fold - ed in Thy peace.
And in our weak - ness Thou dost make us strong.
Where now He plow - eth, wave with gold - en grain. A - men.

170 Come unto Me

HENLEY 11. 10. 11. 10.

Mrs. Catherine H. Esling — Lowell Mason

1. Come un - to me, when shad-ows dark - ly gath - er, When the sad
2. Large are the man - sions in thy Fa-ther's dwell - ing, Glad are the
3. There, like an E - den blos-som - ing in glad - ness, Bloom the fair

heart is wea - ry and dis - tressed, Seek - ing for com - fort
homes that sor - rows nev - er dim; Sweet are the harps in
flow'rs the earth too rude - ly pressed; Come un - to me, all

from your heav'nly Fa - ther, Come un - to me, and I will give you rest.
ho - ly mu - sic swell-ing, Soft are the tones which raise the heav'nly hymn.
ye who droop in sad-ness, Come un - to me, and I will give you rest.

171 I Love to Steal Awhile Away

LELLA C. M.

Phœbe H. Brown, 1818 — Chas. Edw. Pollock

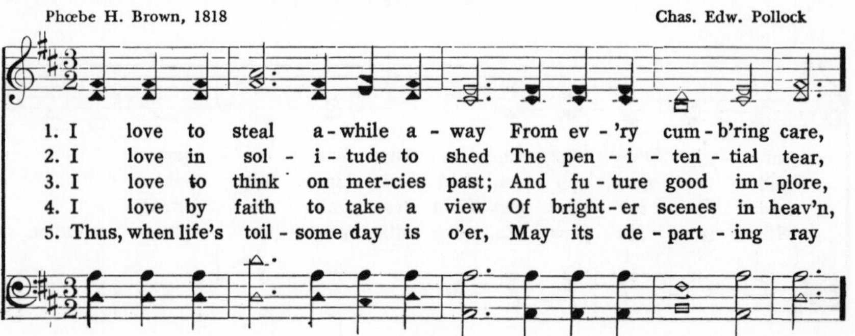

1. I love to steal a-while a - way From ev - 'ry cum - b'ring care,
2. I love in sol - i - tude to shed The pen - i - ten - tial tear,
3. I love to think on mer-cies past; And fu - ture good im - plore,
4. I love by faith to take a view Of bright - er scenes in heav'n,
5. Thus, when life's toil - some day is o'er, May its de - part - ing ray

And spend the hours of set-ting day In hum-ble, grate - ful prayer.
And all His prom-is-es to plead, Where none but God can hear.
And all my cares and sor-rows cast On Him whom I a-dore.
The pros-pect doth my strength re-new, While here by tem - pests driv'n.
Be calm as this im-pres-sive hour, And lead to end - less day.
How Great the Goodness
172
MERIBAH 8. 8. 6. 8. 8. 6.
Psalm 31: 16-19
Lowell Mason
Moderato
1. How great the goodness Thou hast stored In se - cret for Thy saints, O Lord;
2. Thus in the se-cret of Thy face, Shalt find for them a hid-ing place,
3. Oh, let Je-ho-vah bless-ed be, Who showed His wondrous love to me
4. Oh, love the Lord all that Him serve, For He the faith-ful shall pre-serve,
Thy ho-ly name who fear! How great the mer-cies wrought for those
From proud op-press-or's wrongs; A safe re-treat for them pre-pare,
In cit - y for - ti - fied; "Cut off from Thee," I said in fear,
And all the proud re - ward. Be of good cour-age; He with strength
Who do in Thee their trust re - pose, Be - fore men's sons ap - pear.
And keep them in a cov-ert there, Se - cure from strife of tongues.
Yet Thou my suppliant voice didst hear, When un-to Thee I cried.
Will fill your stead-fast hearts at length, All ye who trust the Lord.

173 God Holds My Hand

MAGINES 4. 6. 4. 6. 4. 6. 4. 6.

Rose Magines

Sidney Zook

1. God holds my hand. To walk with Him is sweet.
2. God holds my hand. A prom - ise to His own:

I find in Him A life that is com - plete.
"I'll ne'er for - sake, No, ne'er leave thee a - lone."

And when His will I do not un - der - stand;
His will I'll trust, And on His prom - ise stand.

I can but pray, "Do not let go my hand."
He'll guide my step, He'll not let go my hand.

174 I Need Thee Every Hour

NEED 6. 4. 6. 4. 7. 6. 7. 4.

Mrs. Annie S. Hawks, 1872
Rev. Robert Lowry, 1872
1. I need Thee ev - ery hour, Most gra - cious Lord;
2. I need Thee ev - ery hour, Stay Thou near by;
3. I need Thee ev - ery hour, Teach me Thy will;
4. I need Thee ev - ery hour, Most Ho - ly One;
No ten - der voice like Thine Can peace af - ford.
Temp - ta - tions lose their pow'r When Thou art nigh.
And Thy rich prom - is - es In me ful - fill.
O make me Thine in - deed, Thou bless - ed Son!
I need Thee, O I need Thee, Ev - ery hour I need Thee;
I need Thee, O I need Thee, Ev - ery hour I need Thee;
I need Thee, O I need Thee, Ev - ery hour I need Thee;
I need Thee, O I need Thee, Ev - ery hour I need Thee;
O bless me now, my Sav - iour, I come to Thee.
O bless me now, my Sav - iour, I come to Thee.
O bless me now, my Sav - iour, I come to Thee.
O bless me now, my Sav - iour, I come to Thee. A - men.

175 O Lord, How Happy Should We Be

MERIBAH 8. 8. 8. 6. 8. 8. 6.
Joseph Anstice, 1808-1836
Lowell Mason, 1792-1872
1. O Lord, how hap - py should we be If we could cast our care on Thee,
2. Could we but kneel, and cast our load, E'en while we pray, up - on our God,
3. We can - not trust Him as we should; So chafes weak nature's restless mood
4. Lord, make these faithless hearts of ours Such lessons learn from birds and flowers;
If we from self could rest, And feel at heart that One a - bove,
Then rise with light-ened cheer, Sure that the Fa - ther, who is nigh
To cast its peace a - way; But birds and flow'r - ets round us preach;
Make them from self to cease, Leave all things to a Fa - ther's will,
In per-fect wis-dom, per-fect love, Is work - ing for the best;
To still the fam-ished ra-ven's cry, Will hear, in that we fear.
All, all the pres-ent e - vil teach Suf - fi - cient for the day.
And taste, be - fore Him ly - ing still, E'en in af - flic - tion, peace. A - men.
176 God Moves in a Mysterious Way
DUNFERMLINE C. M.
William Cowper, 1774
Scottish Psalter, 1615
1. God moves in a mys - te - rious way, His won-ders to per - form;
2. Ye fear - ful saints, fresh cour - age take; The clouds ye so much dread
3. Judge not the Lord by fee - ble sense, But trust Him for His grace;
4. His pur - pos - es will rip - en fast, Un - fold - ing ev - ery hour;
5. Blind un - be - lief is sure to err, And scan His work in vain;

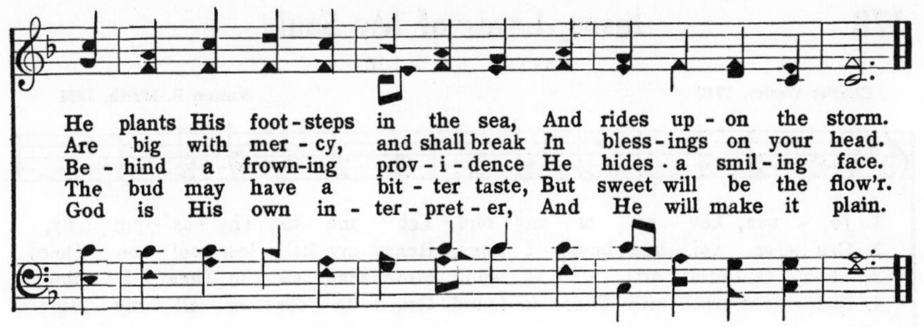
He plants His foot-steps in the sea, And rides up-on the storm.
Are big with mer-cy, and shall break In bless-ings on your head.
Be-hind a frown-ing prov-i-dence He hides a smil-ing face.
The bud may have a bit-ter taste, But sweet will be the flow'r.
God is His own in-ter-pret-er, And He will make it plain.

O Love That Wilt Not Let Me Go 177

ST. MARGARET 8. 8. 8. 8. 6.

George Matheson, 1882 — Albert L. Peace, 1885

1. O Love that wilt not let me go, I rest my wea-ry soul in
2. O Light that fol-l'west all my way, I yield my flick-'ring torch to
3. O Joy that seek-est me thro' pain, I can-not close my heart to
4. O Cross that lift-est up my head, I dare not ask to fly from

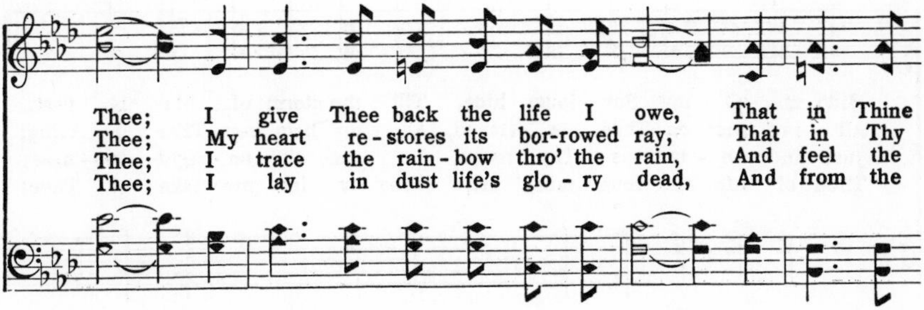

Thee; I give Thee back the life I owe, That in Thine
Thee; My heart re-stores its bor-rowed ray, That in Thy
Thee; I trace the rain-bow thro' the rain, And feel the
Thee; I lay in dust life's glo-ry dead, And from the

o-cean depths its flow May rich-er, full-er be.
sun-shine's blaze its day May bright-er, fair-er be.
prom-ise is not vain That morn shall tear-less be.
ground there blos-soms red Life that shall end-less be. A-men.

178 Jesus, Lover of My Soul

MARTYN 7. 7. 7. 7. D.
Charles Wesley, 1740
Simeon B. Marsh, 1834
1. Je - sus, Lov - er of my soul, Let me to Thy bos - om fly,
2. Oth - er ref - uge have I none, Hangs my help - less soul on Thee;
3. Thou, O Christ, art all I want, More than all in Thee I find;
4. Plen - teous grace with Thee is found, Grace to cov - er all my sin;
While the near - er wa - ters roll, While the tem - pest still is high;
Leave, oh, leave me not a - lone, Still sup - port and com - fort me.
Raise the fall - en, cheer the faint, Heal the sick, and lead the blind.
Let the heal - ing streams a - bound, Make and keep me pure with - in.
Hide me, O my Sav - iour, hide, Till the storm of life is past;
All my trust on Thee is stayed, All my help from Thee I bring;
Just and ho - ly is Thy name, I am all un - right - eous - ness;
Thou of life the foun - tain art, Free - ly let me take of Thee;
Safe in - to the ha - ven guide, O re - ceive my soul at last.
Cov - er my de - fense - less head With the shad - ow of Thy wing.
False and full of sin I am, Thou art full of truth and grace.
Spring Thou up with - in my heart, Rise to all e - ter - ni - ty. A - men.

Lead, Kindly Light

179

SANDON 10. 4. 10. 4. 10. 10.

John H. Newman, 1833

Charles H. Purday, 1799-1885

1. Lead, kind-ly Light, a - mid th'en - cir - cling gloom, Lead Thou me on;
2. I was not ev - er thus, nor prayed that Thou Shouldst lead me on;
3. So long Thy power hath blest me, sure it still Will lead me on,
The night is dark, and I am far from home; Lead Thou me on.
I loved to choose and see my path, but now Lead Thou me on;
O'er moor and fen, o'er crag and tor - rent, till The night is gone,
Keep Thou my feet: I do not ask to see
I loved the gar - ish day, and spite of fears,
And with the morn those an - gel fac - es smile,
The dis - tant scene,— one step e - nough for me.
Pride ruled my will. Re - mem - ber not past years.
Which I have loved long since, and lost a - while. A-men.

180 Rock of Ages

TOPLADY 7. 7. 7. 7. 7. 7.

A. M. Toplady, 1776 — Thomas Hastings, 1830

1. Rock of A-ges, cleft for me, Let me hide my-self in Thee;
2. Not the la-bor of my hands Can ful-fill the law's de-mands;
3. Noth-ing in my hands I bring, Sim-ply to Thy cross I cling;
4. While I draw this fleet-ing breath, When my heart-strings break in death,

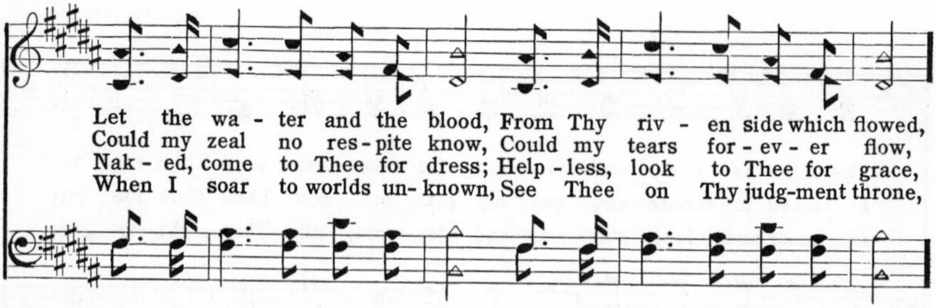

Let the wa-ter and the blood, From Thy riv-en side which flowed,
Could my zeal no res-pite know, Could my tears for-ev-er flow,
Nak-ed, come to Thee for dress; Help-less, look to Thee for grace,
When I soar to worlds un-known, See Thee on Thy judg-ment throne,

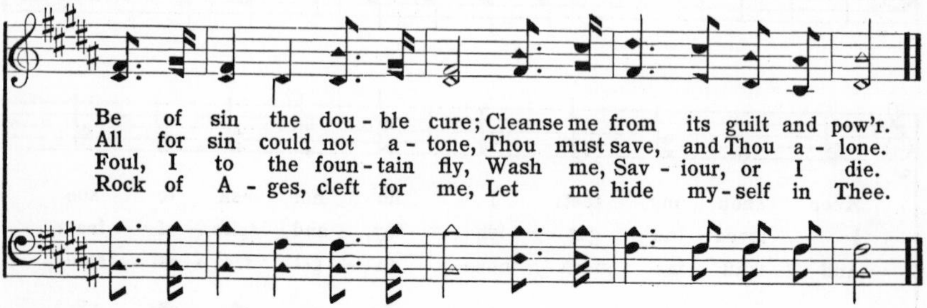

Be of sin the dou-ble cure; Cleanse me from its guilt and pow'r.
All for sin could not a-tone, Thou must save, and Thou a-lone.
Foul, I to the foun-tain fly, Wash me, Sav-iour, or I die.
Rock of A-ges, cleft for me, Let me hide my-self in Thee.

181 O Love Divine, That Stooped to Share

QUEBEC L. M.

Oliver Wendell Holmes, 1859 — Henry W. Baker, 1866

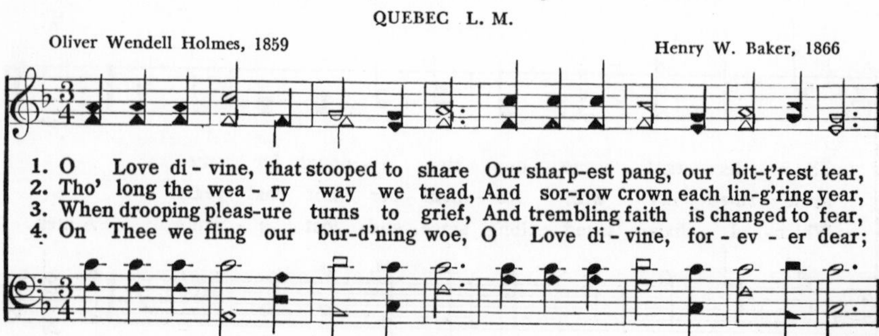
1. O Love di-vine, that stooped to share Our sharp-est pang, our bit-t'rest tear,
2. Tho' long the wea-ry way we tread, And sor-row crown each lin-g'ring year,
3. When drooping pleas-ure turns to grief, And trembling faith is changed to fear,
4. On Thee we fling our bur-d'ning woe, O Love di-vine, for-ev-er dear;

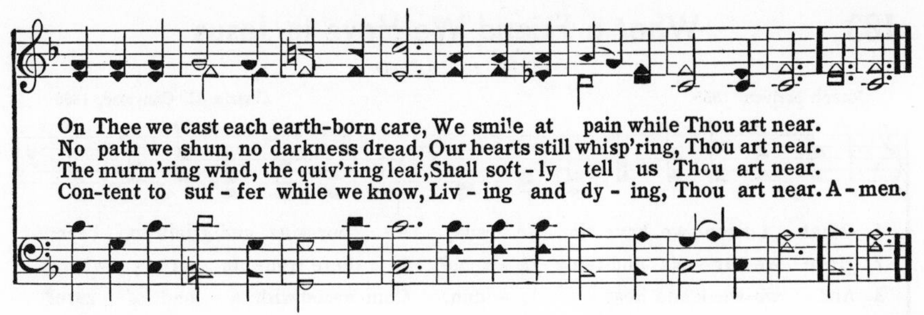
On Thee we cast each earth-born care, We smile at pain while Thou art near.
No path we shun, no darkness dread, Our hearts still whisp'ring, Thou art near.
The murm'ring wind, the quiv'ring leaf, Shall soft - ly tell us Thou art near.
Con-tent to suf - fer while we know, Liv - ing and dy - ing, Thou art near. A - men.

Dear Lord and Father of Mankind 182

REST 8. 6. 8. 8. 6.

John G. Whittier, 1872 — Frederick C. Maker

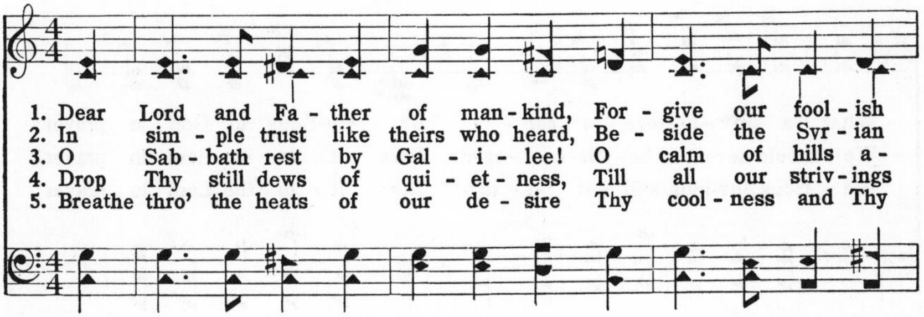

1. Dear Lord and Fa - ther of man - kind, For - give our fool - ish
2. In sim - ple trust like theirs who heard, Be - side the Syr - ian
3. O Sab - bath rest by Gal - i - lee! O calm of hills a -
4. Drop Thy still dews of qui - et - ness, Till all our striv - ings
5. Breathe thro' the heats of our de - sire Thy cool - ness and Thy

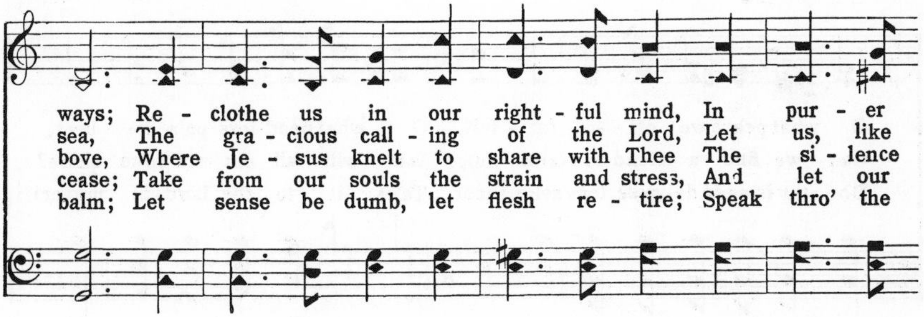

ways; Re - clothe us in our right - ful mind, In pur - er
sea, The gra - cious call - ing of the Lord, Let us, like
bove, Where Je - sus knelt to share with Thee The si - lence
cease; Take from our souls the strain and stress, And let our
balm; Let sense be dumb, let flesh re - tire; Speak thro' the

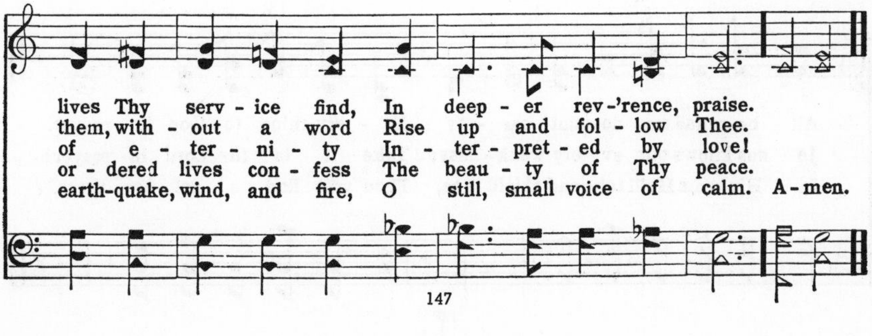

lives Thy serv - ice find, In deep - er rev-'rence, praise.
them, with - out a word Rise up and fol - low Thee.
of e - ter - ni - ty In - ter - pret - ed by love!
or - dered lives con - fess The beau - ty of Thy peace.
earth-quake, wind, and fire, O still, small voice of calm. A - men.

183 What a Friend We Have in Jesus

ERIE 8. 7. 8. 7. D.

Joseph Scriven, 1855
Charles C. Converse, 1868
1. What a friend we have in Je - sus, All our sins and griefs to bear;
2. Have we tri - als and temp - ta - tions? Is there trou - ble an - y - where?
3. Are we weak and heav - y la - den, Cum-bered with a load of care?
What a priv - i - lege to car - ry Ev - ery-thing to God in prayer!
We should nev - er be dis - cour - aged: Take it to the Lord in prayer!
Pre - cious Sav-iour, still our ref - uge; Take it to the Lord in prayer!
O what peace we oft - en for - feit, O what need-less pain we bear,
Can we find a friend so faith - ful, Who will all our sor-rows share?
Do thy friends de-spise, for - sake thee? Take it to the Lord in prayer!
All be-cause we do not car - ry Ev - ery-thing to God in prayer.
Je - sus knows our ev - ery weak - ness; Take it to the Lord in prayer!
In His arms He'll take and shield thee, Thou wilt find a sol - ace there.

Jesus, I My Cross Have Taken

ELLESDIE 8. 7. 8. 7. D.

Henry F. Lyte, 1824

Arr. from W. A. Mozart,
by Hubert P. Main, 1873

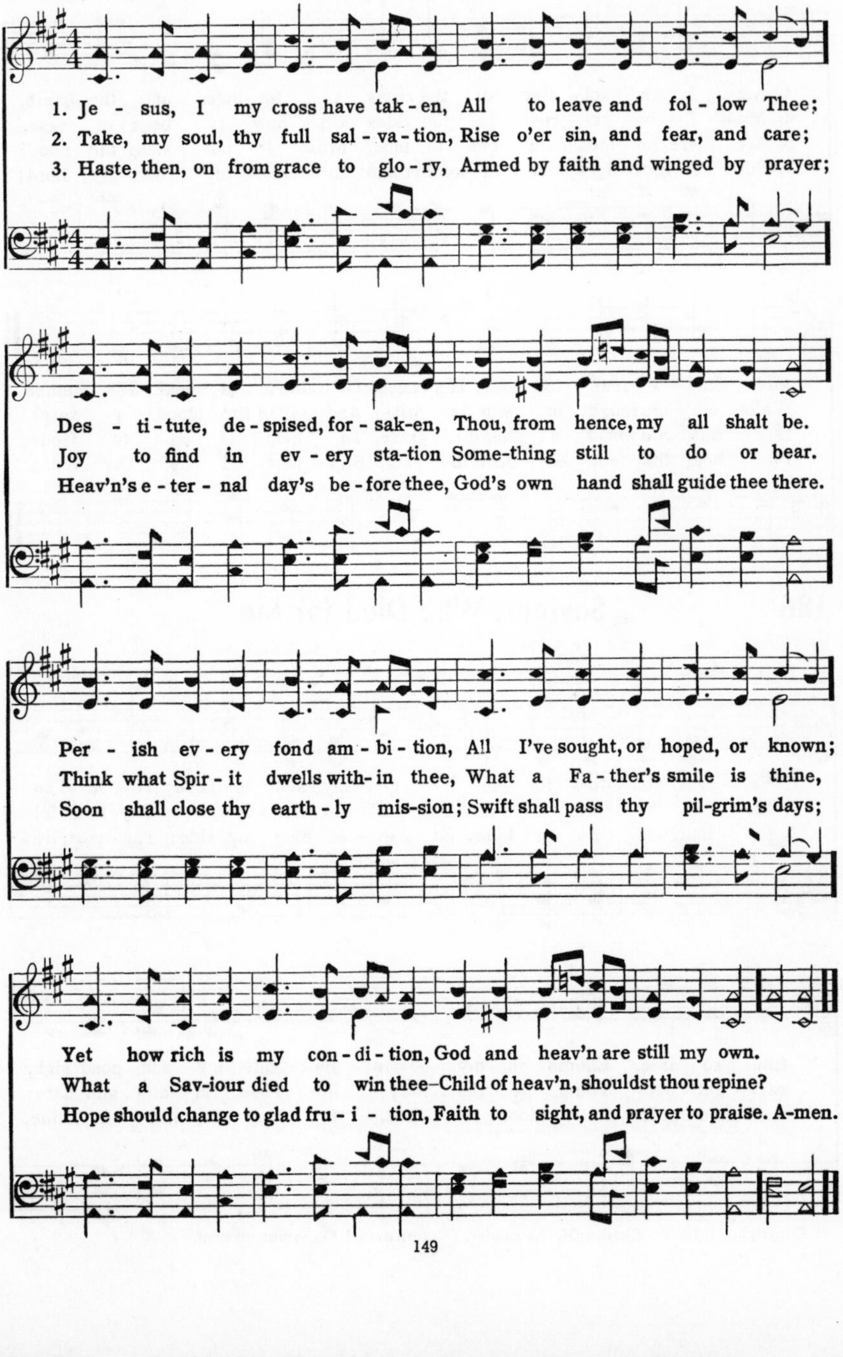

1. Je - sus, I my cross have tak - en, All to leave and fol - low Thee;
2. Take, my soul, thy full sal - va - tion, Rise o'er sin, and fear, and care;
3. Haste, then, on from grace to glo - ry, Armed by faith and winged by prayer;

Des - ti - tute, de - spised, for - sak - en, Thou, from hence, my all shalt be.
Joy to find in ev - ery sta - tion Some - thing still to do or bear.
Heav'n's e - ter - nal day's be - fore thee, God's own hand shall guide thee there.

Per - ish ev - ery fond am - bi - tion, All I've sought, or hoped, or known;
Think what Spir - it dwells with - in thee, What a Fa - ther's smile is thine,
Soon shall close thy earth - ly mis - sion; Swift shall pass thy pil - grim's days;

Yet how rich is my con - di - tion, God and heav'n are still my own.
What a Sav - iour died to win thee—Child of heav'n, shouldst thou repine?
Hope should change to glad fru - i - tion, Faith to sight, and prayer to praise. A - men.

185 Am I a Soldier of the Cross

MARLOW C. M.

Isaac Watts, 1774

Arr. from Rev. John Chetham's Book of Psalmody, 1718

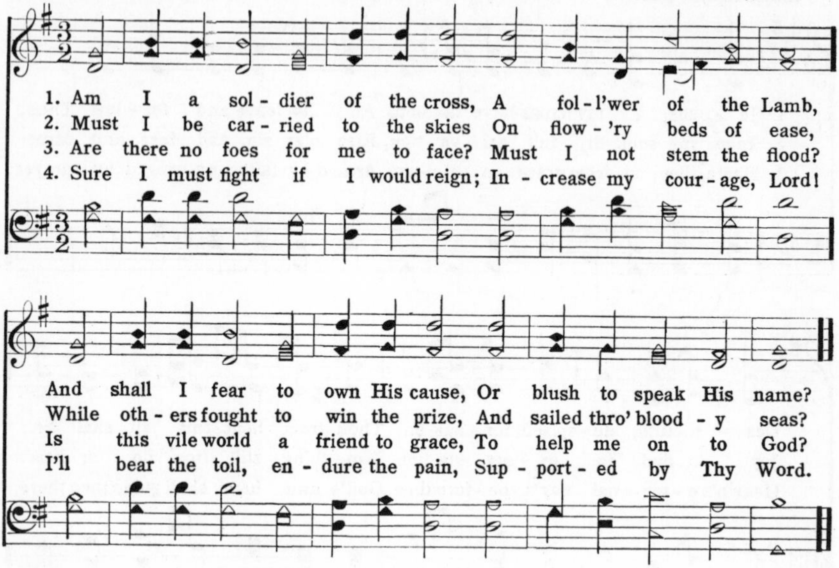

1. Am I a sol - dier of the cross, A fol - l'wer of the Lamb,
2. Must I be car - ried to the skies On flow - 'ry beds of ease,
3. Are there no foes for me to face? Must I not stem the flood?
4. Sure I must fight if I would reign; In - crease my cour - age, Lord!

And shall I fear to own His cause, Or blush to speak His name?
While oth - ers fought to win the prize, And sailed thro' blood - y seas?
Is this vile world a friend to grace, To help me on to God?
I'll bear the toil, en - dure the pain, Sup - port - ed by Thy Word.

186 Saviour, Who Died for Me

I GIVE MYSELF TO THEE 6. 6. 6. 4. 6. 6. 6. 4.

Mary J. Mason

D. B. Towner

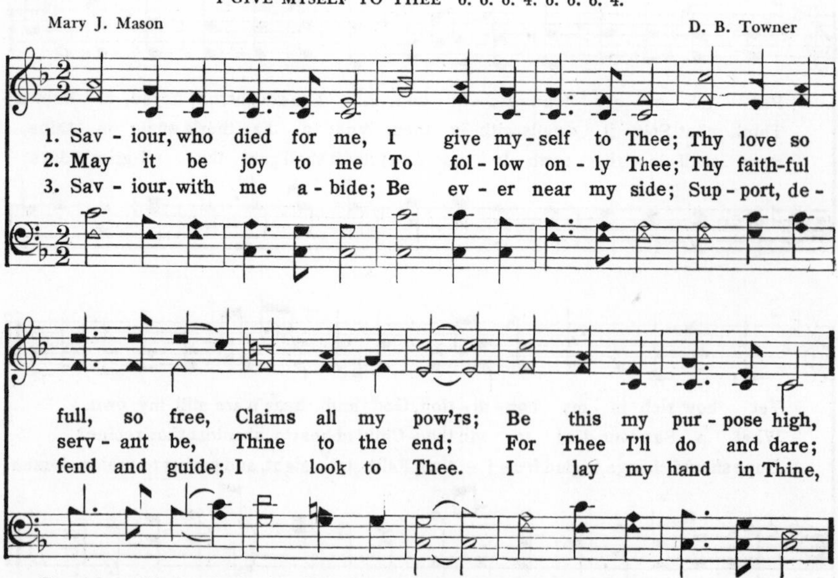
1. Sav - iour, who died for me, I give my - self to Thee; Thy love so
2. May it be joy to me To fol - low on - ly Thee; Thy faith-ful
3. Sav - iour, with me a - bide; Be ev - er near my side; Sup - port, de -
full, so free, Claims all my pow'rs; Be this my pur - pose high,
serv - ant be, Thine to the end; For Thee I'll do and dare;
fend and guide; I look to Thee. I lay my hand in Thine,

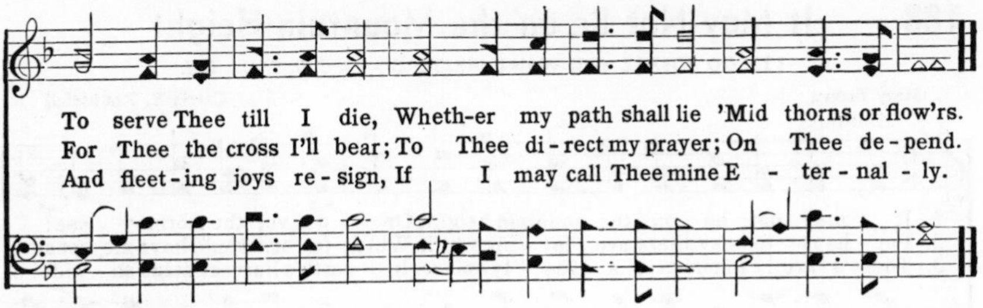

To serve Thee till I die, Wheth-er my path shall lie 'Mid thorns or flow'rs.
For Thee the cross I'll bear; To Thee di-rect my prayer; On Thee de-pend.
And fleet-ing joys re-sign, If I may call Thee mine E - ter-nal-ly.

Sit and Pause Awhile, My Spirit 187

GOLGOTHA 8. 7. 8. 7. 8. 7.

Zion's Harp

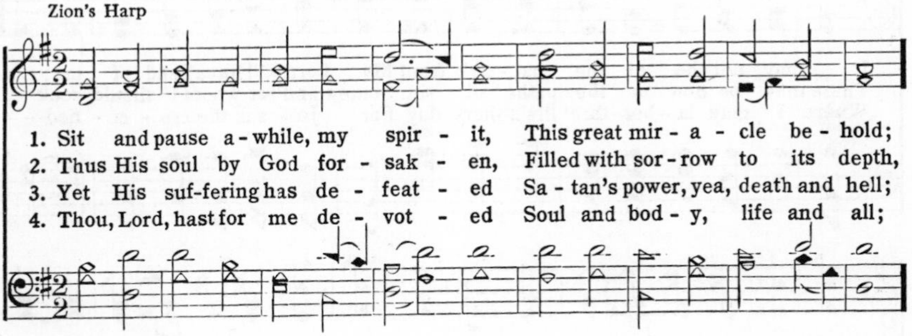

1. Sit and pause a-while, my spir - it, This great mir-a-cle be-hold;
2. Thus His soul by God for-sak - en, Filled with sor-row to its depth,
3. Yet His suf-fering has de - feat - ed Sa-tan's power, yea, death and hell;
4. Thou, Lord, hast for me de - vot - ed Soul and bod-y, life and all;

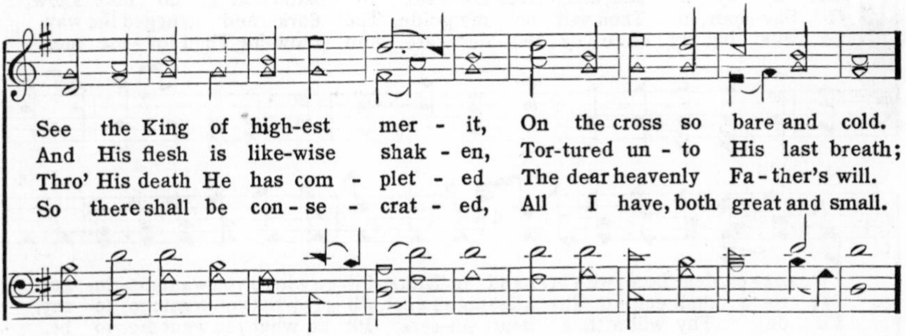

See the King of high-est mer - it, On the cross so bare and cold.
And His flesh is like-wise shak - en, Tor-tured un - to His last breath;
Thro' His death He has com - plet - ed The dear heavenly Fa-ther's will.
So there shall be con - se - crat - ed, All I have, both great and small.

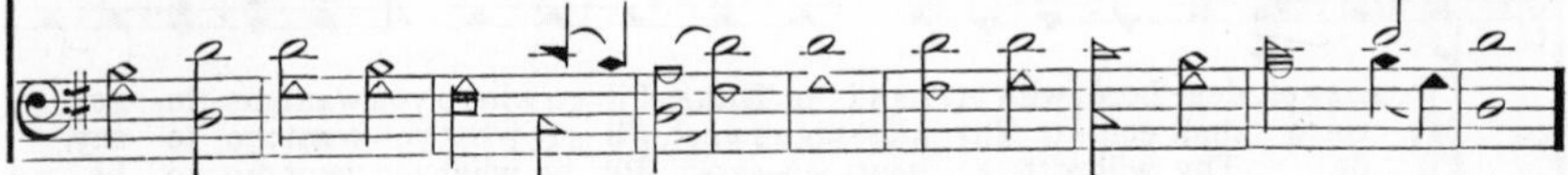

Out of heav-en God has giv-en His own Son in love un - told.
All His vig-or, all His pow-er Is ex-hausted un-to death.
Thus is giv-en to us e-ven Life e-ter-nal to ful - fill.
All my ef-forts and en-deav-or To Thy serv-ice and Thy call.

188 It May Not Be on the Mountain Height

I'LL GO WHERE YOU WANT ME TO GO 9. 7. 9. 7. D. Ref.
Mary Brown
Carrie E. Rounsefell
Andante
1. It may not be on the mountain height, Or o - ver the storm -y sea;
2. Per - haps to - day there are lov - ing words Which Je - sus would have me speak—
3. There's sure-ly somewhere a low - ly place, In earth's harvest fields so wide—
It may not be at the bat - tle's front My Lord will have need of me;
There may be now in the paths of sin Some wand'rer whom I should seek—
Where I may la - bor thro' life's short day For Je - sus the cru - ci - fied—
But if, by a still, small voice He calls To paths that I do not know,
O Sav - iour, if Thou wilt be my guide, Tho' dark and rugged the way,
So trust - ing my all to Thy ten - der care, And know-ing Thou lov - est me,
Fine
I'll answer, dear Lord, with my hand in Thine, I'll go where you want me to go.
My voice shall ech - o Thy mes - sage sweet, I'll say what you want me to say.
I'll do Thy will with a heart sin-cere, I'll be what you want me to be.
D. S.–I'll say what you want me to say, dear Lord, I'll be what you want me to be.
Refrain
D. S.
I'll go where you want me to go, dear Lord, O - ver mountain, or plain, or sea;

Jesus, Come, O Come to Me 189

JESUS, COME 7. 7. 7. 7.

Zion's Harp

1. Je - sus, come, O come to me, Lord, I pray, a - bide with me.
2. Thou - sand times I long for Thee, Noth - ing else can com - fort me;
3. Pleas - ures on this earth a - bound, Yet my heart no joy has found.
4. To no oth - er be it told That I would my heart un - fold;
Come, Thou art my soul's de - light, And with me do Thou a - bide.
Thou - sand times I cry to Thee, Je - sus, Je - sus, come to me.
But Thy pres - ence, Lord, to me Shall my joy for - ev - er be.
On - ly Thou may en - ter in, On - ly Thou may reign with - in.

Just as I Am, Thine Own to Be 190

THERSA L. M.

Marianne Hearn | Thersa Hostetler

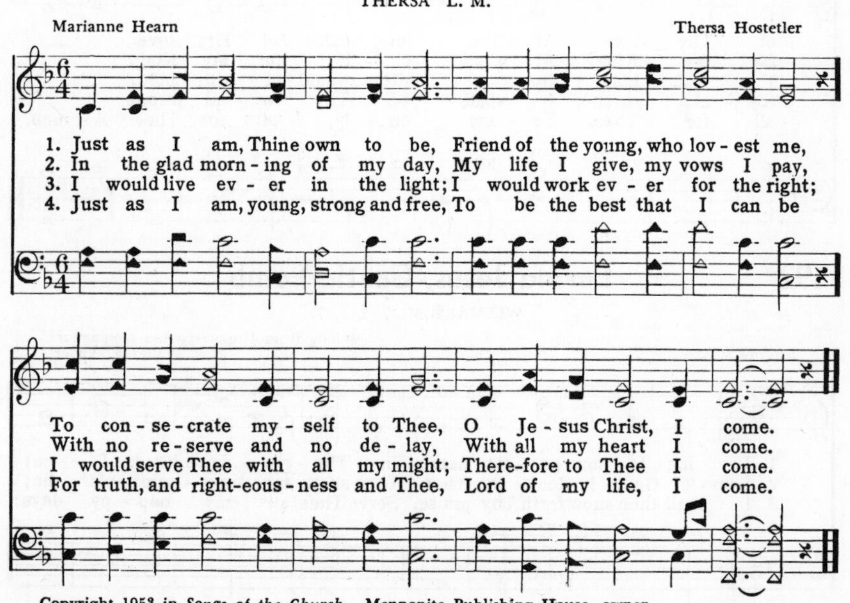
1. Just as I am, Thine own to be, Friend of the young, who lov - est me,
2. In the glad morn - ing of my day, My life I give, my vows I pay,
3. I would live ev - er in the light; I would work ev - er for the right;
4. Just as I am, young, strong and free, To be the best that I can be
To con - se - crate my - self to Thee, O Je - sus Christ, I come.
With no re - serve and no de - lay, With all my heart I come.
I would serve Thee with all my might; There-fore to Thee I come.
For truth, and right - eous - ness and Thee, Lord of my life, I come.

191 Take My Life, and Let It Be

HENDON 7. 7. 7. 7.

Frances R. Havergal | Abraham H. C. Malan

1. Take my life, and let it be Con - se - crat - ed, Lord, to
2. Take my feet, and let them be Swift and beau - ti - ful for
3. Take my lips, and let them be Filled with mes - sag - es from
4. Take my will and make it Thine; It shall be no long - er
5. Take my love; my Lord, I pour At Thy feet its treas - ure -

Thee; Take my hands, and let them move At the im - pulse
Thee; Take my voice, and let me sing Al - ways, on - ly,
Thee; Take my sil - ver and my gold, Not a mite would
mine; Take my heart, it is Thine own! It shall be Thy
store; Take my - self, and I will be, Ev - er, on - ly,

of Thy love, At the im - pulse of Thy love.
for my King, Al - ways, on - ly, for my King.
I with - hold, Not a mite would I with - hold.
roy - al throne, It shall be Thy roy - al throne.
all for Thee, Ev - er, on - ly, all for Thee. A - men.

192 Loving Jesus, Gentle Lamb

WITMARSUM 7. 7. 7. 7.

Charles Wesley | Melody from Unparteyisches Gesangbuch, Har. Walter E. Yoder

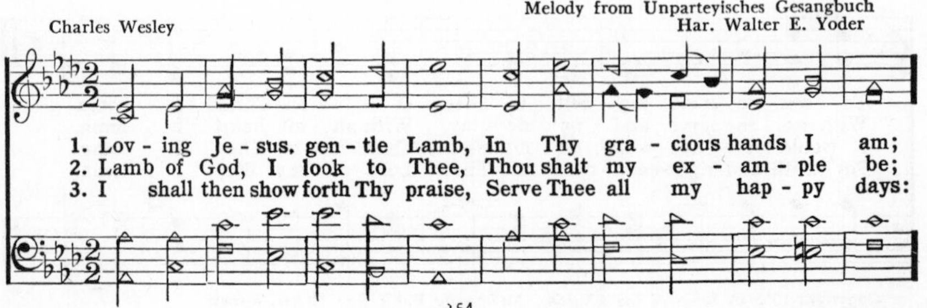
1. Lov - ing Je - sus, gen - tle Lamb, In Thy gra - cious hands I am;
2. Lamb of God, I look to Thee, Thou shalt my ex - am - ple be;
3. I shall then show forth Thy praise, Serve Thee all my hap - py days:

Make me, Sav-iour, what Thou art; Live Thy-self with-in my heart.
Thou didst live to God a-lone, Thou didst nev - er seek Thine own.
Then the world shall al-ways see Christ, the ho - ly child, in me.

Father in Heaven, Hear Us Today 193

SOUTHAMPTON P. M.

Charles G. Ames, 1828-1912 Anonymous, 1870

1. Fa - ther in heav - en, Hear us to - day; Hal - lowed Thy name be;
2. Fa - ther in heav - en, Hear us to - day; Hal - lowed Thy name be;
3. Fa - ther in heav - en, Hear us to - day; Hal - lowed Thy name be;

Hear us, we pray! O let Thy king - dom come, O let Thy
Hear us, we pray! Giv - er of dai - ly food, Foun - tain of
Hear us, we pray! Lead us in paths of right, Save us from

will be done, By all be - neath the sun, As in the skies.
truth and good, Be all our hearts im - bued With love like Thine.
sin and blight, King of all love and might, Glo - rious for aye. A - men.

194 Saviour, While My Heart Is Tender

LILLE 8. 7. 8. 7.
John Burton, the younger, 1803-1877
Old French Melody
1. Sav - iour, while my heart is ten-der, I would yield that heart to Thee;
2. Take me now, Lord Je - sus, take me; Let my youth - ful heart be Thine;
3. Send me, Lord, where Thou wilt send me, On - ly do Thou guide my way;
4. May this sol - emn con - se - cra - tion Nev - er once for - got - ten be;
5. Thine I am, O Lord, for - ev - er, To Thy serv - ice set a - part;
All my pow'rs to Thee sur - ren - der, Thine and on - ly Thine to be.
Thy de - vot - ed serv - ant make me; Fill my soul with love di - vine.
May Thy grace through life at - tend me, Glad - ly then shall I o - bey.
Let it know no rev - o - ca - tion, Reg - is - tered, confirmed by Thee.
Suf - fer me to leave Thee nev - er; Seal Thine im - age on my heart. A - men.
195 The Lord's My Shepherd, I'll Not Want
GRANT C. M.
Psalm 23
David Grant
1. The Lord's my Shep - herd, I'll not want; He makes me down to lie
2. My soul He doth re - store a - gain; And me to walk doth make
3. Yea, though I walk thro' death's dark vale, Yet will I fear no ill;
4. My ta - ble Thou hast fur - nish - ed In pres - ence of my foes;
5. Good - ness and mer - cy all my life Shall sure - ly fol - low me;
In pas - tures green; He lead - eth me The qui - et wa - ters by.
With - in the paths of right - eous - ness, E'en for His own name's sake.
For Thou art with me, and Thy rod, And staff me com - fort still.
My head Thou dost with oil a - noint, And my cup o - ver - flows.
And in God's house for - ev - er - more My dwell - ing place shall be.

Abide with Me

EVENTIDE 10. 10. 10. 10.

Henry F. Lyte, 1847

William H. Monk, 1861

1. A - bide with me; fast falls the e - ven - tide;
2. Swift to its close ebbs out life's lit - tle day;
3. I need Thy pres - ence ev - ery pass - ing hour;
4. I fear no foe, with Thee at hand to bless;
5. Hold Thou Thy cross be - fore my clos - ing eyes;
The dark - ness deep - ens; Lord, with me a - bide;
Earth's joys grow dim, its glo - ries pass a - way;
What but Thy grace can foil the temp - ter's pow'r?
Ills have no weight, and tears no bit - ter - ness;
Shine through the gloom, and point me to the skies;
When oth - er help - ers fail, and com - forts flee,
Change and de - cay in all a - round I see;
Who like Thy - self my guide and stay can be?
Where is death's sting? where, grave, thy vic - to - ry?
Heav'n's morn - ing breaks and earth's vain shad - ows flee;
Help of the help - less, O a - bide with me.
O Thou who chang - est not, a - bide with me.
Through cloud and sun - shine, O a - bide with me.
I tri - umph still, if Thou a - bide with me.
In life, in death, O Lord, a - bide with me. A - men.

197 Christ, Whose Glory Fills the Skies

LUX PRIMA 7. 7. 7. 7. 7. 7.

Charles Wesley, 1740 — Charles F. Gounod, 1872

1. Christ, whose glo - ry fills the skies, Christ, the true, the on - ly Light, Sun of Right - eous - ness, a - rise, Tri - umph o'er the shades of night; Day - spring from on high, be near; Day - star, in my heart ap - pear.
2. Dark and cheer - less is the morn Un - ac - com - pa - nied by Thee; Joy - less is the day's re - turn Till Thy mer - cy's beams I see; Till Thou in - ward life im - part, Glad my eyes, and warm my heart.
3. Vis - it, then, this soul of mine, Pierce the gloom of sin and grief; Fill me, Ra - dian - cy Di - vine, Scat - ter all my un - be - lief; More and more Thy - self dis - play, Shin - ing to the per - fect day. A - men.

I Waited for the Lord 198

BALLERMA C. M.
Psalm 40
Scottish Psalter, 1650
Adapted by Robert Simpson, 1790-1832
1. I wait - ed for the Lord my God, And pa - tient - ly did bear;
2. He took me from a fear - ful pit, And from the mir - y clay,
3. He put a new song in my mouth, Our God to mag - ni - fy:
4. O bless - ed is the man whose trust Up - on the Lord re - lies;
5. O Lord my God, full man - y are The won - ders Thou hast done;
At length to me He did in - cline My voice and cry to hear.
And on a rock He set my feet, Es - tab - lish - ing my way.
Man - y shall see it, and shall fear, And on the Lord re - ly.
Re - spect - ing not the proud, nor such As turn a - side to lies.
Thy gracious thoughts to us - ward far A - bove all thoughts are gone. A-men.
Lord, Thy Mercy Now Entreating 199
STOCKWELL 8. 7. 8. 7.
A. N., in The Scottish Hymnal, 1884
Darius E. Jones, 1851
1. Lord, Thy mer - cy now en - treat - ing, Low be - fore Thy throne we fall;
2. Sin - ful thoughts and words un - lov - ing Rise a - gainst us one by one;
3. Hearts that far from Thee were stray - ing, While in prayer we bowed the knee;
4. Pre - cious mo - ments i - dly wast - ed, Pre - cious hours in fol - ly spent;
5. Lord, Thy mer - cy still en - treat - ing, We with shame our sins would own;
Our mis - deeds to Thee con - fess - ing, On Thy name we hum - bly call.
Acts un - wor - thy, deeds un - think - ing, Good that we have left un - done;
Lips that, while Thy prais - es sounding, Lift - ed not the soul to Thee;
Chris - tian vow and fight un - heed - ed; Scarce a thought to wis - dom lent.
From henceforth, the time re - deeming, May we live to Thee a - lone. A-men.

200 Dear Shepherd of Thy People

DURHAM C. M.

John Newton, 1725-1807 — From Ravenscroft's Psalter, 1621

1. Dear Shep-herd of Thy peo - ple, hear; Thy pres-ence now dis - play;
2. With - in these walls let ho - ly peace And love and con - cord dwell;
3. May we in faith re - ceive Thy word, In faith pre-sent our prayers,
4. The hear - ing ear, the see - ing eye, The hum-bled mind be - stow;
As Thou hast given a place for prayer, So give us hearts to pray.
Here give the trou-bled con-science ease, The wounded spir - it heal.
And in the pres-ence of our Lord Un - bos - om all our cares.
And shine up - on us from on high, To make our grac - es grow. A-men.

201 Hold Thou My Hand

TRUST 11. 10. 11. 10.

Lina Z. Ressler — Thersa Hostetler

1. Hold Thou my hand, my Fa - ther, in life's morn - ing, Bright seems my
2. Hold Thou my hand, I fear the darksome shad - ows, That lurk a -
3. When fi - ery tri - als come a - long my path - way, Keep Thou me
4. And when the eve - ning shad-ows dim my vi - sion, Still keep my

way and I would fain be safe; I fear the snares that all a -
bout my new and un-tried way, Keep me with Thee, and do Thou
near Thy calm un - err - ing way; And in the dark - ness whis - per
hand in Thy own lov - ing hold; Why should I fear while I can

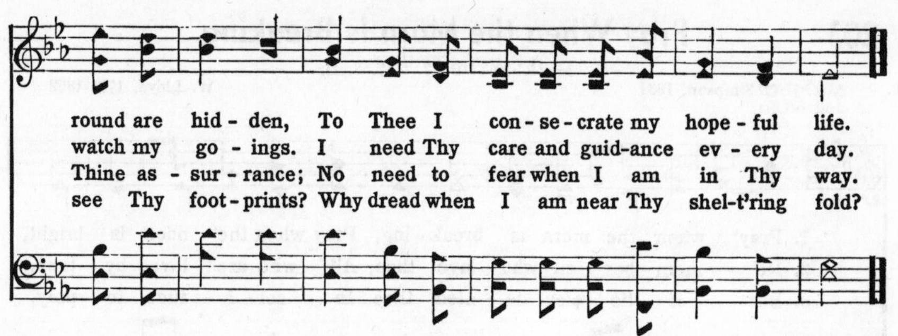
round are hid - den, To Thee I con - se - crate my hope - ful life.
watch my go - ings. I need Thy care and guid-ance ev - ery day.
Thine as - sur - rance; No need to fear when I am in Thy way.
see Thy foot - prints? Why dread when I am near Thy shel-t'ring fold?

For Them Whose Ways Are in the Height 202

MORWELLHAM 8. 6. 8. 6. 8. 6.

Richard Roberts, 1874-1945

Charles Steggall, 1826-1905

1. For them whose ways are in the height, Lord, hear our anx - ious prayer!
2. In cloud and storm be Thou their Friend, O hear our ur - gent cry!
3. By them bid fel - low - ship in - crease, O God in heav - en, hear!

Keep Thou them in the hour of flight In Thine un - sleep - ing care;
By Thy strong arm their lives de - fend In per - ils of the sky;
And speed the hour when wars shall cease And love shall cast out fear;

Their Pi - lot be by day, by night Through the un - chart - ed air.
From jour - ney's start to jour - ney's end Be Thou, good Lord, near by.
A - noint them her - alds of Thy peace To all men far and near. A - men.

203 Pray When the Morn Is Breaking

MEIRIONYDD 7. 6. 7. 6. D.

Mrs. J. C. Simpson, 1831
and others.

W. Lloyd, 1785-1852

1. Pray when the morn is break - ing, Pray when the noon is bright,
2. Re - mem - ber all who love thee, All who are loved by thee,
3. But if 'tis e'er de - nied thee In sol - i - tude to pray,

Pray with the eve's de - clin - ing, Pray in the hush of night:
And next for those who hate thee Pray thou, if such there be:
Should ho - ly thoughts come o'er thee Up - on life's crowd-ed way,

With mind made clear of tu - mult, All mean - er thoughts a - way,
Last for thy - self in meek - ness A bless - ing hum - bly claim,
E'en then the si - lent breath - ing That lifts thy soul a - bove

Make thou thy soul trans-par - ent, Seek thou with God to pray.
And link with each pe - ti - tion Thy great Re - deemer's name.
Shall reach the thron-ed Pres-ence Of mer - cy, truth, and love. A-men.

Pray, O Church, Be Sanctified

POWER OF PRAYER 7. 6. 7. 6. 6. 6. 6.

Zion's Harp

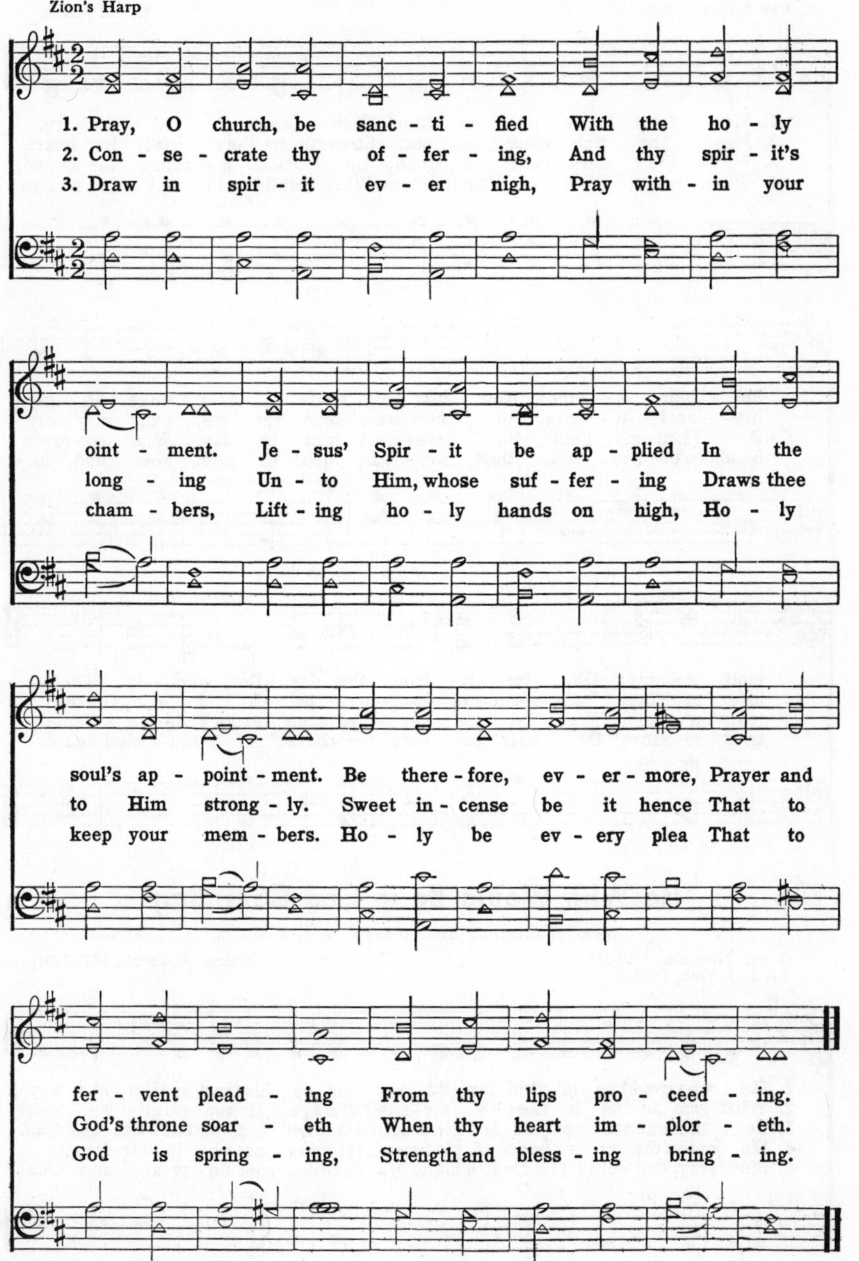
1. Pray, O church, be sanc - ti - fied With the ho - ly
2. Con - se - crate thy of - fer - ing, And thy spir - it's
3. Draw in spir - it ev - er nigh, Pray with - in your
oint - ment. Je - sus' Spir - it be ap - plied In the
long - ing Un - to Him, whose suf - fer - ing Draws thee
cham - bers, Lift - ing ho - ly hands on high, Ho - ly
soul's ap - point - ment. Be there - fore, ev - er - more, Prayer and
to Him strong - ly. Sweet in - cense be it hence That to
keep your mem - bers. Ho - ly be ev - ery plea That to
fer - vent plead - ing From thy lips pro - ceed - ing.
God's throne soar - eth When thy heart im - plor - eth.
God is spring - ing, Strength and bless - ing bring - ing.

205 My Faith Looks Up to Thee

OLIVET 6. 6. 4. 6. 6. 6. 4.
Ray Palmer
Lowell Mason
1. My faith looks up to Thee, Thou Lamb of Cal - va - ry,
2. May Thy rich grace im - part Strength to my faint - ing heart,
3. While life's dark maze I tread, And griefs a - round me spread,
4. When ends life's tran - sient dream, When death's cold, sul - len stream
Sav - iour di - vine! Now hear me while I pray, Take all my
My zeal in - spire; As Thou hast died for me, Oh, may my
Be Thou my guide; Bid dark - ness turn to day, Wipe sor - row's
Shall o'er me roll, Blest Sav - iour, then, in love, Fear and dis -
guilt a - way; Oh, let me from this day Be whol - ly Thine!
love to Thee Pure, warm, and change - less be, A liv - ing fire!
tears a - way, Nor let me ev - er stray From Thee a - side.
trust re - move; Oh, bear me safe a - bove, A ran - somed soul!
206 He Who Would Be in God Confiding
WER NUR DEN LIEBEN GOTT 9. 8. 9. 8. 8. 8.
George Neumark, 1621-1681
Tr. J. J. Voth, 1939
George Neumark, 1621-1681
1. He who would be in God con - fid - ing And put his trust in Him al - ways,
2. What gain to us is heav - y sor - row? What gain, if woe and grief we bear?
3. Be still, and wait up - on His pleas - ure; Do not against God's will con - tend.
4. He knows the ver - y hours of glad - ness; He knows just when it prof - its us.
5. Sing, pray, and walk on God's own highways; Per - form your du - ty kind and true;

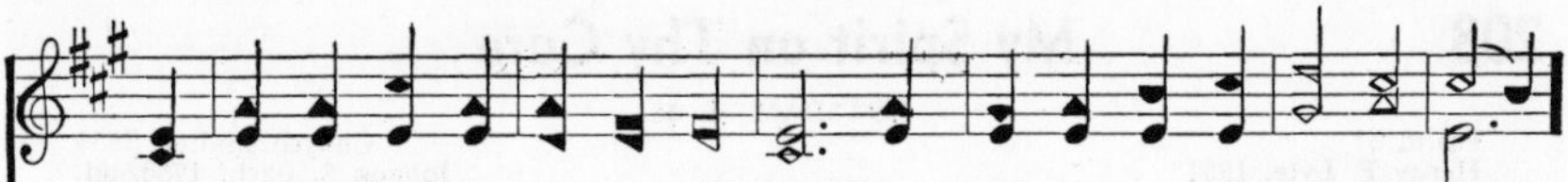

He'll be sustained by love a - bid - ing, Through all the e - vil of his days.
What gain, if we, on ev - ery mor - row, De - plore our hardships and our care?
With loving hands your cares He'll measure And bear you up in all He sends.
If on - ly He can find us blameless, And see no dross and wrong in us:
And trust in heaven's bless - ing al - ways; Then He'll grow dai - ly in you new.

Who trusts in God's al - might - y hand He does not build on sink - ing sand.
We make our cross and sor - ri - ness The great - er by our fret - ful - ness.
To Him, who chose us for His own, Our deep - est hopes and wants are known.
Then He will come be - fore we call And shed His blessing on us all.
For he who trusts in God a - bove Will own His friendship and His love. A-men.

In Sorrow and Pain 207

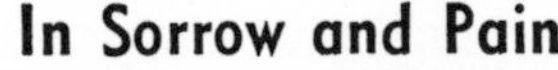

BEST REFUGE 5. 5. 9.

Zion's Harp
1. In sor - row and pain Thy trust do re - tain
2. When bur - dened with care, When thou wouldst de - spair,
3. He'll light - en thy load, And lev - el the road,
4. He's gen - tle and kind, Rich bless - ings thou'lt find,
In Je - sus, the mer - ci - ful Sav - iour.
Then call on thy lov - ing Re - deem - er.
And bear thee on hands of com - pas - sion.
His word gives thee peace ev - er - last - ing.

208 My Spirit on Thy Care

POTSDAM S. M.

Psalm 31
Henry F. Lyte, 1834

Church Psalter, 1854
Johann S. Bach, 1750, ad.

1. My spir - it on Thy care, Blest Sav - iour, I re - cline;
2. In Thee I place my trust, On Thee I calm - ly rest;
3. What - e'er e - vents be - tide, Thy will they all per - form;
4. Let good or ill be - fall, It must be good for me;
Thou wilt not leave me to de-spair, For Thou art Love di - vine.
I know Thee good, I know Thee just, And count Thy choice the best.
Safe in Thy breast my head I hide Nor fear the com - ing storm.
Se - cure of hav - ing Thee in all, Of hav - ing all in Thee. A-men.

209 Lord Jesus Christ, We Seek Thy Face

HOLLEY 8. 8. 8. 8.

Alexander Stewart

George Hews

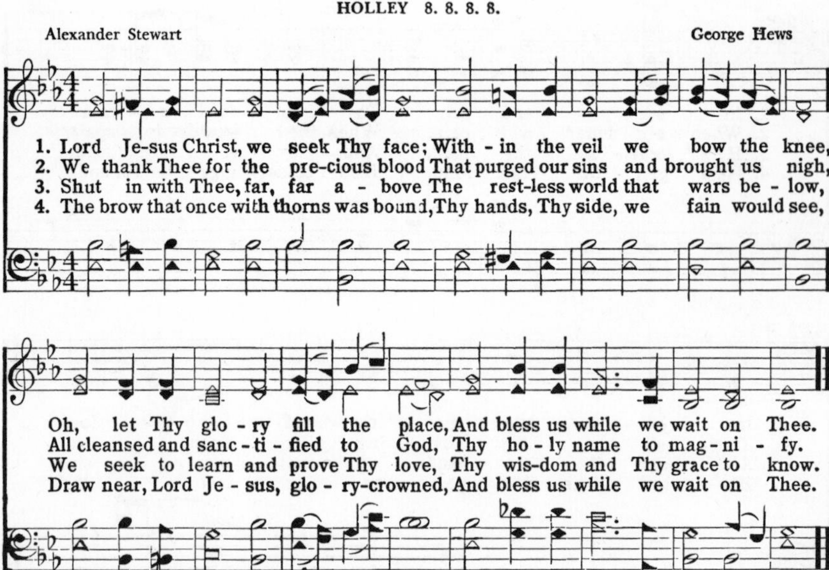

1. Lord Je-sus Christ, we seek Thy face; With - in the veil we bow the knee,
2. We thank Thee for the pre-cious blood That purged our sins and brought us nigh,
3. Shut in with Thee, far, far a - bove The rest-less world that wars be - low,
4. The brow that once with thorns was bound, Thy hands, Thy side, we fain would see,
Oh, let Thy glo - ry fill the place, And bless us while we wait on Thee.
All cleansed and sanc - ti - fied to God, Thy ho - ly name to mag - ni - fy.
We seek to learn and prove Thy love, Thy wis - dom and Thy grace to know.
Draw near, Lord Je - sus, glo - ry-crowned, And bless us while we wait on Thee.

Father, in Thy Mysterious Presence Kneeling 210

HENLEY 11. 10. 11. 10.

Samuel Johnson, 1846

Lowell Mason, 1854

1. Fa - ther, in Thy mys - te - rious pres - ence kneel - ing,
2. Lord, we have wan - dered forth through doubt and sor - row,
3. Now, Fa - ther, now in Thy dear pres - ence kneel - ing,
Fain would our souls feel all Thy kin - dling love;
And Thou hast made each step an on - ward one;
Our spir - its yearn to feel Thy kin - dling love;
For we are weak, and need some deep re - veal - ing
And we will ev - er trust each un - known mor - row;
Now make us strong; we need Thy deep re - veal - ing
Of trust and strength and calm - ness from a - bove.
Thou wilt sus - tain us till its work is done.
Of trust and strength and calm - ness from a - bove. A-men.

211 Teach Me to Pray

PRAYER P. M.

Lina Z. Ressler
Thersa Hostetler
1. Teach me to pray, my Fa - ther, in life's morn - ing,
2. Teach me to pray, my Fa - ther, at the noon - time,
3. Teach me to pray, my Fa - ther, in the eve - ning,
For there are man - y things that I must learn; Help me to
When life is bus - y and there's much to do; I need Thy
My bus - y days are pass - ing like a dream; The shad - ows
find in Thee both help and warn - ing, I need Thy
guid - ance for my du - ties throng me And ev - ery
length - en, and I'm grow - ing wea - ry And ti - red
guid - ing voice at ev - ery turn.
mo - ment I need strength a - new.
as I catch the twi - light's gleam.
Stanzas 1 & 2
And now I trust in Thee,
My Help - er ev - ery day,
For help to Thee I flee.
keep me in Thine own way.
3rd stanza
Still un - done things I

long to do; Oh, keep me calm and strength re - new. A - men.

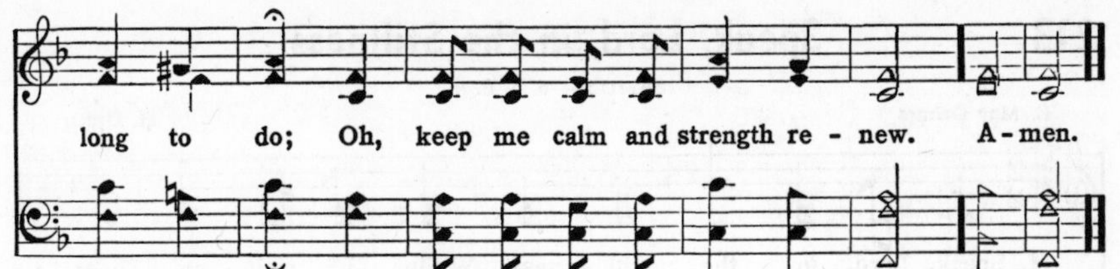

Nearer, My God, to Thee 212

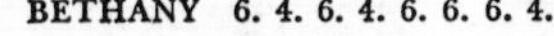

BETHANY 6. 4. 6. 4. 6. 6. 6. 4.

Mrs. Sarah F. Adams, 1840

Lowell Mason

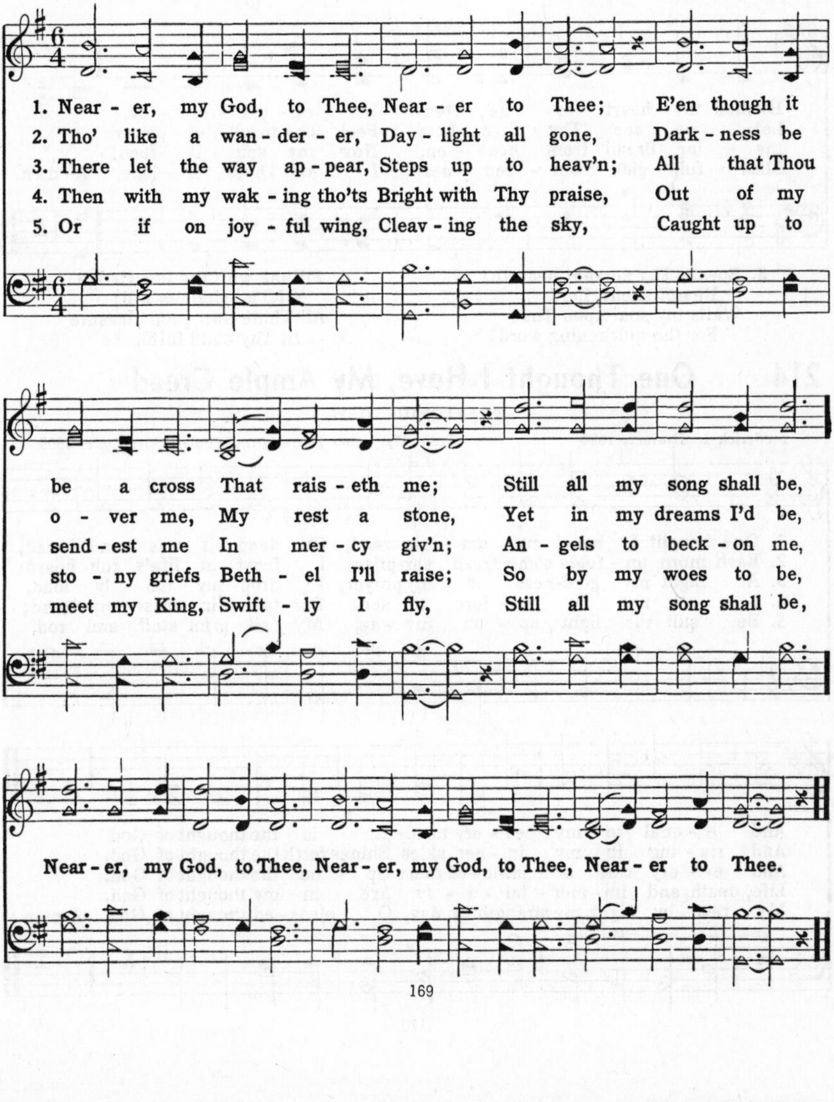

1. Near - er, my God, to Thee, Near - er to Thee; E'en though it
2. Tho' like a wan - der - er, Day - light all gone, Dark - ness be
3. There let the way ap - pear, Steps up to heav'n; All that Thou
4. Then with my wak - ing tho'ts Bright with Thy praise, Out of my
5. Or if on joy - ful wing, Cleav - ing the sky, Caught up to
be a cross That rais - eth me; Still all my song shall be,
o - ver me, My rest a stone, Yet in my dreams I'd be,
send - est me In mer - cy giv'n; An - gels to beck - on me,
sto - ny griefs Beth - el I'll raise; So by my woes to be,
meet my King, Swift - ly I fly, Still all my song shall be,
Near - er, my God, to Thee, Near - er, my God, to Thee, Near - er to Thee.

213 Speak, Lord, in the Stillness

SAMUEL 6. 5. 6. 5.

E. May Grimes H. Green

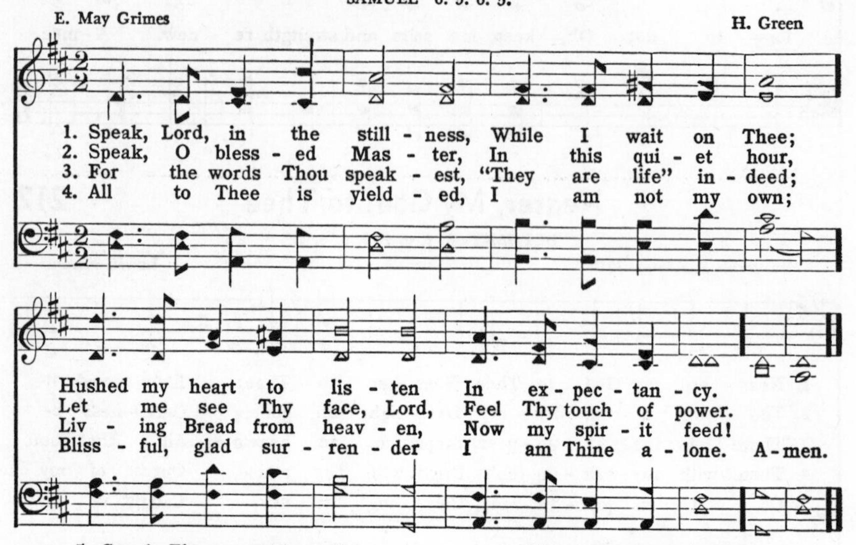
1. Speak, Lord, in the still - ness, While I wait on Thee;
2. Speak, O bless - ed Mas - ter, In this qui - et hour,
3. For the words Thou speak - est, "They are life" in - deed;
4. All to Thee is yield - ed, I am not my own;
Hushed my heart to lis - ten In ex - pec - tan - cy.
Let me see Thy face, Lord, Feel Thy touch of power.
Liv - ing Bread from heav - en, Now my spir - it feed!
Bliss - ful, glad sur - ren - der I am Thine a - lone. A-men.

5. Speak, Thy servant heareth!
Be not silent, Lord:
Waits my soul upon Thee
For the quickening word!

6. Fill me with the knowledge
Of Thy glorious will;
All Thine own good pleasure
In Thy child fulfil.

214 One Thought I Have, My Ample Creed

PRAETORIUS C. M.

Frederick L. Hosmer, 1880 From Harmonai Hymnorum Scholae Gorlicensis, 1599

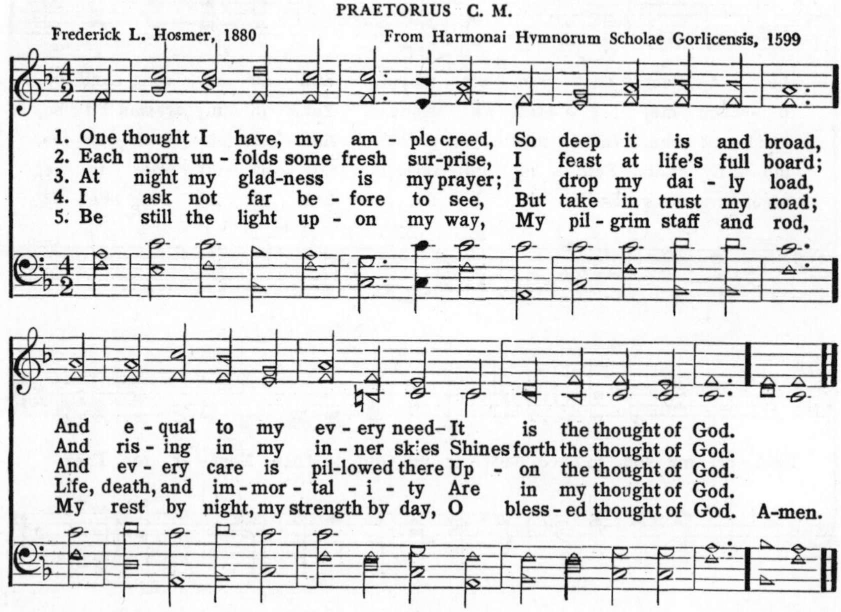
1. One thought I have, my am - ple creed, So deep it is and broad,
2. Each morn un - folds some fresh sur-prise, I feast at life's full board;
3. At night my glad-ness is my prayer; I drop my dai - ly load,
4. I ask not far be - fore to see, But take in trust my road;
5. Be still the light up - on my way, My pil - grim staff and rod,
And e - qual to my ev - ery need- It is the thought of God.
And ris - ing in my in - ner skies Shines forth the thought of God.
And ev - ery care is pil-lowed there Up - on the thought of God.
Life, death, and im - mor - tal - i - ty Are in my thought of God.
My rest by night, my strength by day, O bless - ed thought of God. A-men.

I Think When I Read That Sweet Story 215

SWEET STORY
Greek Folksong
Arr. William B. Bradbury, 1859
Har. Winfred Douglas, 1918
Jemima Luke, 1841
1. I think when I read that sweet story of old, When Jesus was here among men, How He called little children as lambs to His fold, I should like to have been with them then.
2. I wish that His hands had been placed on my head, That His arm had been thrown around me, And that I might have seen His kind look when He said: "Let the little ones come unto me."
3. Yet still to His footstool in prayer I may go, And ask for a share in His love; And if I thus earnestly seek Him below, I shall see Him and hear Him above. A-men.

216 How Firm a Foundation

ADESTE FIDELES 11. 11. 11. 11.
George Keith, 1787
J. Reading
Wade's Cantus Diversi, 1751
1. How firm a foun-da - tion, ye saints of the Lord, Is laid for your faith in His
2. "Fear not, I am with thee, O be not dismayed; For I am thy God, and will
3. "When thro' the deep wa-ters I call thee to go, The riv - ers of sor-rows shall
4. "The soul that on Je - sus hath leaned for re - pose, I will not, I will not de -
ex - cel-lent Word! What more can He say than to you He hath said–Who un - to the
still give thee aid; I'll strengthen thee, help thee, and cause thee to stand, Up-held by my
not o-ver-flow; For I will be with thee, thy trou-bles to bless, And sanc-ti - fy
sert to his foes; That soul, tho' all hell should endeav-or to shake, I'll nev - er, no,
Sav-iour for refuge have fled? Who un - to the Sav - iour for ref-uge have fled?
righteous, om-nip-o-tent hand, Up - held by my righteous, om-nip - o-tent hand.
to thee thy deep-est dis-tress, And sanc - ti - fy to thee thy deep-est dis-tress.
nev - er, no, nev-er for - sake, I'll nev - er, no, nev - er, no, nev - er, for-sake."
217 God's Law Is Perfect
ST. ANDREW C. M.
Psalm 19
Scottish Psalter, 1650
Tans'ur's New Harmony of Zion, 1764
1. God's law is per - fect, and con-verts The soul in sin that lies:
2. The stat - utes of the Lord are right, And do re - joice the heart:
3. Un - spot - ted is the fear of God, And doth en - dure for - e'er:
4. They more than gold, yea, much fine gold, To be de - sir - ed are;
5. More - o - ver, they Thy serv - ant warn How he his life should frame:

God's tes - ti - mo - ny is most sure, And makes the sim - ple wise.
The Lord's com-mand is pure, and doth Light to the eyes im-part.
The judg-ments of the Lord are true And right-eous al - to-gether.
Than hon - ey, hon - ey from the comb That drop-peth, sweet-er far.
A great re - ward pro-vid - ed is For them that keep the same. A-men.

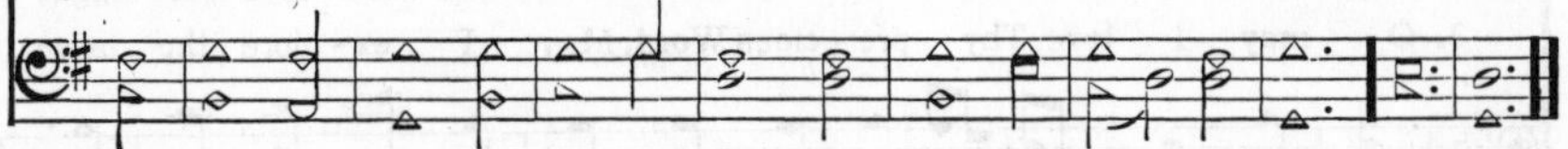

O the Unsearchable Riches 218

UNSEARCHABLE RICHES 10. 7. 10. 7. Ref.

Fanny J. Crosby John R. Sweney

1. O the un-search-a - ble rich - es of Christ! Wealth that can nev-er be told;
2. O the un-search-a - ble rich - es of Christ! Who shall their greatness de -clare!
3. O the un-search-a - ble rich - es of Christ! Free - ly, how free-ly they flow;
4. O the un-search-a - ble rich - es of Christ! Who would not glad-ly en - dure

FINE

Rich - es ex-haust-less of mer - cy and grace, Precious, more precious than gold!
Jew-els whose lus- ter our lives may a - dorn, Pearls that the poor-est may wear.
Mak-ing the souls of the faith-ful and true Hap - py wher-ev - er they go.
Tri - als, af - flic-tions, and cross-es on earth, Rich - es like these to se - cure!

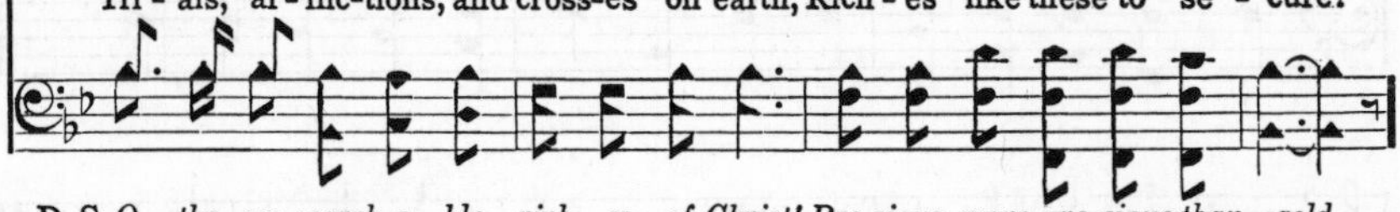

D. S. *O the un-search-a - ble rich - es of Christ! Pre-cious, more pre-cious than gold.*

REFRAIN D.S.

Pre - cious, more pre - cious; Wealth that can nev - er be told; A-men.

219 Thy Word Is Like a Garden, Lord

SERAPH C. M. D.

Edwin Hodder

Old English Melody

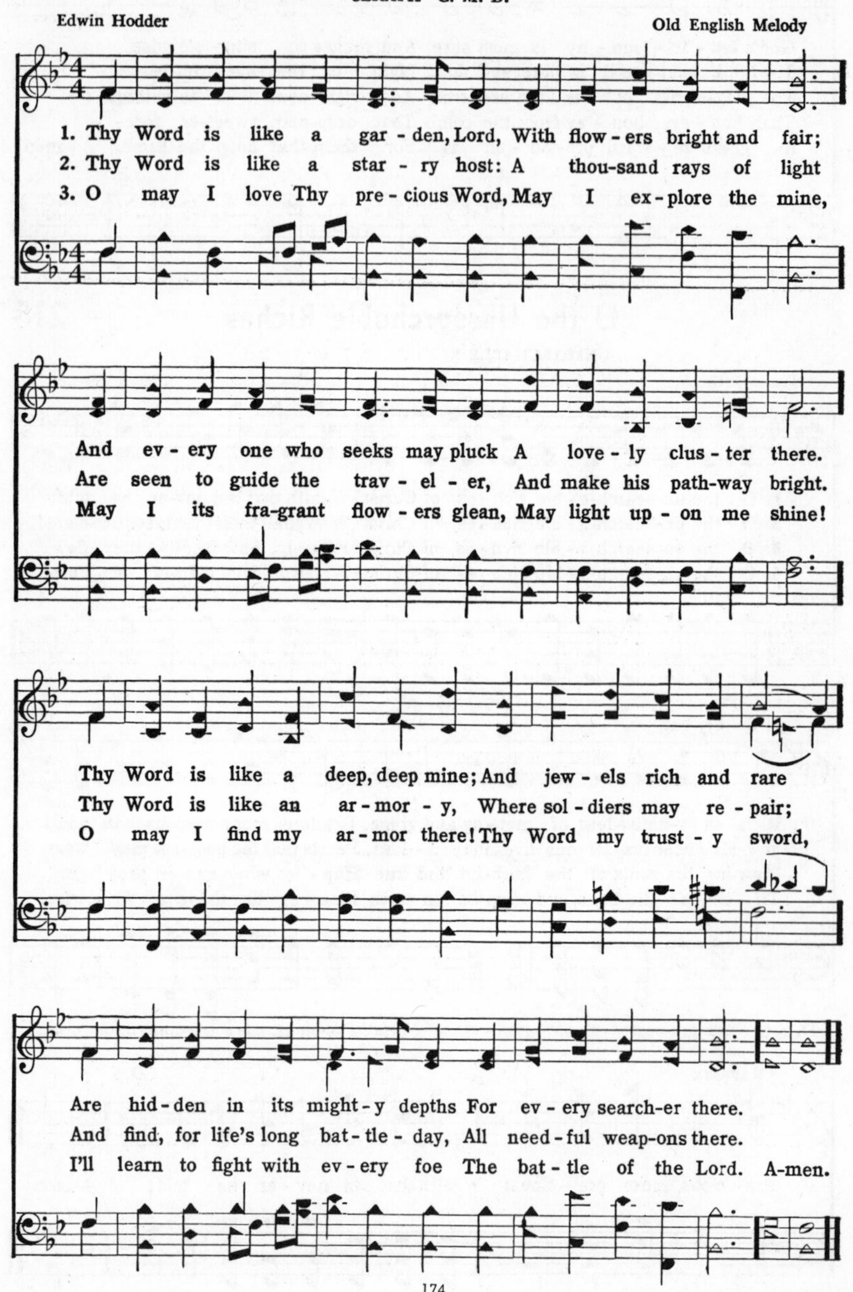
1. Thy Word is like a gar - den, Lord, With flow - ers bright and fair;
2. Thy Word is like a star - ry host: A thou-sand rays of light
3. O may I love Thy pre - cious Word, May I ex - plore the mine,
And ev - ery one who seeks may pluck A love - ly clus - ter there.
Are seen to guide the trav - el - er, And make his path-way bright.
May I its fra-grant flow - ers glean, May light up - on me shine!
Thy Word is like a deep, deep mine; And jew - els rich and rare
Thy Word is like an ar - mor - y, Where sol - diers may re - pair;
O may I find my ar - mor there! Thy Word my trust - y sword,
Are hid - den in its might - y depths For ev - ery search-er there.
And find, for life's long bat - tle - day, All need - ful weap-ons there.
I'll learn to fight with ev - ery foe The bat - tle of the Lord. A-men.

Shine Thou upon Us, Lord 220

BROUGHTON 6. 6. 6. 6. D.

John Ellerton, 1826-1893
Melody by Thomas Hastings, 1784-1872
1. Shine Thou up - on us, Lord, True Light of men, to - day,
2. Breathe Thou up - on us, Lord, Thy Spir - it's liv - ing flame,
3. Speak Thou for us, O Lord, In all we say of Thee;
4. Live Thou with - in us, Lord; Thy mind and will be ours;
And through the writ - ten Word Thy ver - y Self dis - play;
That so with one ac - cord Our lips may tell Thy name.
Ac - cord - ing to Thy Word Let all our teach - ing be;
Be Thou be - lov'd, a - dored, And served with all our pow'rs,
That so, from hearts which burn With gaz - ing on Thy face,
Give Thou the hear - ing ear, Fix Thou the wan-d'ring thought,
That so Thy lambs may know Their own true Shep-herd's voice,
That so our lives may teach Thy chil - dren what Thou art,
Thy lit - tle ones may learn The won-ders of Thy grace.
That those we teach may hear The great things Thou hast wrought.
Wher - e'er He leads them go, And in His love re - joice.
And plead, by more than speech, For Thee with ev - ery heart. A - men.

221 How I Love Thy Law, O Lord!

THY LAW 7. 7. 7. 7. Ref.

Psalm 119

Arr. Benjamin Carr

1. How I love Thy law, O Lord! Dai-ly joy its truths af-ford;
2. Thy commandments in my heart Tru-est wis-dom can im-part;
3. While my heart Thy will o-beys, I am kept from e-vil ways;
In its con-stant light I go, Wise to con-quer ev-ery foe.
To mine eyes Thy pre-cepts show Wis-dom more than sa-ges know.
From Thy law, with Thee to guide, I have nev-er turned a-side.
CHORUS
Sweet-er are Thy words to me Than all oth-er good can be;
Safe I walk, Thy truth my light, Hat-ing false-hood, lov-ing right.

Come, Ye Sinners

222

JEREMIAH 8. 7. 8. 7. D.

Joseph Hart
Jeremiah Ingals
1. Come, ye sin-ners, poor and need-y, Weak and wounded, sick and sore,
2. Let not conscience make you lin-ger, Nor of fit-ness fond-ly dream;
3. Ag-o-niz-ing in the gar-den, Lo, your Sav-iour pros-trate lies!
4. Lo! the ris-ing Lord as-cending, Pleads the vir-tue of His blood;
5. Saints and an-gels, joined in concert, Sing the praises of the Lamb,
Je-sus read-y stands to save you, Full of pit-y, love, and power;
All the fit-ness He re-quir-eth Is to feel your need of Him;
On the bloody tree be-hold Him! Hear Him cry be-fore He dies:
Ven-ture on Him, ven-ture free-ly, Let no oth-er trust in-trude;
While the bliss-ful seats of heav-en Sweet-ly ech-o with His name;
He is a-ble, He is a-ble, He is will-ing-doubt no more;
This He gives you, this He gives you, 'Tis the Sav-iour's ris-ing beam;
"It is fin-ished, it is fin-ished!" Sin-ners, will not this suf-fice?
None but Je-sus, none but Je-sus Can do help-less sin-ners good;
Hal-le-lu-jah! Hal-le-lu-jah! Sin-ners here may do the same;
He is a-ble, He is a-ble, He is will-ing-doubt no more.
This He gives you, this He gives you, 'Tis the Sav-iour's ris-ing beam.
"It is fin-ished, it is fin-ished!" Sin-ners, will not this suf-fice?
None but Je-sus, none but Je-sus Can do help-less sin-ners good.
Hal-le-lu-jah! hal-le-lu-jah! Sin-ners here may do the same.

223 Amazing Grace! How Sweet the Sound

McINTOSH C. M.

John Newton — Arr. Edwin O. Excell

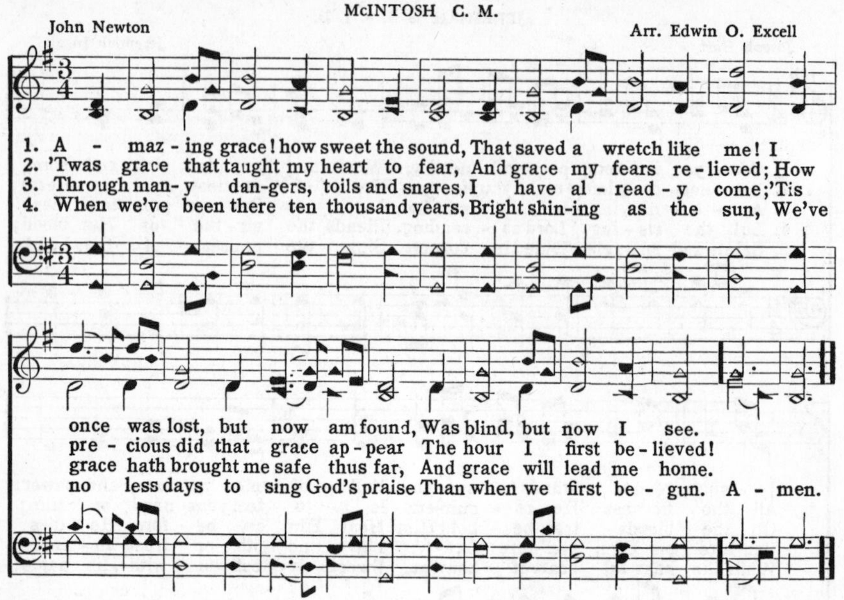
1. A - maz - ing grace! how sweet the sound, That saved a wretch like me! I once was lost, but now am found, Was blind, but now I see.
2. 'Twas grace that taught my heart to fear, And grace my fears re - lieved; How pre - cious did that grace ap - pear The hour I first be - lieved!
3. Through man - y dan - gers, toils and snares, I have al - read - y come; 'Tis grace hath brought me safe thus far, And grace will lead me home.
4. When we've been there ten thousand years, Bright shin - ing as the sun, We've no less days to sing God's praise Than when we first be - gun. A - men.

224 And Can It Be That I Should Gain

WESLEY 8. 8. 8. 8. 8. 8.

Charles Wesley — Jeremiah Ingalls

1. And can it be that I should gain An in - t'rest in the Saviour's blood? Died He for me, who caused His pain? For me, who Him to death pur - sued?
2. 'Tis mys - t'ry all! Th'Im - mortal dies! Who can ex - plore His strange de - sign? In vain the first-born ser - aph tries To sound the depths of love di - vine;
3. He left His Fa - ther's throne a - bove, So free, so in - fi - nite His grace! Emp - tied Him - self of all but love, And bled for Ad - am's help - less race;
4. Long my im - pris - oned spir - it lay, Fast bound in sin and na - ture's night; Thine eye dif - fused a quick - 'ning ray, I woke, the dun - geon flamed with light:
5. No con - dem - na - tion now I dread, Je - sus, with all in Him, is mine; A - live in Him, my liv - ing Head, And clothed in right - eous - ness di - vine,

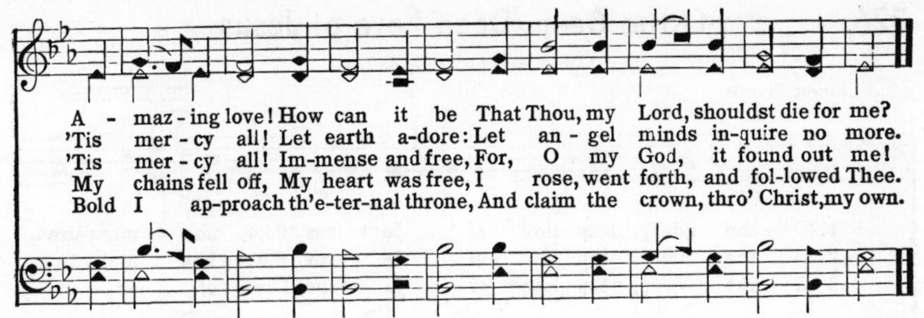
A - maz - ing love! How can it be That Thou, my Lord, shouldst die for me?
'Tis mer - cy all! Let earth a-dore: Let an - gel minds in-quire no more.
'Tis mer - cy all! Im-mense and free, For, O my God, it found out me!
My chains fell off, My heart was free, I rose, went forth, and fol-lowed Thee.
Bold I ap-proach th'e-ter-nal throne, And claim the crown, thro' Christ, my own.

God Loved the World So that He Gave **225**

ST. CRISPIN L. M.

John 3: 16
Also hat Gott die Welt geliebt
Author unknown, 1791, cento
Tr. August Crull, 1923, alt.

George J. Elvey, 1862

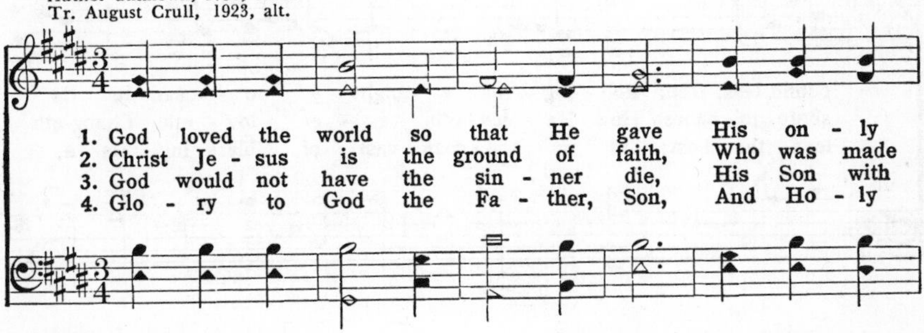

1. God loved the world so that He gave His on - ly
2. Christ Je - sus is the ground of faith, Who was made
3. God would not have the sin - ner die, His Son with
4. Glo - ry to God the Fa - ther, Son, And Ho - ly

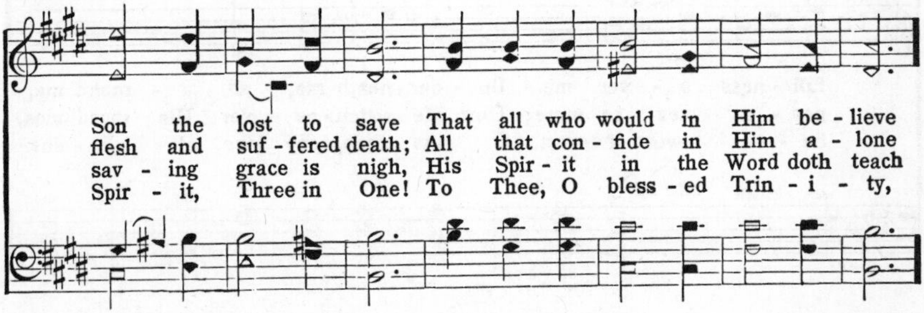

Son the lost to save That all who would in Him be - lieve
flesh and suf - fered death; All that con - fide in Him a - lone
sav - ing grace is nigh, His Spir - it in the Word doth teach
Spir - it, Three in One! To Thee, O bless - ed Trin - i - ty,

Should ev - er - last - ing life re - ceive.
Are built on this chief Cor - ner - stone.
How man the bless - ed goal may reach.
Be praise now and e - ter - nal - ly! A - men.

226 O the Deep, Deep Love of Jesus

TON-Y BOTEL 8. 7. 8. 7. D.

S. Trevor Francis
T. J. Williams
1. O the deep, deep love of Je - sus, Vast, un - meas-ured,
2. O the deep, deep love of Je - sus, Spread His praise from
3. O the deep, deep love of Je - sus, Love of ev - ery
bound-less, free; Roll - ing as a might - y o - cean In its
shore to shore; How He lov - eth, ev - er lov - eth, Chang-eth
love the best; 'Tis an o - cean vast of bless - ing, 'Tis a
full - ness o - ver me. Un - der - neath me, all a - round me,
nev - er, nev - er more; How He watch - es o'er His loved ones,
ha - ven sweet of rest, O the deep, deep love of Je - sus,
Is the cur - rent of Thy love; Lead - ing on - ward, lead - ing
Died to call them all His own; How for them He in - ter -
'Tis a heav'n of heav'ns to me; And it lifts me up to

Music by W. Gwenlyn Evans and Sons.

Lord, I Hear Showers of Blessing 227

EVEN ME 8. 7. 8. 7. 6. 7.

Elizabeth Codner, 1860

William B. Bradbury, 1862

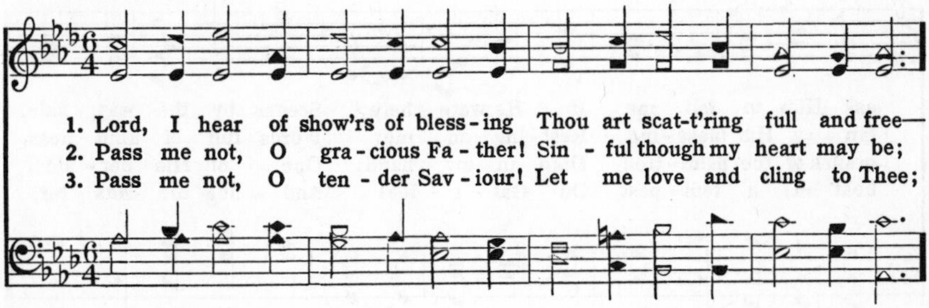

1. Lord, I hear of show'rs of bless - ing Thou art scat - t'ring full and free—
2. Pass me not, O gra - cious Fa - ther! Sin - ful though my heart may be;
3. Pass me not, O ten - der Sav - iour! Let me love and cling to Thee;

Show'rs, the thirst - y land re - fresh - ing; Let Thy bless - ing fall on me—
Thou might'st leave me, but the rath - er Let Thy mer - cy fall on me—
I am long - ing for Thy fa - vor; Whilst Thou'rt calling, O call me—

E - ven me, E - ven me, Let Thy bless - ing fall on me.
E - ven me, E - ven me, Let Thy mer - cy fall on me.
E - ven me, E - ven me, Whilst Thou'rt calling, O call me. A - men.

228 Tell Me the Stories of Jesus

STORIES OF JESUS 8. 4. 8. 4. 5. 4. 5. 4.

W. H. Parker, 1904 F. A. Challinor, 1904

1. Tell me the sto-ries of Je - sus I love to hear; Things I would
2. First let me hear how the chil - dren Stood round His knee; And I shall
3. In - to the cit - y I'd fol - low The chil-dren's band, Wav - ing a
4. Tell me, in ac-cents of won - der, How rolled the sea, Toss - ing the
ask Him to tell me If He were here; Scenes by the way - side,
fan - cy His bless - ing Rest - ing on me: Words full of kind - ness,
branch of the palm - tree High in my hand; One of His her - alds,
boat in a tem - pest On Gal - i - lee! And how the Mas - ter,
Tales of the sea, Sto - ries of Je - sus, Tell them to me.
Deeds full of grace, All in the love - light Of Je - sus' face.
Yes, I would sing Loud - est ho - san - nas! Je - sus is King!
Read - y and kind, Chid - ed the bil - lows, And hushed the wind. A - men.

5. Tell how the sparrow that twitters
   On yonder tree,
And the sweet meadow-side lily
   May speak to me—
Give me their message,
   For I would hear
How Jesus taught us
   Our Father's care.

6. Show me that scene in the garden,
   Of bitter pain;
And of the cross where my Saviour
   For me was slain—
Sad ones or bright ones,
   So that they be
Stories of Jesus,
   Tell them to me.

There Is a Fountain Filled with Blood

CLEANSING FOUNTAIN C. M. D.

William Cowper, 1779

Anonymous

1. There is a foun - tain filled with blood, Drawn from Im - man - uel's veins;
2. The dy - ing thief re - joiced to see That foun - tain in his day;
3. Thou dy - ing Lamb, Thy pre - cious blood Shall nev - er lose its pow'r,
4. And when this fee - ble, fal - t'ring tongue Lies si - lent in the grave,
And sin - ners wash - ing in that flood, Lose all their guilt - y stains;
And may I there, tho' vile as he, Wash all my sins a - way;
Till all the ran - somed church of God Are saved to sin no more;
Then in a nob - ler, sweet - er song I'll sing Thy pow'r to save;
Lose all their guilt - y stains, Lose all their guilt - y stains,
Wash all my sins a - way, Wash all my sins a - way,
Are saved to sin no more, Are saved to sin no more,
I'll sing Thy pow'r to save, I'll sing Thy pow'r to save,
And sin - ners, wash - ing in that flood, Lose all their guilt - y stains.
And may I there, tho' vile as he, Wash all my sins a - way.
Till all the ran - somed church of God Are saved to sin no more.
Then in a no - bler, sweet - er song I'll sing Thy pow'r to save.

230 In Tenderness He Sought Me

GORDON 7. 6. 7. 6. 8. 8. Ref.

W. Spencer Walton
Adoniram J. Gordon
1. In ten-der-ness He sought me, Wea-ry and sick with sin,
2. He washed the bleed-ing sin-wounds, And poured in oil and wine;
3. He point-ed to the nail-prints, For me His blood was shed,
4. I'm sit-ting in His pres-ence, The sun-shine of His face,
5. So while the hours are pass-ing, All now is per-fect rest,
And on His shoul-ders brought me, Back to His fold a-gain.
He whis-pered to as-sure me, "I've found thee, thou art mine";
A mock-ing crown so thorn-y, Was placed up-on His head:
While with a-dor-ing won-der His bless-ing I re-trace.
I'm wait-ing for the morn-ing, The bright-est and the best,
While an-gels in His pres-ence sang Un-til the courts of heav-en rang.
I nev-er heard a sweet-er voice, It made my ach-ing heart re-joice!
I won-dered what He saw in me, To suf-fer such deep ag-o-ny.
It seems as if e-ter-nal days Are far too short to sound His praise.
When He will call us to His side, To be with Him, His spot-less bride.
CHORUS
Oh, the love that sought me! Oh, the blood that bought me, Oh, the grace that

brought me to the fold, Won-drous grace that brought me to the fold!

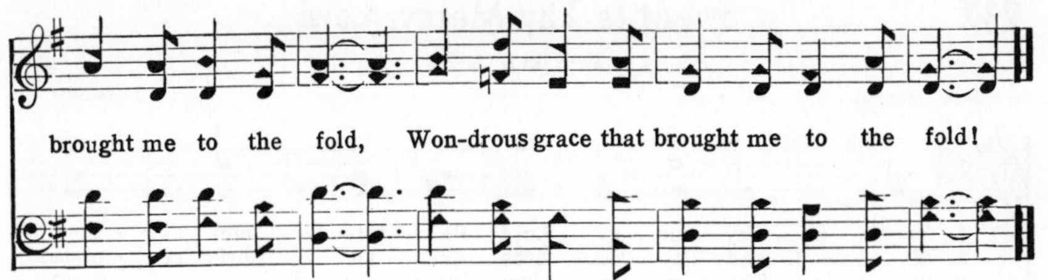

O Listen to Our Wondrous Story

231

WHAT DID HE DO? 9. 7. 9. 7. Ref.

Dr. J. M. Gray

W. Owen

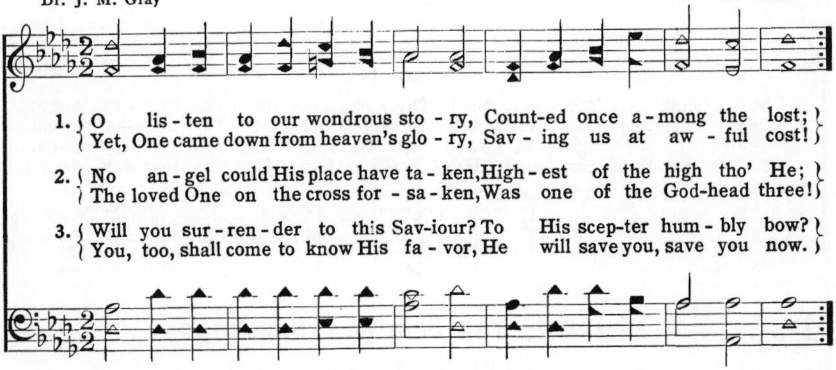

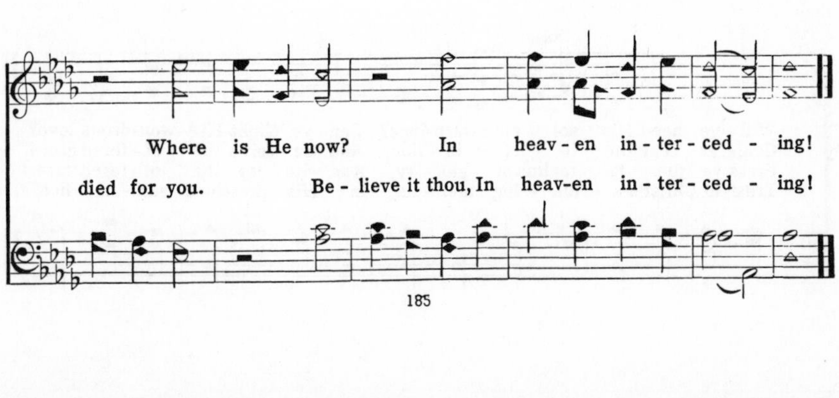

1. { O lis-ten to our wondrous sto - ry, Count-ed once a-mong the lost;
Yet, One came down from heaven's glo - ry, Sav - ing us at aw - ful cost! }
2. { No an-gel could His place have ta - ken, High - est of the high tho' He;
The loved One on the cross for - sa - ken, Was one of the God-head three! }
3. { Will you sur-ren - der to this Sav-iour? To His scep-ter hum - bly bow?
You, too, shall come to know His fa - vor, He will save you, save you now. }

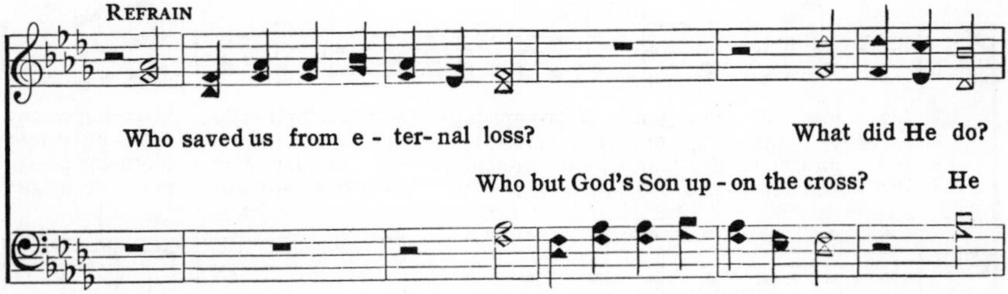

Refrain
Who saved us from e - ter- nal loss? What did He do?
Who but God's Son up - on the cross? He

Where is He now? In heav - en in - ter - ced - ing!
died for you. Be - lieve it thou, In heav-en in - ter - ced - ing!

232 Sweet Is Thy Mercy, Lord

MONSELL S. M.

J. S. Monsell — J. Barnby

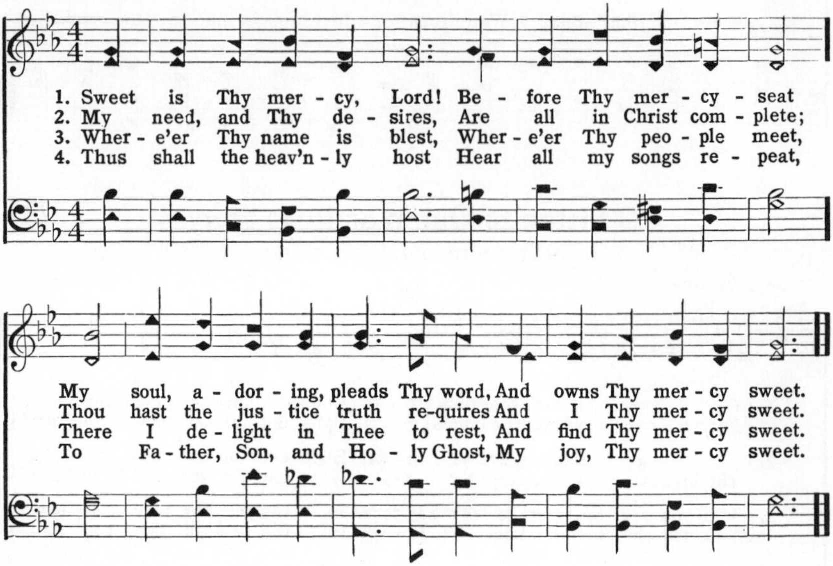

1. Sweet is Thy mer - cy, Lord! Be - fore Thy mer - cy - seat
2. My need, and Thy de - sires, Are all in Christ com - plete;
3. Wher - e'er Thy name is blest, Wher - e'er Thy peo - ple meet,
4. Thus shall the heav'n - ly host Hear all my songs re - peat,

My soul, a - dor - ing, pleads Thy word, And owns Thy mer - cy sweet.
Thou hast the jus - tice truth re - quires And I Thy mer - cy sweet.
There I de - light in Thee to rest, And find Thy mer - cy sweet.
To Fa - ther, Son, and Ho - ly Ghost, My joy, Thy mer - cy sweet.

233 Listen to the Gentle Promptings

WILMOT 8. 7. 8. 7.

James Montgomery — C. M. von Weber

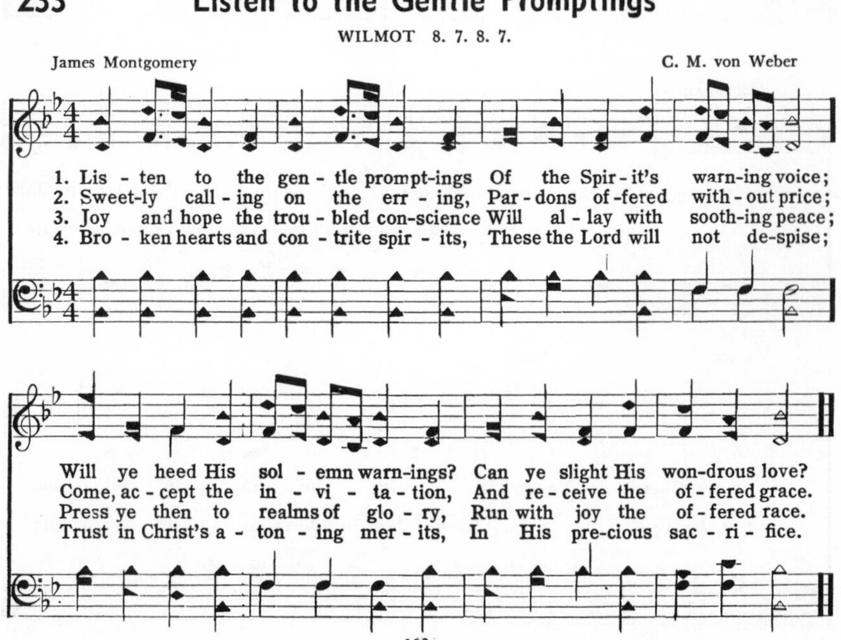
1. Lis - ten to the gen - tle prompt-ings Of the Spir - it's warn-ing voice;
2. Sweet-ly call - ing on the err - ing, Par - dons of - fered with - out price;
3. Joy and hope the trou - bled con-science Will al - lay with sooth-ing peace;
4. Bro - ken hearts and con - trite spir - its, These the Lord will not de - spise;
Will ye heed His sol - emn warn-ings? Can ye slight His won-drous love?
Come, ac - cept the in - vi - ta - tion, And re - ceive the of - fered grace.
Press ye then to realms of glo - ry, Run with joy the of - fered race.
Trust in Christ's a - ton - ing mer - its, In His pre-cious sac - ri - fice.

Just as I Am, Without One Plea 234

WOODWORTH 8. 8. 8. 6.

Charlotte Elliott, 1836 — William B. Bradbury, 1849

1. Just as I am, with - out one plea, But that Thy blood was shed for me, And that Thou bidd'st me come to Thee, O Lamb of God, I come, I come.
2. Just as I am, and wait-ing not To rid my soul of one dark blot, To Thee whose blood can cleanse each spot, O Lamb of God, I come, I come.
3. Just as I am, tho' tossed a-bout With many a con-flict, many a doubt, Fight-ings and fears with-in, with-out, O Lamb of God, I come, I come.
4. Just as I am, poor, wretched, blind; Sight, rich-es, heal - ing of the mind, Yea, all I need, in Thee to find, O Lamb of God, I come, I come.
5. Just as I am! Thou wilt re-ceive, Wilt wel-come, pardon, cleanse, relieve; Be - cause Thy prom-ise I be - lieve, O Lamb of God, I come, I come. A-men.

Jesus, Thou Art the Sinner's Friend 235

I DO BELIEVE C. M.

Richard Burnham

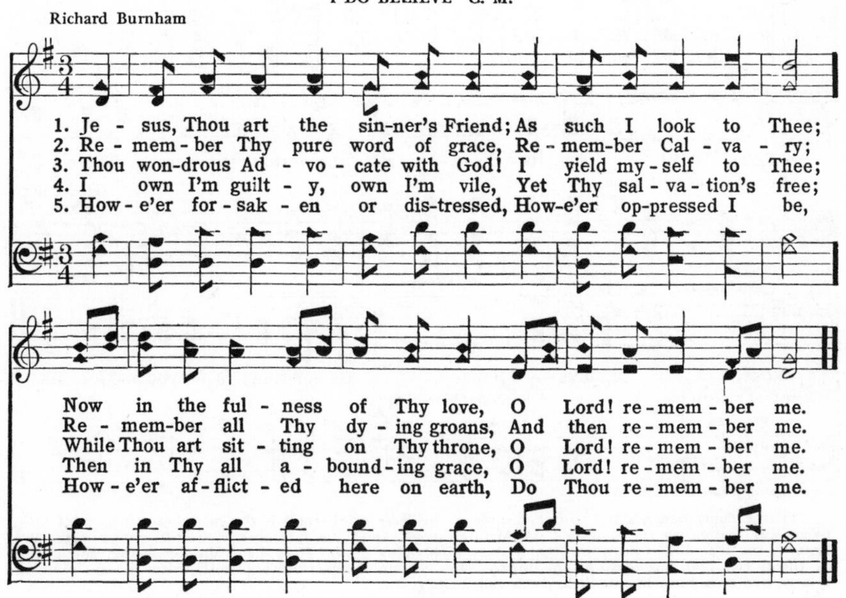

1. Je - sus, Thou art the sin-ner's Friend; As such I look to Thee;
2. Re - mem - ber Thy pure word of grace, Re - mem-ber Cal - va - ry;
3. Thou won-drous Ad - vo - cate with God! I yield my - self to Thee;
4. I own I'm guilt - y, own I'm vile, Yet Thy sal - va - tion's free;
5. How - e'er for - sak - en or dis-tressed, How-e'er op-pressed I be,
Now in the ful - ness of Thy love, O Lord! re - mem - ber me.
Re - mem-ber all Thy dy - ing groans, And then re - mem - ber me.
While Thou art sit - ting on Thy throne, O Lord! re - mem - ber me.
Then in Thy all a - bound - ing grace, O Lord! re - mem - ber me.
How - e'er af - flict - ed here on earth, Do Thou re - mem - ber me.

236 There's a Rose That Is Blooming

ROSE OF SHARON *

H. R. Palmer | H. R. Palmer

1. There's a Rose that is bloom-ing for you, friend, There's a Rose that is bloom-ing for me; Its per-fume is per-vad-ing the world, friend, It's per-fume is for you and for me.
2. Long a-go in the val-ley so fair, friend, Far a-way by the beau-ti-ful sea, This pure Rose in its beau-ty first bloom'd, friend, And it blooms still for you and for me.
3. All in vain did they crush this fair flow'r, friend, All in vain did they shat-ter the tree, For its roots, deep-ly bed-ded, sprang forth, friend, And it blooms still for you and for me.
REFRAIN
There's a Rose, a love-ly Rose, And its beau-ty all the world shall see; There's a Rose, a love-ly Rose, Its per-fume is for you and for me.
Rose that blooms for me, A Rose that blooms for you,
Rose that blooms for me, A Rose that blooms for you,

*Of the many names given to our Saviour, "The Rose of Sharon" is the most beautiful. This little hymn was written on the shores of the Mediterranean, amid the fragrance of ever-blooming roses, and beneath the matchless beauty of Italian skies. Thoughts of the Holy Land on the farther shore, and of the purity and loveliness of the life of our Saviour mingled unconsciously with the surrounding beauty, and took form in this little poem and melody.

We Have Heard the Joyful Sound 237

JESUS SAVES 7. 6. 7. 6. 7. 7. 7. 6.

Priscilla J. Owens — William J. Kirkpatrick

1. We have heard a joy - ful sound, Je - sus saves, Je - sus saves;
2. Waft it on the roll - ing tide, Je - sus saves, Je - sus saves;
3. Sing a - bove the bat - tle's strife, Je - sus saves, Je - sus saves;
4. Give the winds a might - y voice, Je - sus saves, Je - sus saves;
Spread the glad - ness all a - round, Je - sus saves, Je - sus saves.
Tell to sin - ners, far and wide, Je - sus saves, Je - sus saves.
By His death and end - less life, Je - sus saves, Je - sus saves.
Let the na - tions now re - joice, Je - sus saves, Je - sus saves.
Bear the news to ev - ery land, Climb the steeps and cross the waves.
Sing, ye is - lands of the sea, Ech - o back, ye o - cean caves,
Sing it soft - ly thro' the gloom, When the heart for mer - cy craves,
Shout sal - va - tion full and free, High - est hills and deep - est caves,
On - ward, 'tis our Lord's com - mand, Je - sus saves, Je - sus saves.
Earth shall keep her ju - bi - lee, Je - sus saves, Je - sus saves.
Sing in tri - umph o'er the tomb, Je - sus saves, Je - sus saves.
This our song of vic - to - ry, Je - sus saves, Je - sus saves.

238 O Have You Not Heard of That Beautiful Stream

ICH WEISS EINEN STROM 11. 7. 11. 7. Ref.

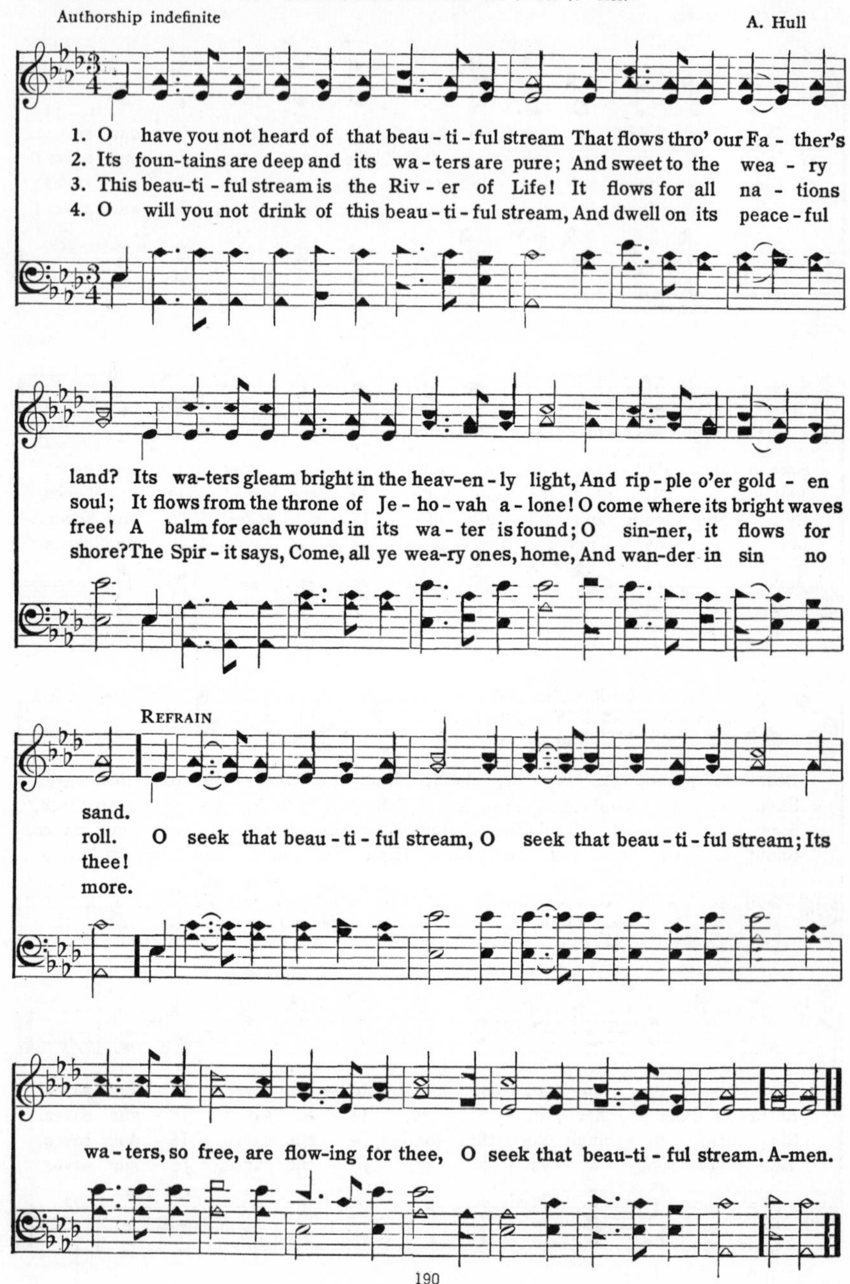
Authorship indefinite
A. Hull
1. O have you not heard of that beau - ti - ful stream That flows thro' our Fa - ther's land? Its wa-ters gleam bright in the heav-en - ly light, And rip - ple o'er gold - en sand.
2. Its foun-tains are deep and its wa - ters are pure; And sweet to the wea - ry soul; It flows from the throne of Je - ho - vah a - lone! O come where its bright waves roll.
3. This beau-ti - ful stream is the Riv - er of Life! It flows for all na - tions free! A balm for each wound in its wa - ter is found; O sin-ner, it flows for thee!
4. O will you not drink of this beau - ti - ful stream, And dwell on its peace - ful shore? The Spir - it says, Come, all ye wea-ry ones, home, And wan-der in sin no more.
Refrain
O seek that beau - ti - ful stream, O seek that beau - ti - ful stream; Its wa - ters, so free, are flow-ing for thee, O seek that beau-ti - ful stream. A-men.

Wonderful Birth, to a Manger He Came 239

WONDERFUL 10. 10. 10. 10. Ref.

A. H. A. — A. H. Ackley

1. Won-der - ful birth, to a man - ger He came, Made in the like-ness of
2. Won-der - ful life, full of serv - ice so free, Friend to the poor and the
3. Won-der - ful death, for it meant not de - feat, Cal - va - ry made His great
4. Won-der - ful hope, He is com - ing a - gain, Com - ing as King o'er the
man, to pro - claim God's boundless love for a world sick with sin, Plead-ing with
need - y was He; Un - fail - ing good-ness on all He bestowed, Un - dy - ing
mis - sion com - plete, Wrought our redemp - tion, and when He a - rose, Ban - ished for-
na - tions to reign; Glo - ri - ous prom - ise, His word can - not fail, His righteous
sin - ners to let Him come in.
faith in the vil - est He showed.
ev - er the last of our foes.
king-dom at last must pre - vail!
Chorus
Won-der - ful name He bears, Won-der - ful
accel.
a tempo
crown He wears, Won-der - ful bless-ings His tri-umphs af - ford; Won - der - ful
Cal - va-ry, Won-der-ful grace for me, Won-der-ful love of my Won-der-ful Lord!

240 My Faith Has Found a Resting Place

NORSE AIR C. M. Ref.

Lidie H. Edmunds

Arr. William J. Kirkpatrick

1. My faith has found a rest-ing place, Not in de-vice nor creed;
2. E-nough for me that Je-sus saves, This ends my fear and doubt;
3. My heart is lean-ing on the Word, The writ-ten Word of God,
4. My great Phy-si-cian heals the sick, The lost He came to save;
I trust the Ev-er-liv-ing One, His wounds for me shall plead.
A sin-ful soul I come to Him, He'll nev-er cast me out.
Sal-va-tion by my Sav-iour's name, Sal-va-tion thro' His blood.
For me His pre-cious blood He shed, For me His life He gave.
CHORUS
I need no oth-er ar-gu-ment, I need no oth-er plea,
It is e-nough that Je-sus died, And that He died for me.

Grace Greater Than Our Sin 241

MARVELOUS GRACE 9. 9. 9. 9. Ref.

Julia H. Johnston
D. B. Towner
1. Mar - vel - ous grace of our lov - ing Lord, Grace that ex - ceeds our
2. Sin and de - spair like the sea waves cold, Threat-en the soul with
3. Dark is the stain that we can - not hide, What can a - vail to
4. Mar - vel - ous, in - fi - nite, match-less grace, Free - ly be - stowed on
sin and our guilt, Yon - der on Cal - va - ry's mount out - poured,
in - fi - nite loss; Grace that is great - er, yes, grace un - told,
wash it a - way? Look, there is flow - ing a crim - son tide;
all who be - lieve; You that are long - ing to see His face,
CHORUS
There where the blood of the Lamb was spilt. Grace, grace,
Points to the Ref - uge, the Might - y Cross.
Whit - er than snow you may be to - day.
Will you this mo - ment His grace re - ceive? Mar - vel - ous grace,
God's grace, Grace that will par - don and cleanse with-in; Grace
In - fi - nite grace, Mar - vel - ous
grace, God's grace, Grace that is great - er than all our sin.
grace, In - fi - nite grace,

242 I Hear the Words of Love

ST. MICHAEL S. M.

Horatius Bonar — From the Genevan Psalter

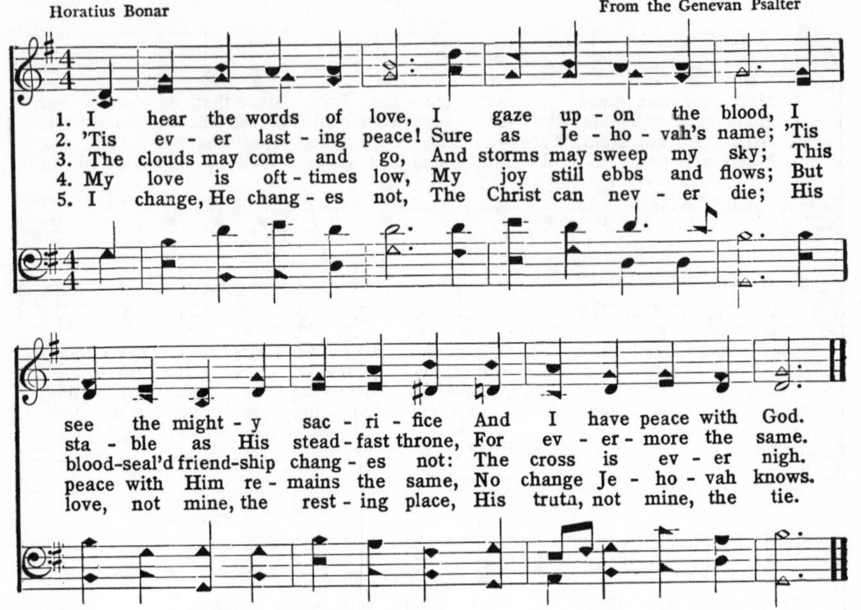

1. I hear the words of love, I gaze up - on the blood, I
2. 'Tis ev - er last - ing peace! Sure as Je - ho - vah's name; 'Tis
3. The clouds may come and go, And storms may sweep my sky; This
4. My love is oft - times low, My joy still ebbs and flows; But
5. I change, He chang - es not, The Christ can nev - er die; His
see the might - y sac - ri - fice And I have peace with God.
sta - ble as His stead - fast throne, For ev - er - more the same.
blood-seal'd friend-ship chang - es not: The cross is ev - er nigh.
peace with Him re - mains the same, No change Je - ho - vah knows.
love, not mine, the rest - ing place, His truth, not mine, the tie.

243 I Am Not Skilled to Understand

GREENWELL 8. 7. 8. 7.

Dora Greenwell — Wm. J. Kirkpatrick

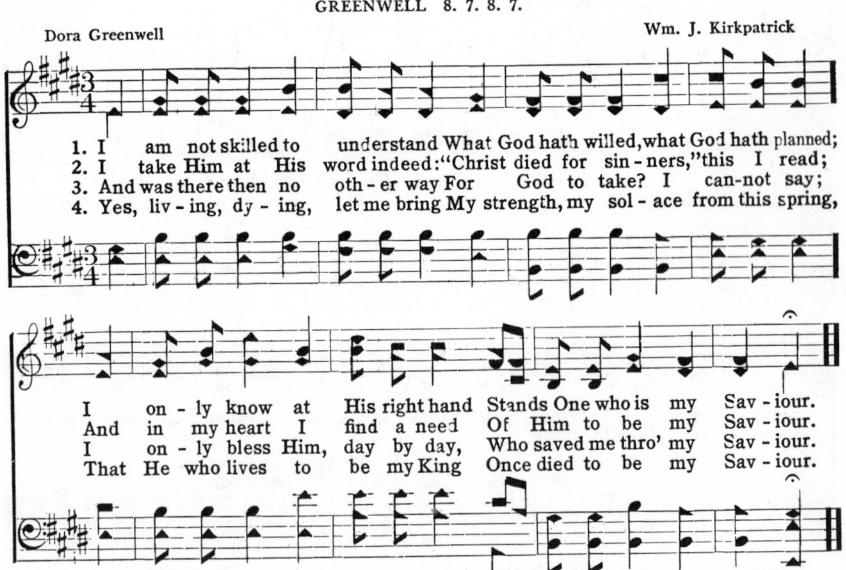

1. I am not skilled to understand What God hath willed, what God hath planned;
2. I take Him at His word indeed: "Christ died for sin - ners," this I read;
3. And was there then no oth - er way For God to take? I can-not say;
4. Yes, liv - ing, dy - ing, let me bring My strength, my sol - ace from this spring,
I on - ly know at His right hand Stands One who is my Sav - iour.
And in my heart I find a need Of Him to be my Sav - iour.
I on - ly bless Him, day by day, Who saved me thro' my Sav - iour.
That He who lives to be my King Once died to be my Sav - iour.

King of My Life I Crown Thee Now

LEAD ME TO CALVARY C. M. Ref.

Jennie Evelyn Hussey

Wm. J. Kirkpatrick

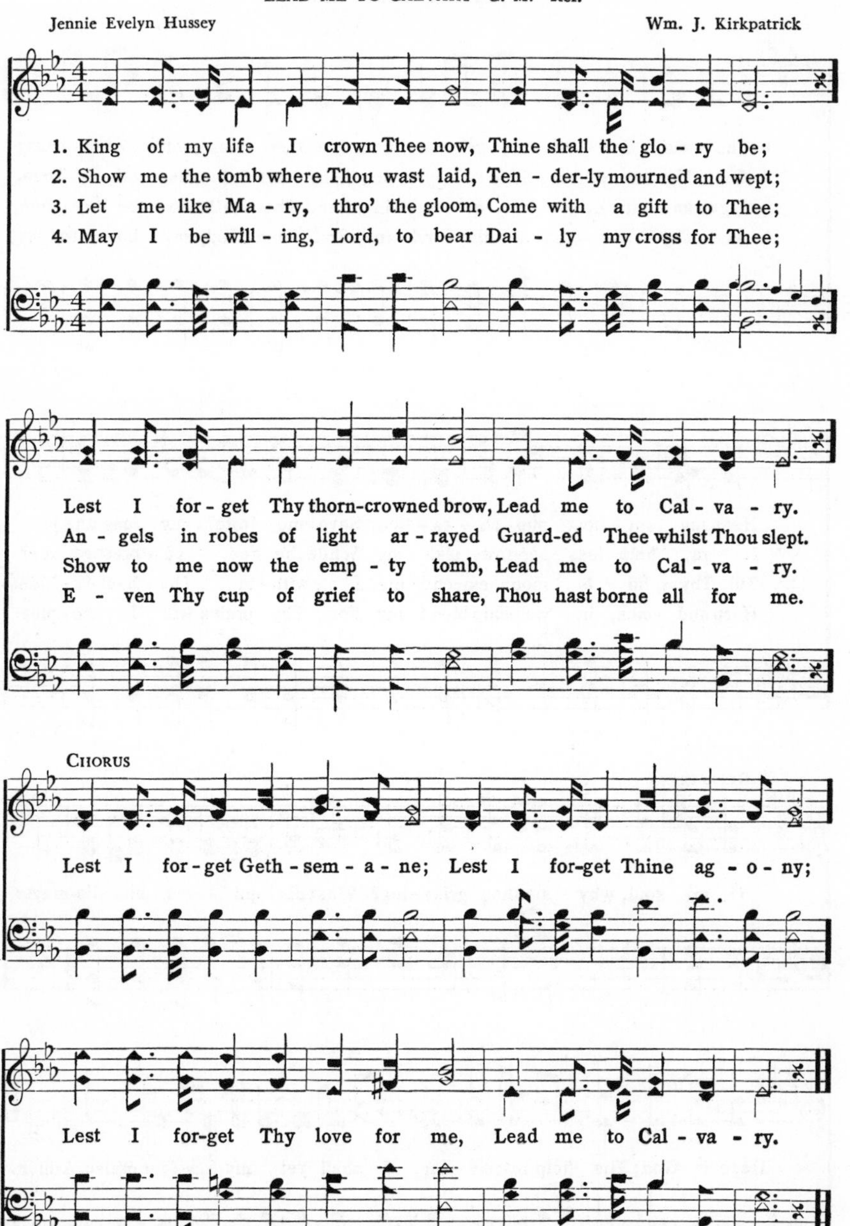
1. King of my life I crown Thee now, Thine shall the glo - ry be;
2. Show me the tomb where Thou wast laid, Ten - der-ly mourned and wept;
3. Let me like Ma - ry, thro' the gloom, Come with a gift to Thee;
4. May I be will - ing, Lord, to bear Dai - ly my cross for Thee;
Lest I for - get Thy thorn-crowned brow, Lead me to Cal - va - ry.
An - gels in robes of light ar - rayed Guard-ed Thee whilst Thou slept.
Show to me now the emp - ty tomb, Lead me to Cal - va - ry.
E - ven Thy cup of grief to share, Thou hast borne all for me.
Chorus
Lest I for - get Geth - sem - a - ne; Lest I for - get Thine ag - o - ny;
Lest I for - get Thy love for me, Lead me to Cal - va - ry.

245 Judge Me, God of My Salvation

AMARA 8. 7. 8. 7. Ref.

Psalm 43

William O. Perkins

1. Judge me, God of my sal-va-tion, Plead my cause, for Thee I trust;
2. On Thy strength a-lone re-ly-ing, Why am I cast off by Thee,
3. Light and truth, my way at-tend-ing, Send Thou forth to be my guide,
4. At Thy sa-cred al-tar bend-ing, God, my God, my boundless Joy,
Hear my ear-nest sup-pli-ca-tion, Save me from my foes un-just.
In my help-less sor-row sigh-ing, While the foe op-presses me?
Till Thy ho-ly mount as-cend-ing, I with-in Thy house a-bide.
Harp and voice, in wor-ship blend-ing, For Thy praise will I em-ploy.
Refrain
O my soul, why art thou griev-ing? What dis-qui-ets and dis-mays?
Hope in God; His help re-ceiv-ing, I shall yet my Sav-iour praise. A-men.

246 In Loving Kindness Jesus Came

HE LIFTED ME 8. 8. 8. 6. Ref.

Charlotte G. Homer — Chas. H. Gabriel

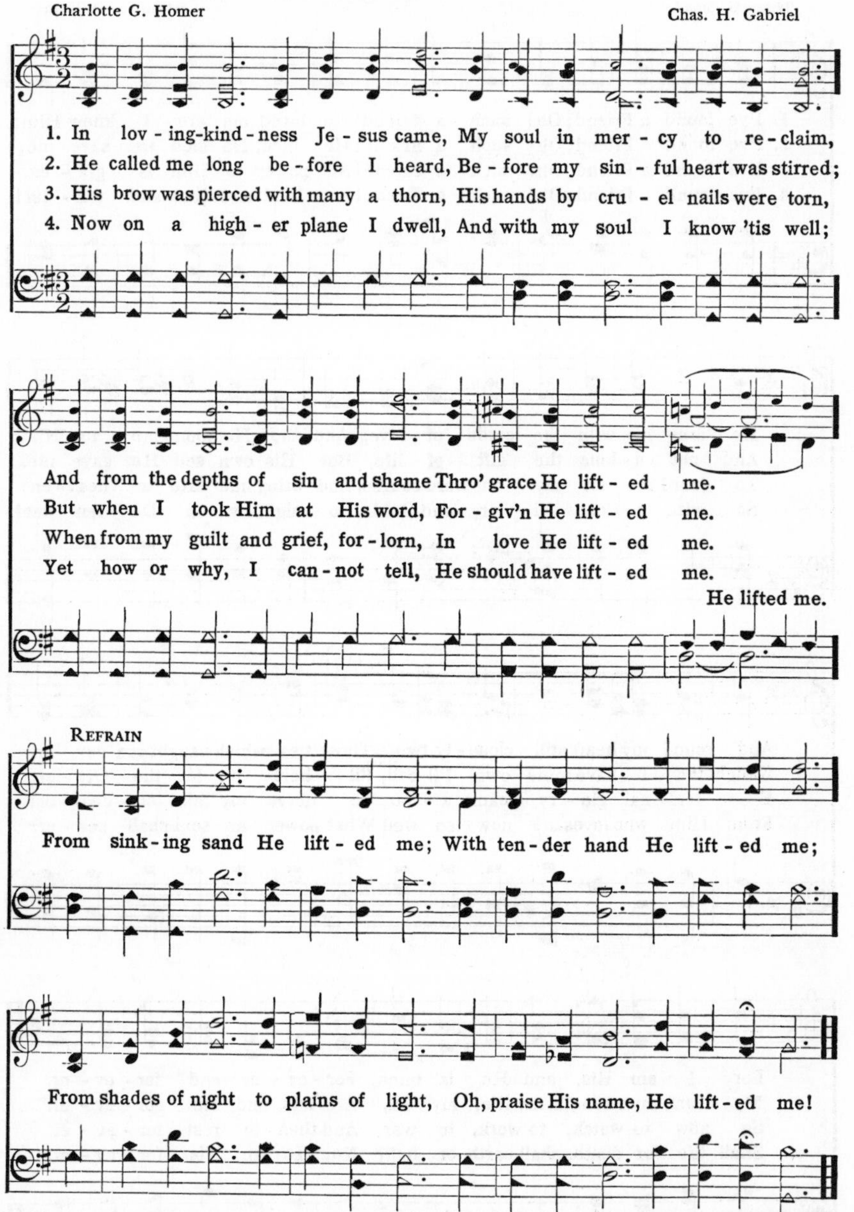
1. In lov-ing-kind-ness Je-sus came, My soul in mer-cy to re-claim,
2. He called me long be-fore I heard, Be-fore my sin-ful heart was stirred;
3. His brow was pierced with many a thorn, His hands by cru-el nails were torn,
4. Now on a high-er plane I dwell, And with my soul I know 'tis well;
And from the depths of sin and shame Thro' grace He lift-ed me.
But when I took Him at His word, For-giv'n He lift-ed me.
When from my guilt and grief, for-lorn, In love He lift-ed me.
Yet how or why, I can-not tell, He should have lift-ed me.
He lifted me.
Refrain
From sink-ing sand He lift-ed me; With ten-der hand He lift-ed me;
From shades of night to plains of light, Oh, praise His name, He lift-ed me!

The verse can be sung as a duet by Soprano and Tenor (singing the Contralto an octave higher).

247 I've Found a Friend; O Such a Friend!

CONSTANCE 8. 7. 8. 7. D.
James G. Small
Arthur S. Sullivan
1. I've found a Friend; Oh! such a Friend! He loved me ere I knew Him;
2. I've found a Friend; Oh! such a Friend! He bled, He died to save me;
3. I've found a Friend; Oh! such a Friend! All power to Him is giv - en,
4. I've found a Friend; Oh! such a Friend! So kind and true and ten - der!
He drew me with the cords of love, And thus He bound me to Him;
And not a - lone the gift of life, But His own self He gave me.
To guard me on my on- ward course, And bring me safe to heav - en:
So wise a Coun - sel - lor and Guide, So might - y a De - fen - der!
And round my heart still close - ly twine Those ties which naught can sev - er,
Naught that I have mine own I'll call, I'll hold it for the Giv - er;
E - ter - nal glo - ry gleams a - far, To nerve my faint en - deav - or:
From Him who loves me now so well What power my soul shall sev - er?
For I am His, and He is mine, For - ev - er and for - ev - er.
My heart, my strength, my life, my all, Are His, and His for - ev - er.
So now to watch, to work, to war; And then to rest for - ev - er.
Shall life or death, shall earth or hell? No: I am His for - ev - er.

My Days Are Gliding Swiftly By

SHINING SHORE 8. 7. 8. 7. Ref.

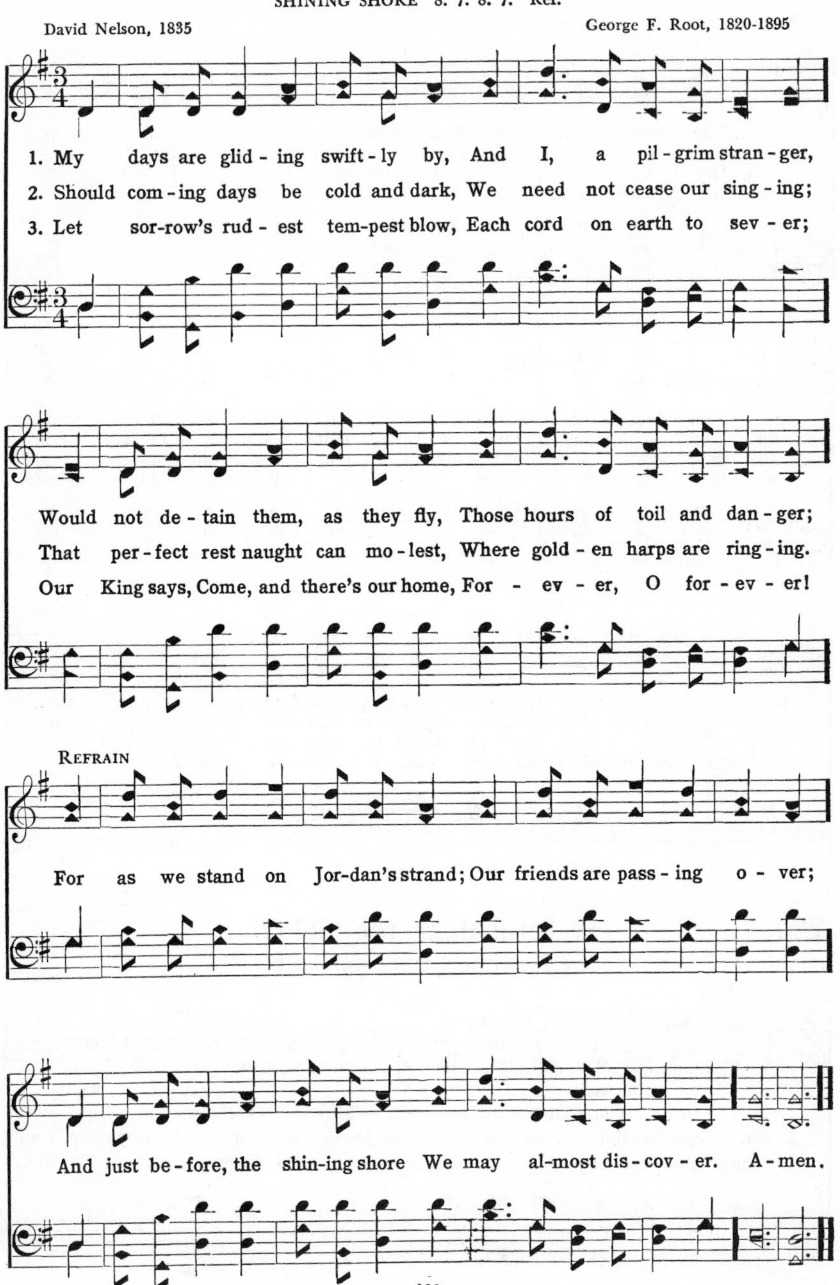
David Nelson, 1835
George F. Root, 1820-1895
1. My days are glid - ing swift - ly by, And I, a pil - grim stran - ger,
2. Should com - ing days be cold and dark, We need not cease our sing - ing;
3. Let sor - row's rud - est tem - pest blow, Each cord on earth to sev - er;
Would not de - tain them, as they fly, Those hours of toil and dan - ger;
That per - fect rest naught can mo - lest, Where gold - en harps are ring - ing.
Our King says, Come, and there's our home, For - ev - er, O for - ev - er!
Refrain
For as we stand on Jor - dan's strand; Our friends are pass - ing o - ver;
And just be - fore, the shin - ing shore We may al - most dis - cov - er. A - men.

249 Come, Come, Sweet Death

YEARNING FOR HOME 8. 9. 8. 11.

Zion's Harp

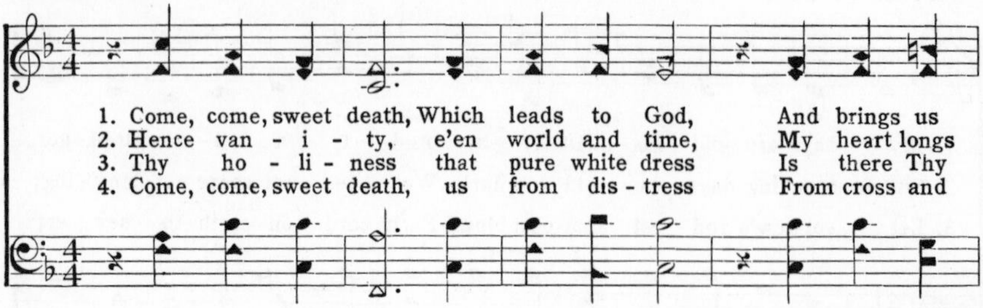

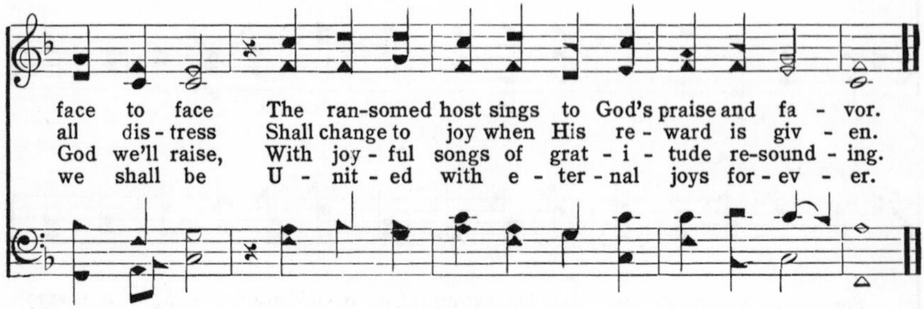

1. Come, come, sweet death, Which leads to God, And brings us to our bless-ed Sav-iour. In that blest place where face to face The ran-somed host sings to God's praise and fa-vor.
2. Hence van-i-ty, e'en world and time, My heart longs for its home in heav-en. Here tears op-press, but all dis-tress Shall change to joy when His re-ward is giv-en.
3. Thy ho-li-ness that pure white dress Is there Thy host with grace a-dorn-ing. Our thanks and praise to God we'll raise, With joy-ful songs of grat-i-tude re-sound-ing.
4. Come, come, sweet death, us from dis-tress From cross and sor-row to de-liv-er. E-ter-ni-ty where we shall be U-nit-ed with e-ter-nal joys for-ev-er.

250 O Jerusalem, the Golden

PASSIONATE LONGING 8. 7. 8. 7. 7. 7.

Zion's Harp

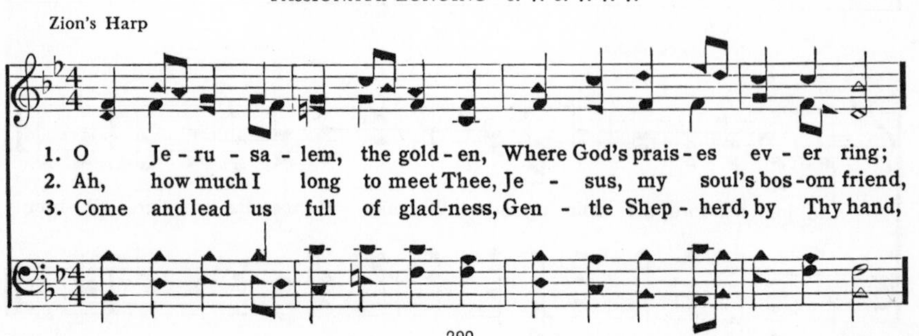

1. O Je-ru-sa-lem, the gold-en, Where God's prais-es ev-er ring;
2. Ah, how much I long to meet Thee, Je-sus, my soul's bos-om friend,
3. Come and lead us full of glad-ness, Gen-tle Shep-herd, by Thy hand,

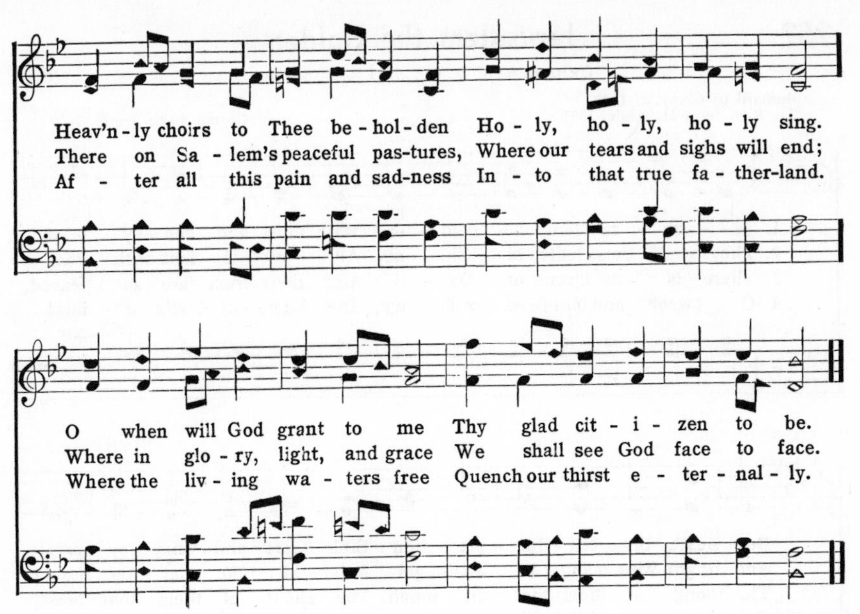

Heav'n-ly choirs to Thee be-hol-den Ho-ly, ho-ly, ho-ly sing.
There on Sa-lem's peaceful pas-tures, Where our tears and sighs will end;
Af-ter all this pain and sad-ness In-to that true fa-ther-land.
O when will God grant to me Thy glad cit-i-zen to be.
Where in glo-ry, light, and grace We shall see God face to face.
Where the liv-ing wa-ters free Quench our thirst e-ter-nal-ly.

No Shadows Yonder

251

HOLY CITY 5. 4. 5. 4. 5. 4.

Horatius Bonar

Fr. Alfred R. Gaul

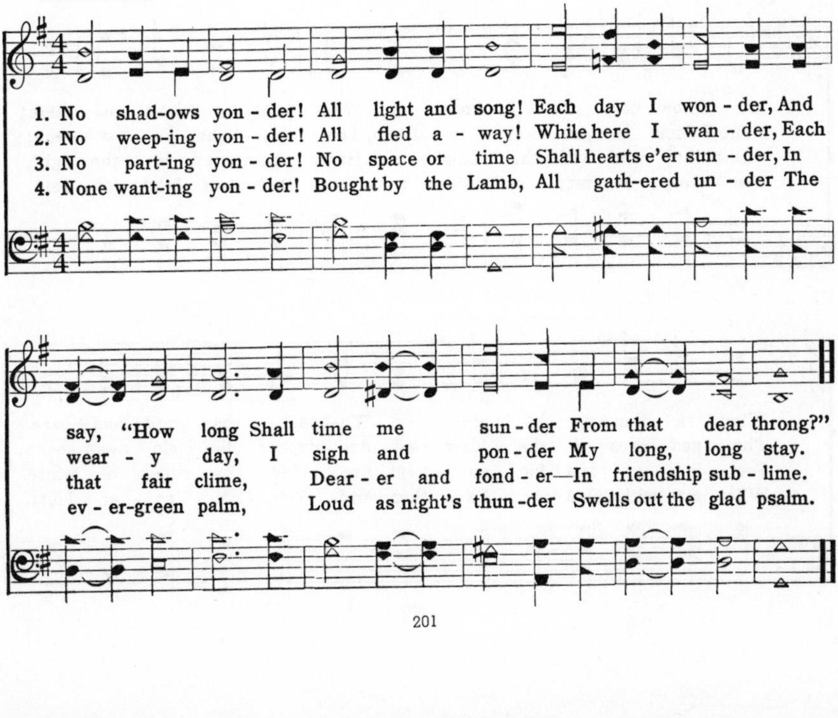

1. No shad-ows yon-der! All light and song! Each day I won-der, And say, "How long Shall time me sun-der From that dear throng?"
2. No weep-ing yon-der! All fled a-way! While here I wan-der, Each wear-y day, I sigh and pon-der My long, long stay.
3. No part-ing yon-der! No space or time Shall hearts e'er sun-der, In that fair clime, Dear-er and fond-er—In friendship sub-lime.
4. None want-ing yon-der! Bought by the Lamb, All gath-ered un-der The ev-er-green palm, Loud as night's thun-der Swells out the glad psalm.

252 Jerusalem the Golden

URBS BEATA 7. 6. 7. 6. 7. 6. 7. 6. Ref.

Bernard of Cluny, c. 1145
Tr. Rev. John M. Neale, 1851
George F. Le Jeune, 1887
1. Je - ru - sa - lem the gold - en, With milk and hon - ey blest,
2. They stand, those halls of Zi - on, All ju - bi - lant with song,
3. There is the throne of Da - vid; And there, from care re - leased,
4. O sweet and bless - ed coun - try, The home of God's e - lect!
Be - neath thy con - tem - pla - tion Sink heart and voice op - prest;
And bright with many an an - gel And all the mar - tyr throng.
The song of them that tri - umph, The shout of them that feast;
O sweet and bless - ed coun - try That ea - ger hearts ex - pect!
I know not, O I know not, What joys a - wait us there;
The Prince is ev - er in them, The day - light is se - rene;
And they who with their Lead - er Have con-quered in the fight,
Je - sus, in mer - cy bring us To that dear land of rest;
What ra - dian - cy of glo - ry, What bliss be - yond com - pare.
The pas - tures of the bless - ed Are decked in glo - rious sheen.
For ev - er and for ev - er Are clad in robes of white.
Who art, with God the Fa - ther, And Spir - it, ev - er blest.

REFRAIN
Je - ru - sa - lem, Je - ru - sa - lem,
Je - ru - sa - lem the gold - en, With milk and hon - ey blest;
Be - neath
Be - neath thy con - tem - pla - tion Sink heart and voice op - prest. A-men.
Org.

Sunset and Evening Star

253

CROSSING THE BAR 6. 6. 8. 6.

Alfred Tennyson, arr. — Geo. F. Root

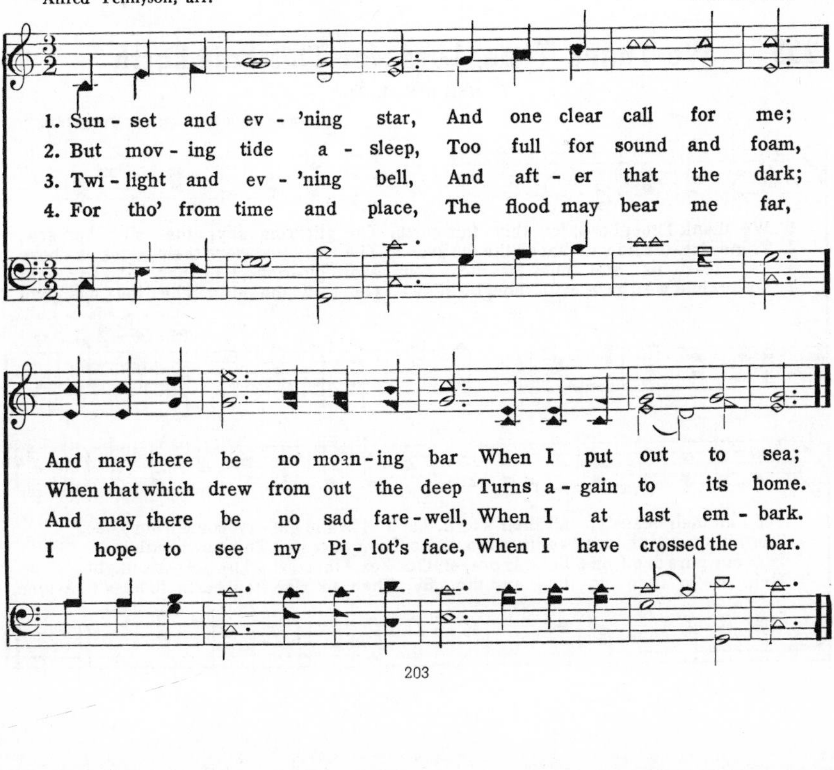

1. Sun - set and ev - 'ning star, And one clear call for me;
And may there be no moan - ing bar When I put out to sea;

2. But mov - ing tide a - sleep, Too full for sound and foam,
When that which drew from out the deep Turns a - gain to its home.

3. Twi - light and ev - 'ning bell, And aft - er that the dark;
And may there be no sad fare - well, When I at last em - bark.

4. For tho' from time and place, The flood may bear me far,
I hope to see my Pi - lot's face, When I have crossed the bar.

254 The Year Is Swiftly Waning

WAS KANN ES SCHON'RES GEBEN 7. 6. 7. 6.
W. W. How, 1823-1897
From Gesangbuch mit Noten
1. The year is swift - ly wan - ing, The sum-mer days are past;
2. The ev - er-chang-ing sea - sons In si-lence come and go;
3. O pour Thy grace up - on us, That we may wor-thier be,
4. O by each mer - cy sent us, And by each grief and pain,
5. Our bar - ren hearts make fruit - ful With ev - ery good - ly grace,
And life, brief life, is speed - ing; The end is near - ing fast.
But Thou, e - ter - nal Fa - ther, No time or change canst know.
Each year that pass - es o'er us, To dwell in heav'n with Thee.
By bless-ings like the sun - shine, And sor-rows like the rain,
That we Thy name may hal - low, And see at last Thy face. A - men.
255 We Thank Thee, Lord, for This Fair Earth
MENDON L. M.
G. E. L. Cotton, 1856
German Melody. Arr. S. Dyer, 1814
1. We thank Thee, Lord, for this fair earth, The glitt'ring sky, the sil - ver sea;
2. Thine are the flow'rs that clothe the ground, The trees that wave their arms a - bove,
3. Yet teach us still how far more fair, More glo-rious, Fa - ther, in Thy sight,
4. So while we gaze with thoughtful eye On all the gifts Thy love has giv'n,
For all their beau-ty, all their worth, Their light and glo - ry, come from Thee.
The hills that gird our dwellings round, As Thou dost gird Thine own with love.
Is one pure deed, one ho - ly prayer, One heart that owns Thy Spir-it's might.
Help us in Thee to live and die, By Thee to rise from earth to heav'n. A-men.

Ring Out, Wild Bells

256

WILD BELLS L. M.

Alfred Tennyson, 1850

Henry Lahee, 1826-1912

1. Ring out, wild bells, to the wild, wild sky, The
2. Ring out the old, ring in the new, Ring,
3. Ring out a slow - ly dy - ing cause, And
4. Ring in the val - iant man and free, The

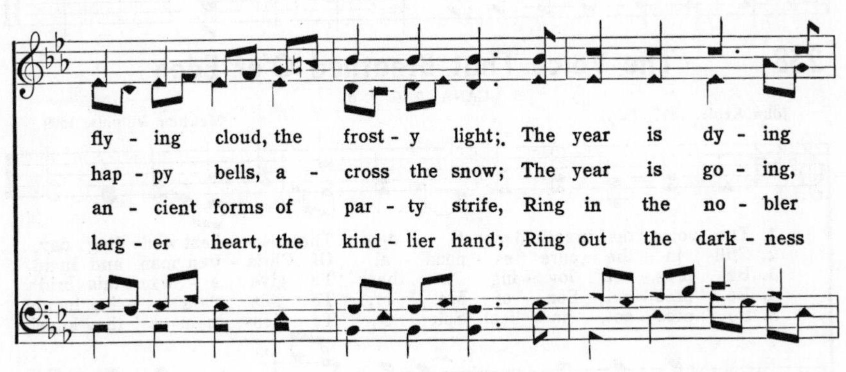
fly - ing cloud, the frost - y light;. The year is dy - ing
hap - py bells, a - cross the snow; The year is go - ing,
an - cient forms of par - ty strife, Ring in the no - bler
larg - er heart, the kind - lier hand; Ring out the dark - ness

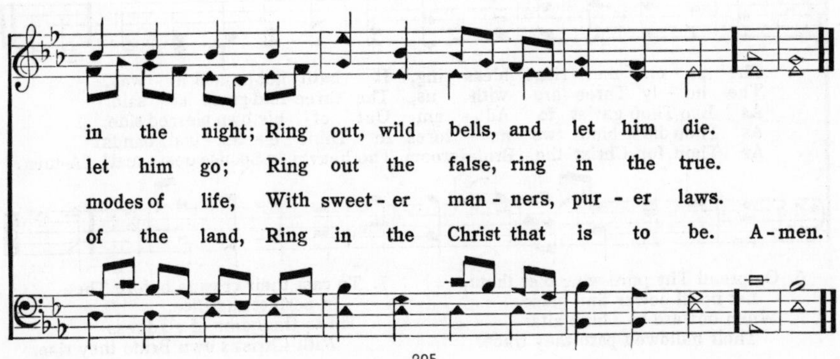
in the night; Ring out, wild bells, and let him die.
let him go; Ring out the false, ring in the true.
modes of life, With sweet - er man - ners, pur - er laws.
of the land, Ring in the Christ that is to be. A - men.

257 Since Jesus Freely Did Appear

WEDDING GUEST C. M.

Flora H. Good

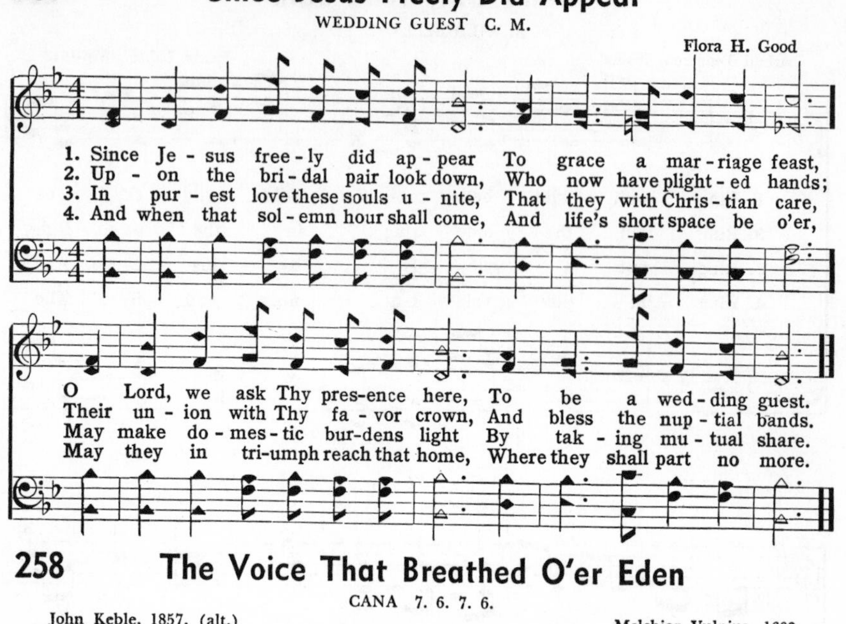

1. Since Je - sus free - ly did ap - pear To grace a mar - riage feast,
2. Up - on the bri - dal pair look down, Who now have plight - ed hands;
3. In pur - est love these souls u - nite, That they with Chris - tian care,
4. And when that sol - emn hour shall come, And life's short space be o'er,
O Lord, we ask Thy pres - ence here, To be a wed - ding guest.
Their un - ion with Thy fa - vor crown, And bless the nup - tial bands.
May make do - mes - tic bur - dens light By tak - ing mu - tual share.
May they in tri - umph reach that home, Where they shall part no more.

258 The Voice That Breathed O'er Eden

CANA 7. 6. 7. 6.

John Keble, 1857, (alt.)

Melchior Vulpius, 1609

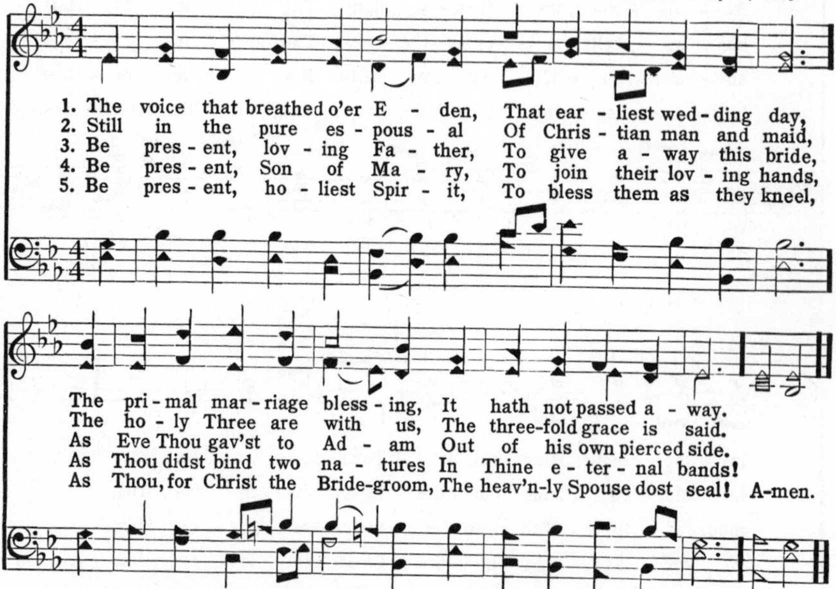

1. The voice that breathed o'er E - den, That ear - liest wed - ding day,
2. Still in the pure es - pous - al Of Chris - tian man and maid,
3. Be pres - ent, lov - ing Fa - ther, To give a - way this bride,
4. Be pres - ent, Son of Ma - ry, To join their lov - ing hands,
5. Be pres - ent, ho - liest Spir - it, To bless them as they kneel,

The pri - mal mar - riage bless - ing, It hath not passed a - way.
The ho - ly Three are with us, The three-fold grace is said.
As Eve Thou gav'st to Ad - am Out of his own pierced side.
As Thou didst bind two na - tures In Thine e - ter - nal bands!
As Thou, for Christ the Bride-groom, The heav'n-ly Spouse dost seal! A-men.

6. O spread Thy pure wing o'er them,
Let no ill power find place,
When onward to Thine altar
Their hallowed path they trace.

7. To cast their crowns before Thee
In perfect sacrifice,
Till to the home of gladness
With Christ's own Bride they rise.

Awake, My Heart

AWAKE 7. 6. 7. 6. D.

Zion's Harp

1. A - wake, my heart, and hon - or With praise and thanks and might,
2. To all parts un - der heav - en Thy truth and faith ex - tend;
3. My heart - felt thanks I bring Thee, Sal - va - tion I have found.
Thy God and thy Cre - a - tor And sen - ti - nel at night.
We see each morn and e - ven Thy grace of cov - e - nant.
As Thou hast suf - fered for me, In love to Thee I'm bound.
The morn - ing sun with splen - dor Pro - claims its Mak - er's fame;
Let us this day con - sid - er, O Lord, Thy kind - li - ness;
And what Thou, Lord, hast giv - en I con - se - crate to Thee,
An - thems of praise do ren - der, All ye who bear His name.
Our heart and soul to - geth - er In - spire with thank - ful - ness.
O lead us, Lord, to heav - en, Where we Thy glo - ry see.

260 When Morning Gilds the Skies

LAUDES DOMINI 6. 6. 6. 6. 6. 6.

From the German
Tr. Edward Caswall, 1853

Joseph Barnby, 1868

1. When morn - ing gilds the skies, My heart a - wak - ing cries:
May Je - sus Christ be praised! A - like at work or prayer
To Je - sus I re - pair: May Je - sus Christ be praised!

2. Does sad - ness fill my mind, A sol - ace here I find:
May Je - sus Christ be praised! Or fades my earth - ly bliss,
My com-fort now is this: May Je - sus Christ be praised!

3. In heaven's e - ter - nal bliss The lov - liest strain is this,
May Je - sus Christ be praised! The powers of dark - ness fear,
When this sweet chant they hear: May Je - sus Christ be praised!

4. Be this, while life is mine, My can - ti - cle di - vine,
May Je - sus Christ be praised! Be this th'e - ter - nal song,
Through all the a - ges long: May Je - sus Christ be praised! A-men.

261 As the Sun Doth Daily Rise

INNOCENTS 7. 7. 7. 7.

Anonymous

Old French Melody
Arr. W. H. Monk

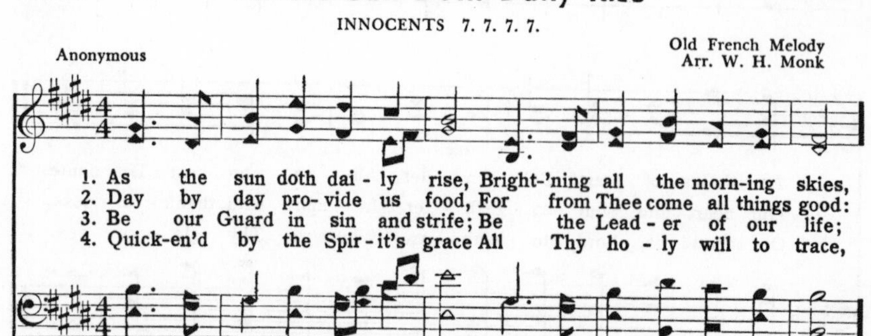
1. As the sun doth dai - ly rise, Bright-'ning all the morn-ing skies,
2. Day by day pro- vide us food, For from Thee come all things good:
3. Be our Guard in sin and strife; Be the Lead - er of our life;
4. Quick-en'd by the Spir - it's grace All Thy ho - ly will to trace,

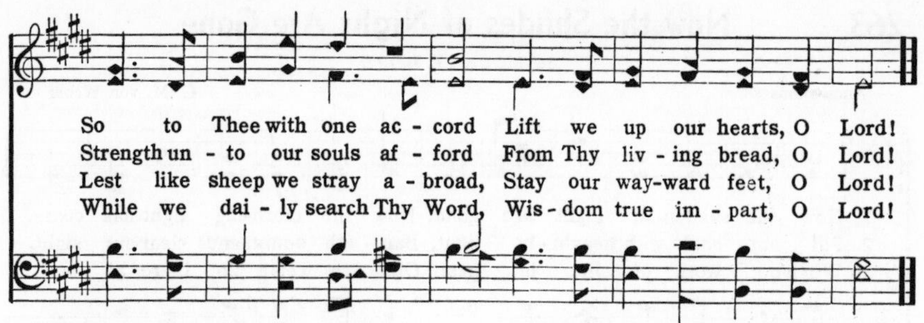
So to Thee with one ac - cord Lift we up our hearts, O Lord!
Strength un - to our souls af - ford From Thy liv - ing bread, O Lord!
Lest like sheep we stray a - broad, Stay our way-ward feet, O Lord!
While we dai - ly search Thy Word, Wis - dom true im - part, O Lord!

5. When the sun withdraws his light,
When we seek our beds at night,
Thou, by sleepless hosts adored,
Hear the prayer of faith, O Lord!

6. Praise we, with the heavenly host,
Father, Son, and Holy Ghost;
Thee would we with one accord
Praise and magnify, O Lord!

Still, Still with Thee 262

GERRISH CHANT

Harriet B. Stowe

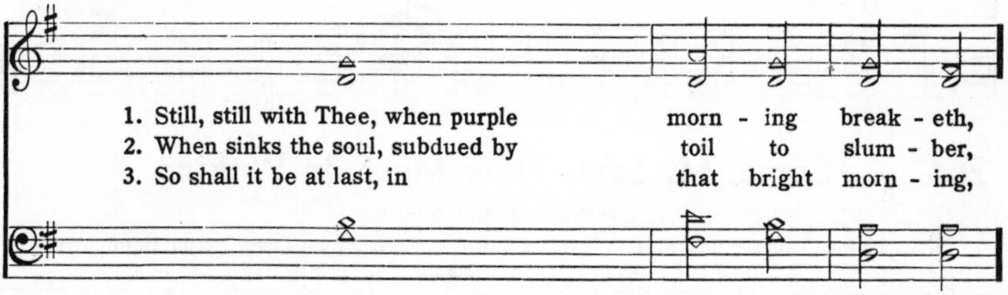

1. Still, still with Thee, when purple morn - ing break - eth,
2. When sinks the soul, subdued by toil to slum - ber,
3. So shall it be at last, in that bright morn - ing,

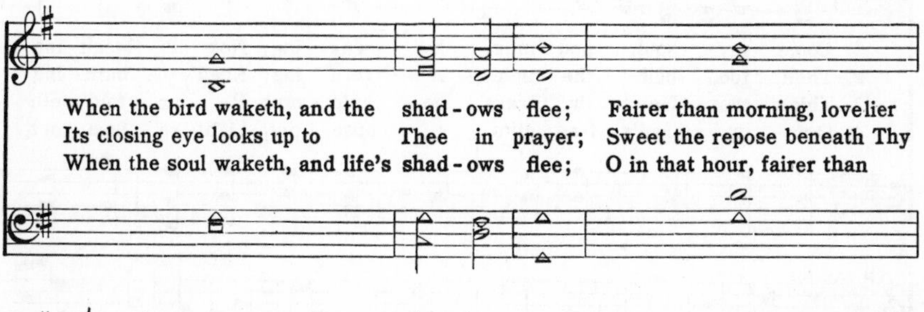

When the bird waketh, and the shad - ows flee; Fairer than morning, lovelier
Its closing eye looks up to Thee in prayer; Sweet the repose beneath Thy
When the soul waketh, and life's shad - ows flee; O in that hour, fairer than

than the day - light, Dawns the sweet con - scious - ness, I am with Thee!
wings o'er - shad - ing, But sweet - er still to wake and find Thee there.
day - light dawn - ing, Shall rise the glo - rious thought, I am with Thee.

263 Now the Shades of Night Are Gone

SEYMOUR 7. 7. 7. 7.

Anonymous — C. M. von Weber

1. Now the shades of night are gone, Now the morn-ing light has come,
2. Fill our souls with heav'n-ly light, Ban - ish doubt, and clear our sight,
3. When our work of life is past, Oh, re - ceive us there at last.
Lord, may we be Thine to - day, Drive the shades of night a - way.
In Thy serv - ice, Lord, to - day, May we stand, and watch and pray.
Night and sin will be no more, When we reach the heav'n-ly shore.

264 Come, My Soul, Thou Must Be Waking

HAYDN 8. 4. 7. 8. 4. 7.

F. R. L. von Canitz, publ., 1700 — Arr. from Franz Joseph Haydn, 1791

1. Come, my soul, thou must be wak - ing; Now is break - ing
2. Thou, too, hail the light re - turn - ing; Read - y burn - ing
3. Think that He thy ways be - hold - eth; He un - fold - eth
4. On - ly God's free gifts a - buse not, Light re - fuse not,

O'er the earth an - oth - er day; Come to Him who made this
Be the in - cense of thy pow'rs; For the night is safe - ly
Ev - ery fault that lurks with - in; Ev - ery stain of shame glossed
But His Spir - it's voice o - bey; Thou with Him shalt dwell, be -

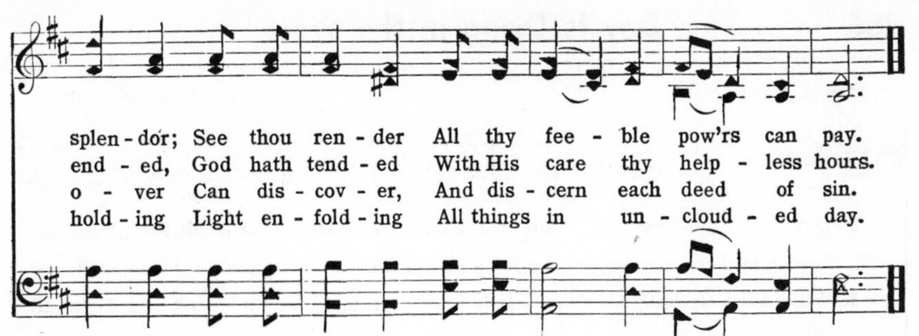
splen - dor; See thou ren - der All thy fee - ble pow'rs can pay.
end - ed, God hath tend - ed With His care thy help - less hours.
o - ver Can dis - cov - er, And dis - cern each deed of sin.
hold - ing Light en - fold - ing All things in un - cloud - ed day.

My God, How Endless Is Thy Love 265

GRATITUDE L. M.

Isaac Watts | Harmonia Sacra

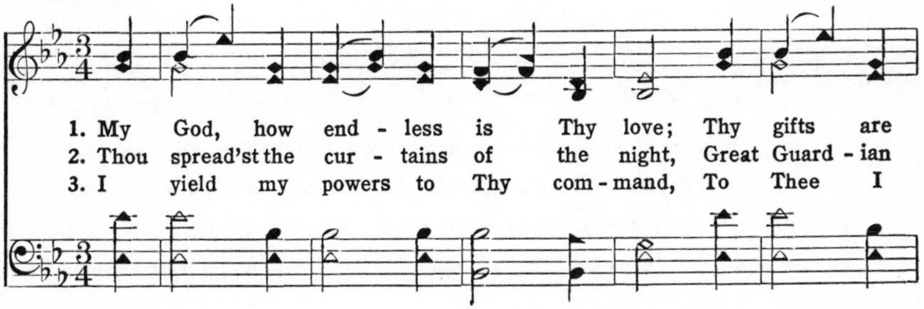

1. My God, how end - less is Thy love; Thy gifts are
2. Thou spread'st the cur - tains of the night, Great Guard - ian
3. I yield my powers to Thy com - mand, To Thee I

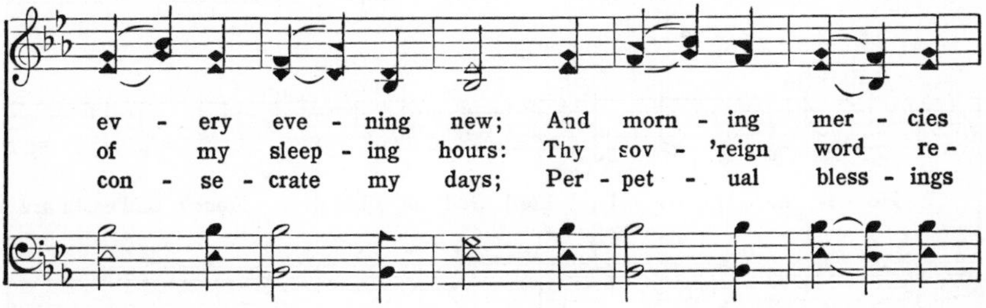

ev - ery eve - ning new; And morn - ing mer - cies
of my sleep - ing hours: Thy sov - 'reign word re -
con - se - crate my days; Per - pet - ual bless - ings

from a - bove Gen - tly dis - til like ear - ly dew.
stores the light, And quick - ens all my drow - sy powers.
from Thy hand De - mand per - pet - ual songs of praise.

266 Day Is Dying in the West

CHAUTAUQUA 7. 7. 7. 7. 4. Ref.

Mary A. Lathbury, 1877 William F. Sherwin, 1877

1. Day is dy - ing in the west; Heav'n is touch-ing earth with rest; Wait and
2. Lord of life, be-neath the dome Of the u - ni-verse, Thy home, Gath - er
3. While the deep-'ning shad - ows fall, Heart of love, en - fold - ing all, Thro' all
4. When for - ev - er from our sight Pass the stars, the day, the night, Lord of

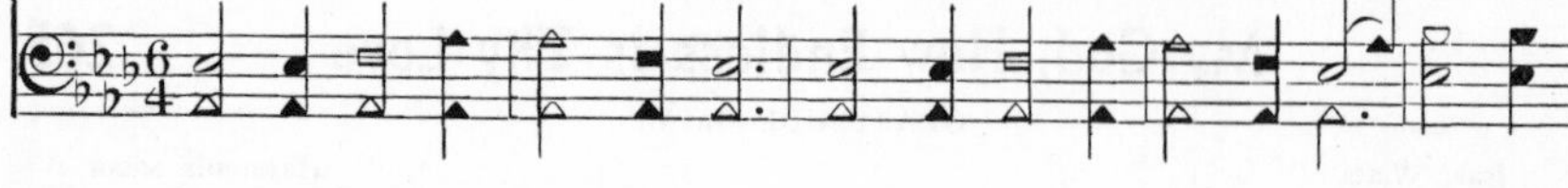

wor-ship while the night Sets her eve-ning lamps a - light Thro' all the sky.
us who seek Thy face To the fold of Thy em-brace, For Thou art nigh.
glo - ry and the grace Of the stars that veil Thy face, Our hearts as - cend.
an - gels, on our eyes Let e - ter - nal morn-ing rise, And shad-ows end.

Ho - ly, ho - ly, ho - ly, Lord God of hosts! Heav'n and earth are

full of Thee; Heav'n and earth are prais-ing Thee, O Lord most high. A-men.

Unheard the Dews Around Me Fall 267

WINDSOR C. M.

Anonymous — Damon's Psalmes, 1591

Saviour, Breathe an Evening Blessing 268

EVEN SONG 8. 7. 8. 7.

J. Edmeston — George C. Stebbins

1. Un - heard the dews a - round me fall, And heav'n - ly in-fluence shed;
2. Night moves in si - lence round the pole, The stars sing on un - heard,
3. In qui - e - tude Thy Spir - it grows In man from hour to hour;
4. Lord, grant my soul to hear at length Thy deep and si - lent voice:
And si - lent on this earth - ly ball, Ce - les - tial foot-steps tread.
Their mu - sic pierc - es to the soul, Yet bor-rows not a word.
In calm e - ter - nal on-ward flows Thine all - re-deem-ing power.
To work in still-ness, wait in strength, With calm-ness to re - joice. A - men.
1. Sav - iour, breathe an eve-ning bless-ing Ere re - pose our spir - its seal;
2. Tho' de - struc-tion walk a - round us, Tho' the ar - rows past us fly,
3. Tho' the night be dark and drear - y, Darkness can - not hide from Thee;
4. Should swift death this night o'er-take us, And com - mand us to the tomb,
rit.
Sin and want we come con - fess - ing; Thou canst save and Thou canst heal.
An - gel-guards from Thee sur - round us; We art safe if Thou art nigh.
Thou art He, who, nev - er wear - y, Watchest where Thy peo - ple be.
May the morn in heav'n a - wake us, Clad in bright e - ter - nal bloom.

269 We Feel Thy Calm at Evening's Hour

VERDURE 8. 8. 8. 8. 8. 8.

Samuel Longfellow

Arr. from Haydn's Creation

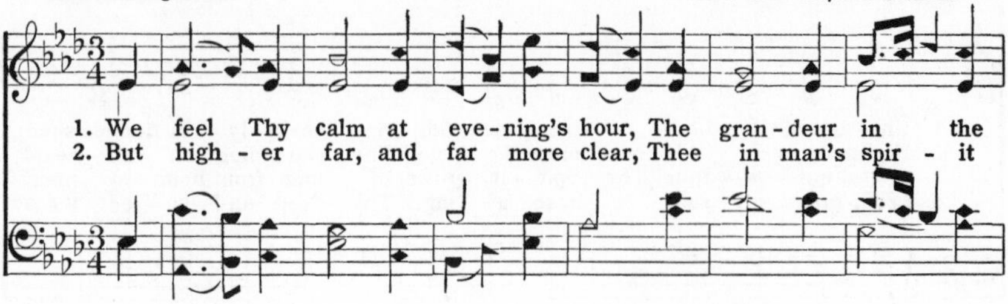

1. We feel Thy calm at eve - ning's hour, The gran - deur in the
2. But high - er far, and far more clear, Thee in man's spir - it

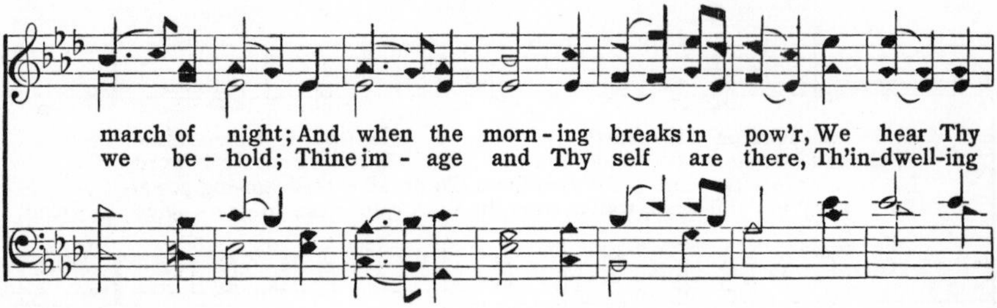

march of night; And when the morn - ing breaks in pow'r, We hear Thy
we be - hold; Thine im - age and Thy self are there, Th'in-dwell-ing

word, "Let there be light," We hear Thy word, "Let there be light."
God pro - claim'd of old, Th'in - dwell - ing God, pro - claim'd of old.

270 Now the Day Is Over

MERRIAL 6. 5. 6. 5.

Rev. Sabine Baring-Gould, 1865

Sir Joseph Barnby, 1868

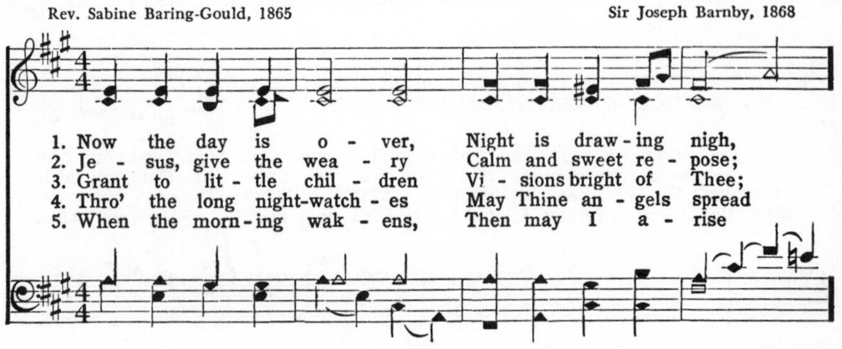

1. Now the day is o - ver, Night is draw - ing nigh,
2. Je - sus, give the wea - ry Calm and sweet re - pose;
3. Grant to lit - tle chil - dren Vi - sions bright of Thee;
4. Thro' the long night-watch - es May Thine an - gels spread
5. When the morn - ing wak - ens, Then may I a - rise

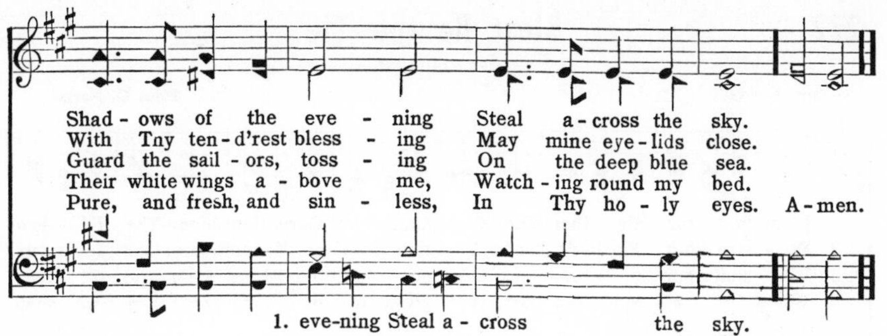
Shad - ows of the eve - ning Steal a - cross the sky.
With Thy ten - d'rest bless - ing May mine eye - lids close.
Guard the sail - ors, toss - ing On the deep blue sea.
Their white wings a - bove me, Watch - ing round my bed.
Pure, and fresh, and sin - less, In Thy ho - ly eyes. A - men.
1. eve-ning Steal a - cross the sky.

Saviour, Again to Thy Dear Name 271

ELLERS 10. 10. 10. 10.

John Ellerton

Edward J. Hopkins

1. Sav - iour, a - gain to Thy dear name we raise With one ac-
2. Grant us Thy peace up - on our home-ward way; With Thee be -
3. Grant us Thy peace, Lord, through the com - ing night, Turn Thou for
4. Grant us Thy peace through - out our earth - ly life, Our balm in

cord our part - ing hymn of praise; We stand to bless Thee ere our
gan, with Thee shall end the day; Guard Thou the lips from sin, the
us its dark-ness in - to light; From harm and dan - ger keep Thy
sor - row, and our stay in strife; Then, when Thy voice shall bid our

wor - ship cease; Then, low - ly kneel - ing, wait Thy word of peace.
hearts from shame, That in this house have called up - on Thy name.
chil - dren free, For dark and light are both a - like to Thee.
con - flict cease, Call us, O Lord, to Thine e - ter - nal peace. A-men.

272 Blest Be the Tie

DENNIS S. M.

John Fawcett — Hans G. Naegeli

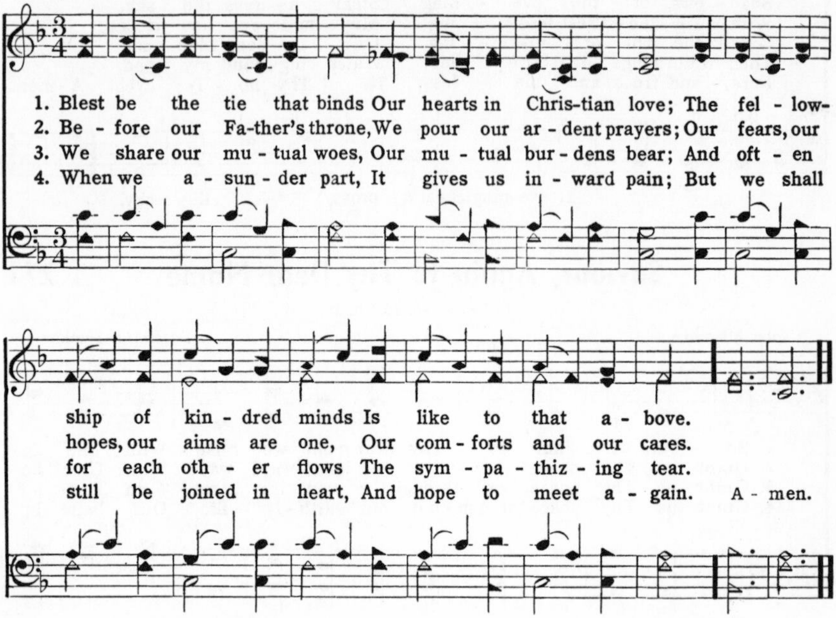

1. Blest be the tie that binds Our hearts in Chris-tian love; The fel - low- ship of kin - dred minds Is like to that a - bove.
2. Be - fore our Fa-ther's throne, We pour our ar - dent prayers; Our fears, our hopes, our aims are one, Our com - forts and our cares.
3. We share our mu - tual woes, Our mu - tual bur - dens bear; And oft - en for each oth - er flows The sym - pa - thiz - ing tear.
4. When we a - sun - der part, It gives us in - ward pain; But we shall still be joined in heart, And hope to meet a - gain. A - men.

273 Praise God from Whom All Blessings Flow

OLD HUNDRED L. M.

Thomas Ken, 1695 — Guillaume Franc, 1543; Genevan Psalter, 1551

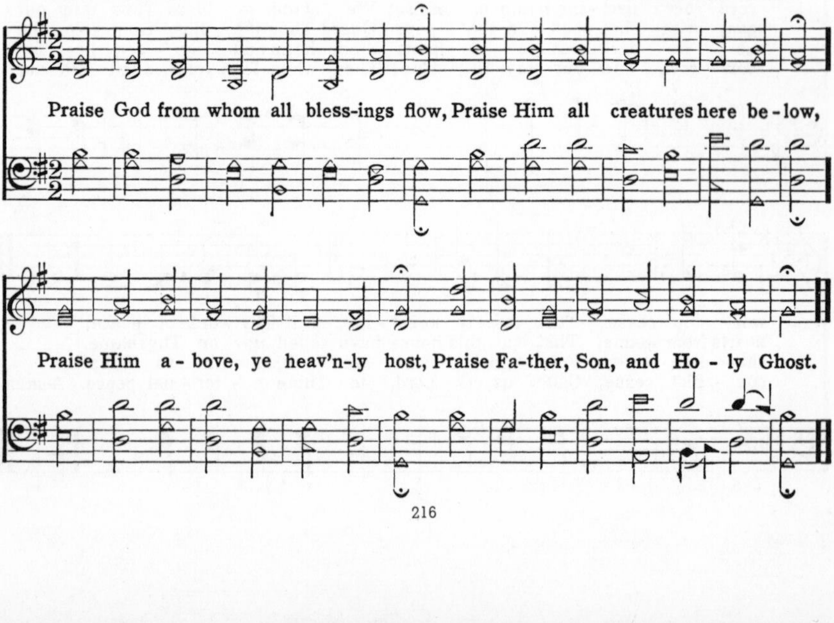

Praise God from whom all bless-ings flow, Praise Him all creatures here be - low,

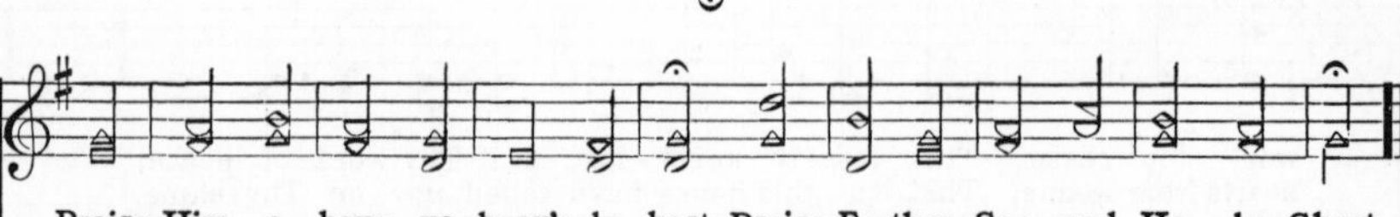

Praise Him a - bove, ye heav'n-ly host, Praise Fa-ther, Son, and Ho - ly Ghost.

The Lord Bless You and Keep You 274

BENEDICTION P. M.

Arr. from Numbers 6: 24-26 Peter C. Lutkin, 1858-1931

The Lord bless you and keep you; The Lord lift His coun - te-nance up-

The
on you, and give you peace, and give you peace; The Lord
and give you peace, and give you peace; the Lord

Lord make His face and be gra - - cious un - to
make His face to shine up - on you, and be gra-cious,

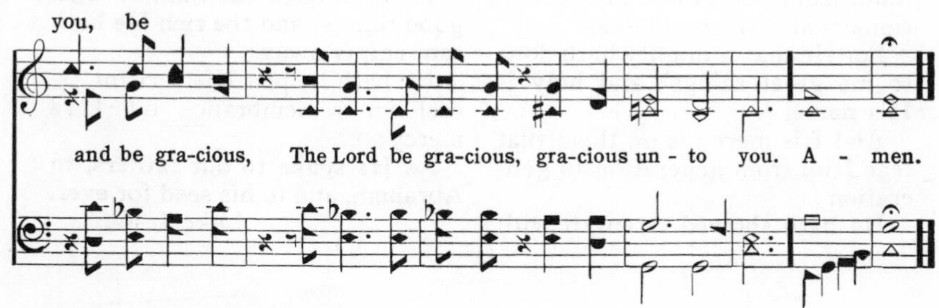
you, be
and be gra-cious, The Lord be gra-cious, gra-cious un - to you. A - men.

Used by permission of H. C. Lutkin.

Worship Services

275 GRATITUDE

I love the Lord, because He hath heard my voice and my supplications.

Because He hath inclined His ear unto me, therefore will I call upon Him as long as I live.

The sorrows of death compassed me, and the pains of hell gat hold upon me: I found trouble and sorrow.

Then called I upon the name of the Lord: O Lord, I beseech Thee, deliver my soul.

Gracious is the Lord, and righteous; yea, our God is merciful.

The Lord preserveth the simple: I was brought low, and He helped me.

Return unto thy rest, O my soul; for the Lord hath dealt bountifully with thee.

For Thou hast delivered my soul from death, mine eyes from tears, and my feet from falling.

I will walk before the Lord in the land of the living.

What shall I render unto the Lord for all His benefits toward me?

I will take the cup of salvation, and call upon the name of the Lord.

I will pay my vows unto the Lord now in the presence of all His people.

Precious in the sight of the Lord is the death of His saints.

O Lord, truly I am Thy servant; I am Thy servant, and the son of Thine handmaid: Thou hast loosed my bonds.

I will offer to Thee the sacrifice of thanksgiving, and will call upon the name of the Lord.

I will pay my vows unto the Lord now in the presence of all His people. Psalm 116:1-9, 12-18.

276 THE MAGNIFICAT

And Mary said, My soul doth magnify the Lord.

And my spirit hath rejoiced in God my Saviour.

For He hath regarded the low estate of His handmaiden; for, behold, from henceforth all generations shall call me blessed.

For He that is mighty hath done to me great things; and holy is His name.

And His mercy is on them that fear Him from generation to generation.

He hath showed strength with His arm; He hath scattered the proud in the imagination of their hearts.

He hath put down the mighty from their seats, and exalted them of low degree.

He hath filled the hungry with good things; and the rich He hath sent empty away.

He hath holpen His servant Israel in remembrance of His mercy;

As He spake to our fathers, to Abraham, and to his seed for ever.

Luke 1:46-55.

We thank Thee, God,
for the universal Church, Thy Bride;
for the denominational fellowship in which we find a common faith and a channel for service;
for the brotherhood in this congregation which warms our hearts;
for this building, the center of our Christian community;
for the privilege to worship Thee, here, today.

We confess to Thee, O Lord,
our constant dependence upon Thy grace;
our slips and faults of character;
our lack of love and compassion;
our failures in zeal and earnestness;
our coming short of Thy perfect will.

We petition Thee, our God,
that Thou wilt look upon us in merciful forgiveness;
that Thou wilt renew us in Christian truth and righteousness;
that Thou wilt teach us, and help us to perform that which we know;
that we may be enabled to exemplify the Christian way among our neighbors;
that the power of the world, the flesh, and the devil may be broken as they conspire to defeat our testimony in this community.

We ask Thy blessing, O God,
upon those who preach Thy Word to us today;
upon all of us who reverently receive it;
upon those among us who stand in need of the atoning blood;
upon those whom unconcern has kept from this house;
upon those who look up to Thee from hospitals and sickrooms;
upon all those who represent us on the world front of missions and relief.

Be with us today
to open up the Word by Thy Spirit;
to convict of sin and every manifestation of the worldly spirit;
to pour the balm of Gilead into wounded hearts;
to bind us together as a truly Christian brotherhood.

For Jesus' sake. Amen.

THE TEN COMMANDMENTS 278

Thou shalt have no other gods before me.

Thou shalt not make unto thee any graven image; thou shalt not bow down to it nor serve it.

Thou shalt not take the name of the Lord the God in vain.

Remember the Sabbath day to keep it holy.

Honor thy father and thy mother.

Thou shalt not kill.

Thou shalt not commit adultery.

Thou shalt not steal.

Thou shalt not bear false witness against thy neighbor.

Thou shalt not covet anything that is thy neighbor's.

Selections from Exodus 20.

279 GLAD WORSHIP

I was glad when they said unto me, Let us go into the house of the Lord.

Our feet shall stand within thy gates, O Jerusalem.

Jerusalem is builded as a city that is compact together:

Whither the tribes go up, the tribes of the Lord, unto the testimony of Israel, to give thanks unto the name of the Lord.

For there are set thrones of judgment, the thrones of the house of David.

Pray for the peace of Jerusalem: they shall prosper that love thee.

Peace be within thy walls, and prosperity within thy palaces.

For my brethren and companions' sakes I will now say, Peace be within thee.

Because of the house of the Lord our God I will seek thy good.

I was glad when they said unto me: Let us go into the house of the Lord. Psalm 122.

280 A CALL TO STEWARDSHIP

Blessed be the Lord, who daily loadeth us with benefits, even the God of our salvation.

What shall I render unto the Lord for all His benefits toward me?

I will take the cup of salvation, and call upon the name of the Lord.

I will pay my vows unto the Lord, yea, in the presence of all His people.

I will offer to Thee the sacrifice of thanksgiving and will call upon the name of the Lord.

Remember the words of the Lord Jesus, that He Himself said, It is more blessed to give than to receive.

He that soweth sparingly shall reap also sparingly: and he that soweth bountifully shall reap also bountifully.

Let each man do according as he hath purposed in his heart; not grudgingly, or of necessity: for the Lord loveth a cheerful giver.

Selections from Psalms, Acts, and II Corinthians.

281 O GOD OUR HELP

If it had not been the Lord who was on our side, now may Israel say;

If it had not been the Lord who was on our side, when men rose up against us:

Then they had swallowed us up quick, when their wrath was kindled against us:

Then the waters had overwhelmed us, the stream had gone over our soul:

Then the proud waters had gone over our soul.

Blessed be the Lord, who hath not given us as a prey to their teeth.

Our soul is escaped as a bird out of the snare of the fowlers: the snare is broken, and we are escaped.

Our help is in the name of the Lord, who made heaven and earth.

Psalm 124.

THE MERCY OF THE LORD 282

They have cast away the law of the Lord of hosts, and despised the Word of the Holy One of Israel.

For all this His anger is not turned away, but His hand is stretched out still.

Their heart was not right with Him, neither were they steadfast in their covenant.

But He, being full of compassion, forgave their iniquity, and destroyed them not; yea, many a time turned He His anger away.

This is a rebellious people, lying children, children that will not hear the law of the Lord.

In returning and rest shall ye be saved; in quietness and confidence shall be your strength.

Ephraim is joined to idols. Israel slideth back as a backsliding heifer.

Come, and let us return unto the Lord. I will heal their backsliding, I will love them freely.

They have forsaken me the fountain of living waters and hewed them out cisterns that can hold no water.

Ho, every one that thirsteth, come ye to the waters, and he that hath no money; come ye, buy and eat; yea, come, buy wine and milk without money and without price.

The whole head is sick, and the whole heart faint. From the sole of the foot even unto the head there is no soundness in it; but wounds, and bruises, and putrifying sores: they have not been closed, neither bound up, neither mollified with ointment.

Come now, and let us reason together, saith the Lord: though your sins be as scarlet, they shall be as white as snow; though they be red like crimson, they shall be as wool. If ye be willing and obedient, ye shall eat the good of the land.

Selections from Isaiah, Psalms, Hosea, and Jeremiah.

OUR HEAVENLY FATHER'S CARE 283

Be not anxious for your life, what ye shall eat, or what ye shall drink; nor yet for your body what ye shall put on.

Is not our life more than meat and our body than raiment?

Consider the fowls of the air, for they sow not, neither do they reap, nor gather into barns,

Yet our heavenly Father feedeth them. Are we not much better than they?

Why take ye thought for raiment? Consider the lilies of the field, how they grow; they toil not, neither do they spin;

And yet Solomon in all his glory was not arrayed like one of these.

Wherefore if God so clothe the grass of the field, which today is, and tomorrow is cast into the oven,

Shall He not much more clothe us?

Therefore be not anxious, saying, What shall we eat? or What shall we drink? or, Wherewithal shall we be clothed?

Our heavenly Father knoweth we have need of all these things.

Seek ye first the kingdom of God, and His righteousness; and all these things shall be added unto you.

Matthew 6:25-33, adapted.

The law of the Lord is perfect, converting the soul: the testimony of the Lord is sure, making wise the simple.

The statutes of the Lord are right, rejoicing the heart: the commandment of the Lord is pure, enlightening the eyes.

The fear of the Lord is clean, enduring for ever: the judgments of the Lord are true and righteous altogether.

Man doth not live by bread only, but by every word that proceedeth out of the mouth of the Lord doth man live.

But the word is very nigh unto thee, in thy mouth, and in thy heart, that thou mayest do it.

So shall my word be that goeth forth out of my mouth: it shall not return unto me void, but it shall accomplish that which I please, and it shall prosper in the thing whereto I sent it.

The grass withereth, the flower fadeth: but the word of our God shall stand for ever.

Thy word is a lamp unto my feet, and a light unto my path. I have sworn, and I will perform it, that I will keep Thy righteous judgments.

And the Word was made flesh, and dwelt among us, and we beheld His glory, the glory as of the only begotten of the Father, full of grace and truth.

It is the spirit that quickeneth; the flesh profiteth nothing: the words that I speak unto you, they are spirit, and they are life.

Therefore whosoever heareth these words of mine, and doeth them, I will liken him unto a wise man, which built his house upon a rock: and the rain descended, and the floods came, and the winds blew, and beat upon that house; and it fell not: for it was founded upon a rock.

Selections from Psalms, Deuteronomy, Isaiah, John, and Matthew.

285 UNDERSTANDING THROUGH THE WORD

Teach me, O Lord, the way of Thy statutes; and I shall keep it unto the end.

Give me understanding, and I shall keep Thy law; yea, I shall observe it with my whole heart.

Make me to go in the path of Thy commandments; for therein do I delight.

Incline my heart unto Thy testimonies, and not to covetousness.

Turn away mine eyes from beholding vanity; and quicken Thou me in Thy way.

Stablish Thy Word unto Thy servant, who is devoted to Thy fear.

Turn away my reproach which I fear: for Thy judgments are good.

Behold, I have longed after Thy precepts: quicken me in Thy righteousness.

Let Thy mercies come also unto me, O Lord, even Thy salvation, according to Thy Word.

So shall I keep Thy law continually for ever and ever.

And I will walk at liberty: for I seek Thy precepts.

Psalm 119:33-41, 44, 45.

Blessed are the undefiled in the way, who walk in the law of the Lord.

Blessed are they that keep His testimonies, and that seek Him with the whole heart.

Thou hast commanded us to keep Thy precepts diligently.

O that my ways were directed to keep Thy statutes!

Then shall I not be ashamed, when I have respect unto all Thy commandments.

I will praise Thee with uprightness of heart, when I shall have learned Thy righteous judgments.

Wherewithal shall a young man cleanse his way? by taking heed thereto according to Thy Word.

Blessed art Thou, O Lord: teach me Thy statutes.

I will meditate in Thy precepts, and have respect unto Thy ways.

Deal bountifully with Thy servant, that I may live, and keep Thy Word.

Open Thou mine eyes, that I may behold wondrous things out of Thy law.

Incline my heart unto Thy testimonies, and not covetousness.

Turn away mine eyes from beholding vanity; and quicken Thou me in Thy way.

Teach me good judgment and knowledge: for I have believed Thy commandments.

Before I was afflicted I went astray: but now have I kept Thy Word.

Thou art good, and doest good; teach me Thy statutes.

It is good for me that I have been afflicted; that I might learn Thy statutes.

Thy hands have made me and fashioned me: give me understanding, that I may learn Thy commandments.

The entrance of Thy words giveth light; it giveth understanding unto the simple.

Great peace have they which love Thy law: and nothing shall offend them.

Selections from Psalm 119.

THE BEATITUDES OF JESUS 287

Blessed are the poor in spirit: for theirs is the kingdom of heaven.

Blessed are they that mourn: for they shall be comforted.

Blessed are the meek: for they shall inherit the earth.

Blessed are they that hunger and thirst after righteousness: for they shall be filled.

Blessed are the merciful: for they shall obtain mercy.

Blessed are the pure in heart: for they shall see God.

Blessed are the peacemakers: for they shall be called sons of God.

Blessed are they that have been persecuted for righteousness' sake: for theirs is the kingdom of heaven.

Blessed are ye when men shall reproach you, and persecute you,

And say all manner of evil against you falsely, for my sake.

Rejoice, and be exceeding glad; for great is your reward in heaven:

For so persecuted they the prophets that were before you.

Matthew 5.

As many as are led by the Spirit of God, they are the sons of God.

For ye have not received the spirit of bondage again to fear: but ye have received the Spirit of adoption, whereby we cry, Abba, Father.

The Spirit itself beareth witness with our spirit, that we are the children of God:

And if children, then heirs: heirs of God, and joint-heirs with Christ; if so be that we suffer with Him, that we may also be glorified together.

For I reckon that the sufferings of this present time are not worthy to be compared with the glory which shall be revealed in us.

And we know that all things work together for good to them that love God, to them who are the called according to His purpose.

What shall we say then to these things? If God be for us, who can be against us?

He that spareth not His own Son, but delivered Him up for us all, how shall He not with Him also freely give us all things?

Who shall separate us from the love of Christ? Shall tribulation, or distress, or persecution, or famine, or nakedness, or peril, or sword?

Nay, in all these things we are more than conquerors through Him that loved us.

For I am persuaded, that neither death, nor life, nor angels, nor principalities, nor powers, nor things present, nor things to come,

Nor height, nor depth, nor any other creature, shall be able to separate us from the love of God, which is in Christ Jesus our Lord.

Selections from Romans 8.

289 HOLY BIBLE, BOOK DIVINE

Thy testimonies are wonderful: therefore doth my soul keep them.

The entrance of Thy words giveth light; it giveth understanding unto the simple.

Order my steps in Thy Word: and let not any iniquity have dominion over me.

Uphold me according unto Thy Word, that I may live: and let me not be ashamed of my hope.

Hold Thou me up, and I shall be safe: and I will have respect unto Thy statutes continually.

Teach me, O Lord, the way of Thy statutes; and I shall keep it unto the end.

Give me understanding, and I shall keep Thy law; yea, I shall observe it with my whole heart.

Make me to go in the path of Thy commandments; for therein do I delight.

Incline my heart unto Thy testimonies, and not to covetousness.

Turn away mine eyes from beholding vanity; and quicken thou me in Thy way.

Stablish Thy Word unto Thy servant, who is devoted to Thy fear.

Turn away my reproach which I fear: for Thy judgments are good.

Behold, I have longed after Thy precepts: quicken me in Thy righteousness.

Selections from Psalm 119

Who can find a virtuous woman? for her price is far above rubies.

The heart of her husband doth safely trust in her, so that he shall have no need of spoil.

She will do him good and not evil all the days of her life.

She seeketh wool and flax, and worketh willingly with her hands.

She is like the merchants' ships; she bringeth her food from afar.

She riseth also while it is yet night, and giveth meat to her household, and a portion to her maidens.

She considereth a field, and buyeth it; with the fruit of her hands she planteth a vineyard.

She girdeth her loins with strength, and strengtheneth her arms.

She perceiveth that her merchandise is good: her candle goeth not out by night.

She layeth her hands to the spindle, and her hands hold the distaff.

She stretcheth out her hand to the poor; yea, she reacheth forth her hands to the needy.

She is not afraid of the snow for her household; for all her household are clothed with scarlet.

She maketh herself coverings of tapestry; her clothing is silk and purple.

Her husband is known in the gates, when he sitteth among the elders of the land.

She maketh fine linen and selleth it; and delivereth girdles unto the merchant.

Strength and honor are her clothing; and she shall rejoice in time to come.

She openeth her mouth with wisdom; and in her tongue is the law of kindness.

She looketh well to the ways of her household, and eateth not the bread of idleness.

Her children arise up, and call her blessed; her husband also, and he praiseth her.

Many daughters have done virtuously, but thou excellest them all.

Favor is deceitful, and beauty is vain; but a woman that feareth the Lord, she shall be praised.

Give her of the fruit of her hands: and let her own works praise her in the gates.

Proverbs 31:10-31.

BEATITUDES IN THE OLD TESTAMENT 291

Blessed is the man that walketh not in the counsel of the ungodly.

Blessed is that man that maketh the Lord his trust, and respecteth not the proud.

Blessed is the man that feareth the Lord, that delighteth greatly in His commandments.

Blessed is he whose transgression is forgiven, whose sin is covered.

Blessed is he that considereth the poor: the Lord will deliver him in time of trouble.

Blessed are they that keep judgment, and he that doeth righteousness at all times.

Blessed are they that dwell in Thy house: they will be still praising Thee.

Selections from Psalms.

292 LIBERTY FROM GOD

Proclaim liberty throughout all the land unto all the inhabitants thereof.

Stand fast therefore in the liberty wherewith Christ hath made us free, and be not entangled again with the yoke of bondage.

For the law of the Spirit of life in Christ Jesus hath made me free from the law of sin and death.

And ye shall know the truth, and the truth shall make you free.

Behold how good and how pleasant it is for brethren to dwell together in unity!

For as the body is one, and hath many members, and all the members of that one body, being many, are one body: so also is Christ.

Now I beseech you, brethren, by the name of our Lord Jesus Christ, that ye all speak the same thing, and that there be no divisions among you; but that ye be perfectly joined together in the same mind and in the same judgment.

And other sheep I have, which are not of this fold: them also I must bring, and they shall hear my voice; and there shall be one fold, and one shepherd.

That in the dispensation of the fullness of times He might gather together in one all things in Christ, both which are in heaven, and which are on earth; even in Him.

Finally, brethren, whatsoever things are true, whatsoever things are honest, whatsoever things are just, whatsoever things are pure, whatsoever things are lovely, whatsoever things are of good report; if there be any virtue, and if there be any praise, think on these things.

Selections from Leviticus, Galatians, Romans, John, Psalms, I Corinthians, Ephesians, and Philippians.

293 BEHOLD, YOUR GOD

O thou that tellest good tidings to Zion, get thee up into the high mountain; O thou that tellest good tidings to Jerusalem, lift up thy voice with strength; lift it up, be not afraid; say unto the cities of Judah, behold, your God!

Behold, the Lord God will come as a mighty one, and His arm shall rule for Him: behold, His reward is with Him, and His recompense before Him.

He shall feed His flock like a shepherd, He shall gather the lambs in His arm, and carry them in His bosom, and shall gently lead those that have their young.

Hast thou not known? hast thou not heard? the everlasting God, the Lord, the Creator of the ends of the earth, fainteth not, neither is weary; there is no searching of His understanding.

He giveth power to the faint; and to him that hath no might He increaseth strength.

Even the youths shall faint and be weary, and the young men shall utterly fall.

But they that wait upon the Lord shall renew their strength;

They shall mount up with wings as eagles; they shall run, and not be weary; they shall walk, and not faint.

Isaiah 40:9-11, 25-31.

There is a spirit in man: and the inspiration of the Almighty giveth them understanding.

Great men are not always wise: neither do the aged understand judgment.

Who hath put wisdom in the inward parts? or who hath given understanding to the heart?

The fear of the Lord is the beginning of wisdom: and the knowledge of the Holy is understanding.

James saith, If any of you lack wisdom, let him ask of God, that giveth to all men liberally, and upbraideth not; and it shall be given him.

Search the Scriptures; for in them ye think ye have eternal life: and these are they which testify of me.

And ye will not come to me, that ye might have life.

For had ye believed Moses, ye would have believed me: for he wrote of me.

But if ye believe not his writings, how shall ye believe my words?

Whosoever therefore shall break one of these least commandments, and shall teach men so, he shall be called the least in the kingdom of heaven:

But whosoever shall do and teach them, the same shall be called great in the kingdom of heaven.

But these are written, that ye might believe that Jesus is the Christ, the Son of God; and that believing ye might have life through His name.

Selections from Job, Proverbs, John and Matthew.

JESUS OUR SAVIOUR 295

Thou shalt call His name Jesus: for He shall save His people from their sins.

For God sent not His Son into the world to condemn the world; but that the world through Him might be saved.

This is a faithful saying, and worthy of all acceptation, that Christ Jesus came into the world to save sinners.

For the Son of man is come to seek and to save that which was lost.

For there is one God, and one mediator between God and men, the man Christ Jesus.

Who gave Himself a ransom for all.

Ye know that ye were not redeemed with corruptible things, as silver and gold, from your vain conversation received by tradition from your fathers;

But with the precious blood of Christ, as of a lamb without blemish and without spot.

God forbid that I should glory save in the cross of our Lord Jesus Christ, by whom the world is crucified unto me, and I unto the world.

The blood of Jesus Christ, His Son, cleanseth us from all sin.

The Lord hath done great things for us; whereof we are glad.

I will praise Thee, O Lord my God, with all my heart; and I will glorify Thy name for evermore.

Selections from Matthew, John, I Timothy, Luke, I Peter, Galatians, I John, and the Psalms.

296 LOVE NEVER FAILETH

If I speak with the tongues of men and of angels, but have not love, I am become sounding brass, or a clanging cymbal.

And if I have the gift of prophecy, and know all mysteries and all knowledge; and if I have all faith, so as to remove mountains, but have not love, I am nothing.

And if I bestow all my goods to feed the poor, and if I give my body to be burned, but have not love, it profiteth me nothing.

Love suffereth long, and is kind; love envieth not; love vaunteth not itself, is not puffed up,

Doth not behave itself unseemly, seeketh not its own, is not provoked, taketh not account of evil;

Rejoiceth not in unrighteousness, but rejoiceth with the truth;

Beareth all things, believeth all things, hopeth all things, endureth all things.

Love never faileth: but whether there be prophecies, they shall be done away; whether there be tongues, they shall cease; whether there be knowledge, it shall be done away.

For we know in part, and we prophecy in part;

But when that which is perfect is come, that which is in part shall be done away.

When I was a child, I spake as a child, I felt as a child, I thought as a child: now that I am become a man, I have put away childish things.

For now we see in a mirror, darkly; but then face to face:

Now I know in part; but then shall I know fully even as also I was fully known.

But now abideth faith, hope, love, these three; and the greatest of these is love.

I Corinthians 13.

297 BY FAITH

By faith Abraham, when he was called to go out into a place which he should after receive for an inheritance, obeyed; and he went out, not knowing whither he went.

By faith Abraham, when he was tried, offered up Isaac: and he that had received the promises offered up his only begotten son.

By faith Isaac blessed Jacob and Esau concerning things to come.

By faith Jacob, when he was a dying, blessed both the sons of Joseph; and worshiped, leaning upon the top of his staff.

By faith Joseph, when he died, made mention of the departing of the children of Israel; and gave commandment concerning his bones.

By faith Moses, when he was come to years, refused to be called the son of Pharaoh's daughter.

Choose rather to suffer affliction with the people of God, than to enjoy the pleasures of sin for a season;

By faith they passed through the Red sea as by dry land: which the Egyptians assaying to do were drowned.

By faith the walls of Jericho fell down, after they were compassed about seven days.

But without faith it is impossible to please Him.

Selections from Hebrews 11.

THE GOOD SHEPHERD

298

Jesus saith unto them: I am the good shepherd. The good shepherd layeth down his life for the sheep.

I came that they may have life and may have it abundantly.

I am the good shepherd and I know mine own and mine own know me.

And other sheep have I, which are not of this fold; them also must I bring, and they shall hear my voice; and they shall become one flock, one shepherd.

What man of you, having a hundred sheep, and having lost one of them, doth not leave the ninety and nine in the wilderness and go out after that which is lost, until he find it?

And when he hath found it he layeth it on his shoulder, rejoicing.

And when he cometh home he calleth together his friends and neighbors, saying unto them,

Rejoice with me for I have found my sheep which was lost.

When Jesus saw the multitude He was moved with compassion for them, because they were distressed and scattered, as sheep not having a shepherd.

And He called unto Him His twelve disciples. . . saying, Go to the lost sheep of the house of Israel. And as ye go, preach, saying, The kingdom of heaven is at hand.

Ye were going astray like sheep, but are now returned unto the Shepherd and Bishop of your souls.

And when the chief Shepherd shall be manifested, ye shall receive the crown of glory that fadeth not away.

Selections from John, Luke, Matthew and I Peter.

OUR REFUGE AND STRENGTH

299

God is our refuge and strength, a very present help in trouble.

Therefore will not we fear, though the earth do change, and though the mountains be shaken into the heart of the seas;

Though the waters thereof roar and be troubled, though the mountains tremble with the swelling thereof.

There is a river, the streams whereof make glad the city of God, the holy place of the tabernacles of the Most High.

God is in the midst of her; she shall not be moved: God will help her, and that right early.

The nations raged, the kingdoms were moved: He uttered His voice, the earth melted.

The Lord of hosts is with us; the God of Jacob is our refuge.

Come, behold the works of the Lord, what desolations He hath made in the earth.

He maketh wars to cease unto the end of the earth; He breaketh the bow, and cutteth the spear in sunder; He burneth the chariots in the fire.

Be still, and know that I am God:

I will be exalted among the nations, I will be exalted in the earth.

The Lord of hosts is with us; the God of Jacob is our refuge.

Psalm 46.

300 COMFORT FROM GOD

Comfort ye, comfort ye my people, saith your God.

Speak ye comfortably to Jerusalem, and cry unto her, that her warfare is accomplished, that her iniquity is pardoned: for she hath received of the Lord's hand double for all her sins.

The voice of him that crieth in the wilderness, Prepare ye the way of the Lord, make straight in the desert a highway for our God.

Every valley shall be exalted, and every mountain and hill shall be made low: and the crooked shall be made straight, and the rough places plain:

And the glory of the Lord shall be revealed, and all flesh shall see it together: for the mouth of the Lord hath spoken it.

The voice said, Cry. And he said, What shall I cry? All flesh is grass, and all the goodliness thereof is as the flower of the field:

The grass withereth, the flower fadeth: because the Spirit of the Lord bloweth upon it: surely the people is grass.

The grass withereth, the flower fadeth: but the Word of our God shall stand for ever.

O Zion, that bringest good tidings, get thee up into the high mountain; O Jerusalem, that bringest good tidings, lift up thy voice with strength; lift it up, be not afraid; say unto the cities of Judah, Behold your God!

Behold, the Lord God will come with strong hand, and His arm shall rule for Him; behold, His reward is with Him, and His work before Him.

He shall feed His flock like a shepherd, He shall gather the lambs with His arm, and carry them in His bosom, and shall gently lead those that are with young.

He giveth power to the faint; and to them that have no might, He increaseth strength.

Even the youths shall faint and be weary, and the young men shall utterly fall:

But they that wait upon the Lord shall renew their strength; they shall mount up with wings as eagles; they shall run, and not be weary; and they shall walk and not faint.

Isaiah 40:1-11, 29-31.

301 THE SHEPHERD PSALM

The Lord is my shepherd; I shall not want.

He maketh me to lie down in green pastures: He leadeth me beside the still waters.

He restoreth my soul: He leadeth me in the paths of righteousness for His name's sake.

Yea, though I walk through the valley of the shadow of death, I will fear no evil:

For Thou art with me; Thy rod and Thy staff they comfort me.

Thou preparest a table before me in the presence of mine enemies:

Thou anointest my head with oil; my cup runneth over.

Surely goodness and mercy shall follow me all the days of my life; and I will dwell in the house of the Lord for ever.

Psalm 23.

THE GREAT COMMISSION 302

Then the eleven disciples went away into Galilee, into a mountain where Jesus had appointed them.

And when they saw Him, they worshiped Him: but some doubted.

And Jesus came and spake unto them saying, All power is given unto me in heaven and in earth.

Go ye therefore, and teach all nations, baptizing them in the name of the Father, and of the Son, and of the Holy Ghost;

Teaching them to observe all things whatsoever I have commanded you: and, lo, I am with you alway, even unto the end of the world.

Jesus said unto them, Thus it is written, and thus it behooved Christ to suffer, and to rise from the dead the third day:

And that repentance and remission of sins should be preached in His name among all nations, beginning at Jerusalem,

And ye are witnesses of these things.

And, behold, I send the promise of my Father upon you: but tarry ye in the city of Jerusalem, until ye be endued with power from on high.

They asked of Him, saying, Lord wilt Thou at this time restore again the kingdom to Israel?

And He said unto them, It is not for you to know the times or the seasons, which the Father hath put in His own power.

But ye shall receive power, after that the Holy Ghost is come upon you:

And ye shall be witnesses unto me both in Jerusalem, and in all Judaea, and in Samaria, and unto the uttermost part of the earth.

And when He had spoken these things, while they beheld, He was taken up and a cloud received Him out of their sight.

Selections from Matthew, Luke, and Acts.

THE WORKS OF GOD 303

O Lord, how manifold are Thy works! In wisdom hast Thou made them all: the earth is full of Thy riches.

The heavens declare the glory of God; and the firmament showeth His handiwork.

Thou visitest the earth and waterest it; Thou greatly enrichest it.

The river of God is full of water. Thou preparest them corn when Thou hast so provided for it.

Thou crownest the year with Thy goodness; and Thy paths drop fatness.

They drop upon the pastures of the wilderness; and the little hills rejoice on every side.

The pastures are clothed with flocks; the valleys also are covered over with corn.

O Lord, how manifold are Thy works! In wisdom hast Thou made them all.

O bless our God, ye people, and make the voice of His praise to be heard.

I will sing unto the Lord as long as I live: I will sing praise to my God while I have my being.

Praise ye the Lord! O give thanks unto the Lord, for he is good; for His mercy endureth forever.

Selections from the Psalms.

The heavens declare the glory of God; and the firmament showeth His handiwork.

By the Word of the Lord were the heavens made; and all the host of them by the breath of His mouth.

Praise ye the Lord. Praise God in His sanctuary: praise Him in the firmament of His power.

Praise ye Him, all His angels; Praise ye Him, all His hosts.

Let them praise the name of the Lord; for He commanded, and they were created.

The earth is the Lord's and the fullness thereof; the world, and they that dwell therein.

He hath also stablished them for ever and ever: He hath made a decree which shall not pass.

For the Word of the Lord is right; and all His works are done in truth.

He loveth righteousness and judgment: the earth is full of the goodness of the Lord.

Let them praise the name of the Lord: for His name alone is excellent; His glory is above the earth and heaven.

For by Him were all things created, that are in heaven, and that are in earth, visible and invisible, whether they be thrones, or dominions, or principalities, or powers: all things were created by Him, and for Him.

And He is before all things, and by Him all things consist.

Praise Him for His mighty acts: praise Him according to His excellent greatness.

He also exalteth the horn of His people, the praise of all His saints . . . . Praise ye the Lord.

Blessed is the nation whose God is the Lord. . . .

Let everything that hath breath praise the Lord. Praise ye the Lord.

Selections from the Psalms and Colossians.

305 THE LORD IS GOOD

The Lord is good to all: and His tender mercies are over all His works.

The Lord is good to all.

The Lord preserveth all that love Him.

The Lord is good to all.

The Lord upholdeth all that fall, and raiseth up all those that be bowed down.

The Lord is good to all.

He will fulfill the desire of them that fear Him: He also will hear their cry, and will save them.

The Lord is good to all.

The eyes of all wait upon Thee and Thou givest them their meat in due season.

The Lord is good to all.

Thou openest Thine hand, and satisfiest the desire of every living thing.

The Lord is good to all.

The Lord is nigh unto all that call upon Him, to all that call upon Him in truth.

The Lord is good to all.

The Lord is gracious, and full of compassion; slow to anger, and of great mercy.

The Lord is good to all.

My mouth shall speak the praise of the Lord: and let all flesh bless His holy name for ever and ever.

Selections from Psalm 145.

But I would not have you to be ignorant, brethren, concerning them which are asleep, that ye sorrow not, even as others which have no hope.

For if we believe that Jesus died and rose again, even so them also which sleep in Jesus will God bring with Him.

For this we say unto you by the word of the Lord, that we which are alive, and remain unto the coming of the Lord, shall not precede them which are asleep.

For the Lord Himself shall descend from heaven with a shout, with the voice of the archangel, and with the trump of God: and the dead in Christ shall rise first.

Then we which are alive and remain, shall be caught up together with them in the clouds, to meet the Lord in the air: and so shall we ever be with the Lord.

Wherefore comfort one another with these words.

But of the times and the seasons, brethren, ye have no need that I write unto you.

For yourselves know perfectly that the day of the Lord so cometh as a thief in the night.

For when they shall say, Peace and safety; then sudden destruction cometh upon them, as travail upon a woman with child; and they shall not escape.

But ye, brethren, are not in darkness, that that day should overtake you as a thief.

Ye are all the children of light, and the children of the day: we are not of the night, nor of darkness.

Therefore let us not sleep, as do others; but let us watch and be sober.

For they that sleep, sleep in the night; and they that be drunken are drunken in the night.

But let us, who are of the day, be sober, putting on the breastplate of faith and love; and for an helmet, the hope of salvation.

For God hath not appointed us to wrath, but to obtain salvation by our Lord Jesus Christ.

Who died for us, that, whether we wake or sleep, we should live together with Him.

I Thessalonians 4:13-18; 5:1-10.

FOR THE LORD'S DAY 307

This is the day the Lord hath made: We will rejoice and be glad in it.

I was glad when they said unto me, Let us go into the house of the Lord.

Surely the Lord is in this place.

The Lord is nigh unto all them that call upon Him, to all that call upon Him in truth.

Come before His presence with singing.

I will sing of lovingkindness and justice; unto Thee, O Lord, will I sing praises.

Know ye that the Lord, he is God; it is He that hath made us, and not we ourselves.

We are His people and the sheep of His pasture.

Give thanks unto Him and bless His name.

Bless the Lord, O my soul; and all that is within me, bless His holy name.

Selections from Psalms and Genesis.

Index to Hymns

WORSHIP AND PRAISE

Meter	Author	Composer
L. M.	Warren La Pree	Omer S. Garber
C. M. Ref.	Anne Shepherd	H. E. Mathews
7. 7. 7. 7.	Joachim Neander	Freylinghausen's Gesangbuch
	Bible	Harmonia Sacra
C. M. Ref.	W. H. Clark	Wm. J. Kirkpatrick
C. M. Ref.	E. Perronet	James Ellor
C. M.	E. Perronet	Wm. Shrubsole
6. 5. 6. 5.	London Hymn Book	Thersa Hostetler
7. 8. 7. 8. 7. 7.	Te Deum—tr. C. Walworth	Katholisches Gesangbuch
L. M.	Thomas Ken	Harmonia Sacra
6. 6. 6. 6. 8. 8.	Tr. John Chandler	John Darwall
C. M. D.	Psalm 105	English Tune
6. 6. 8. 6. 6. 8. 6. 6. 6.	W. T. Matson	Joachim Neander
6. 7. 8. 7. 8. 9. 6.	Psalm 148	Wm. J. Kirkpatrick
8. 7. 8. 7. D. Ref.	Isaac Watts	Reuben Brooks
L. M.	Anonymous	Johann Schmidt
P. M.	J. Franck—tr. C. Winkworth	J. Crüger—har. J. S. Bach
8. 7. 8. 7. 4. 7.	Thomas Kelly	Wm. H. Monk
P. M.	G. K. Pfeffel	Johann C. Gerold
L. M.	Bernard of Clairvaux	Josquin des Pres
8. 7. 8. 7. D.	D. A. McGregor	Thomas Hastings
C. M. Ref.	Tate and Brady	Adapted from Haydn
8. 7. 8. 7.	Anonymous	C. G. Hoover
S. M.	Anonymous	Harmonia Sacra
6. 6. 6. 6. 8. 8.	Isaac Watts	Parish Choir
C. M.	Chas. Wesley	Joseph Funk
8. 7. 8. 7. 8. 8. 7.	Leonard Clock—tr. J. C. Wenger	German Chorale—har. W. E. Yoder
6. 7. 6. 7. 6. 6. 6. 6.	John Heerman—tr. C. Winkworth	Har. J. S. Bach
P. M.	Fanny Crosby	Chester G. Allen
L. M.	Henry Burton	Johann Mozart
7. 7. 7. 7.	Anonymous	Henry Pollard
C. M.	Chas. Wesley	Ebenezer Beesley
C. M.	Anna L. Price	Scotch Psalter
C. M.	Rollin Pease	Dwight Weldy
L. M.	Isaac Watts	John D. Brunk
C. M.	Samuel Stennett	Thomas Hastings
6. 4. 6. 4. D.	Mary A. Lathbury	Wm. F. Sherwin
6. 6. 4. 6. 6. 6. 4.	Anonymous	Felice de Giardini
C. M.	Bernard of Clairvaux—tr. Edward Caswall	John B. Dykes
12. 13. 12. 10.	Reginald Heber	John B. Dykes
L. M.	Isaac Watts	John Hatton
P. M.	Münster	Richard S. Willis
7. 7. 7. 7. 8. 7. 8. 7.	S. F. Coffman	John D. Brunk
11. 11. 11. 11.	Wm. R. Featherstone	A. J. Gordon
10. 10. 11. 11.	Robert Grant	J. Michael Haydn
P. M.	Anonymous	Anonymous
7. 7. 7. 7. D.	Anonymous	Harmonia Sacra
12. 11. 12. 11.	Julia B. Cady	Old Netherlands
L. M.	Isaac Watts	John D. Brunk
10. 10. 11. 11.	Anonymous	Anonymous
S. M.	Isaac Watts	Aaron Williams
7. 6. 7. 6. D.	Wm. G. Tarrant	Berthold Tours
P. M.	Martin Luther	Martin Luther
7. 7. 7. 7. D.	Henry Alford	Geo. J. Elvey
7. 6. 7. 6. D.	Ada Cross	Salvatore Ferretti
S. M.	John Ellerton	König's Choralbuch
7. 7. 7. 7. 7. 7.	F. S. Pierpont	Conrad Kocher
C. M.	Joseph Addison	John Cole

CHRIST'S BIRTH, CHRISTMAS

No.	*First Line*	*Tune*
59.	A child is born in Bethlehem	Ein Kind Geboren zu Bethlehem
60.	I heard the bells on Christmas day	Waltham
61.	All my heart this night rejoices	Frölich
62.	A child is born in Bethlehem	Christmas Carol
63.	Come, all ye shepherds	Kommet Ihr Hirten
64.	Angels we have heard on high	Westminster Carol
65.	Hark! what mean those holy voices	Shields
66.	Joy to the world	Antioch
67.	How brightly shines the morning star	Wie schön Leuchtet der Morgenstern
68.	Our song of praise	Carol
69.	Silent night, Holy night	Stille Nacht
70.	While shepherds watched	Christmas
71.	Hark! the herald angels sing	Mendelssohn
72.	To us a child of hope is born	Zerah
73.	O come, all ye faithful	Adeste Fideles
74.	Watchman, tell us of the night	Watchman
75.	Lift up your heads, rejoice	Blessed Home
76.	Lo, how a Rose e'er blooming	Es ist Ein Ros'
77.	O come, O come, Emmanuel	Veni Emmanuel
78.	Once in royal David's city	Irby
79.	We three kings of Orient are	Kings of Orient
80.	Veiled in darkness Judah lay	Ebeling

CHRIST'S PASSION AND COMMUNION

No.	*First Line*	*Tune*
81.	Ride on, ride on in majesty	St. Drostane
82.	When I survey the wondrous cross	Hamburg
83.	Into the woods my Master went	Lanier
84.	Beneath the cross of Jesus	St. Christopher
85.	Christ, we do all adore Thee	Adoramus Te
86.	On a hill far away	Old Rugged Cross
87.	Ask ye what great thing I know	Crucified and Glorified
88.	O come and mourn with me awhile	St. Cross
89.	In the cross of Christ I glory	Rathbun
90.	Out onto Calvary's hill	Calvary
91.	Draw nigh and take the body	Morecambe
92.	The Gospel shows the Father's grace	Herr Jesu Christ, dich
93.	Bread of the world in mercy broken	Eucharistic Hymn
94.	Come, risen Lord	Birmingham
95.	Built on a rock	Kirken den er et
96.	Blessed Saviour, Thee I love	Spanish Hymn
97.	A parting hymn we sing	Olmutz

CHRIST'S RESURRECTION, EASTER

No.	*First Line*	*Tune*
98.	Christ, the Lord, is risen today	Resurrexit
99.	Here, O my Lord, I see Thee	Penitentia
100.	Christ, the Lord, is risen again	Mache Dich, Mein Geist, Bereit
101.	Christ who left His home in glory	Christ Is Risen
102.	Thine be the glory	Handel
103.	Alleluia! sing to Jesus	Alleluia
104.	Ye sons and daughters of the King	Gelobet sei Gott
105.	Jesus, o'er the grave victorious	Talmar
106.	I am the Lord, O hear my voice	Christ's Voice

CHRISTIAN LIFE, DISCIPLESHIP

No.	*First Line*	*Tune*
107.	All for Jesus	James
108.	Abide with us, our Saviour	Ach bleib mit Deiner Gnade
109.	By cool Siloam's shady rill	Siloam
110.	A charge to keep I have	St. Thomas
111.	Eternal God, we look to Thee	Winchester Old
112.	Deck thyself, my soul	Crüger
113.	Faith of our fathers	St. Catherine
114.	Help me to be holy	Daniel
115.	Jesus! how much Thy name unfolds	Thy Name

Meter	*Author*	*Composer*
8. 4. 8. 4. 4. 4.	Tr. W. E. Yoder	Har. W. E. Yoder
L. M.	H. W. Longfellow	J. B. Calkin
8. 6. 6. 8. 6. 6.	Paul Gerhardt–tr. C. Winkworth	Johann Ebeling
8. 4. 8. 4. 4. 4.	Anonymous	Esther Musselman
10. 10. 10. 10. 4.	Tr. Mari Hofer	Bohemian Tune
7. 7. 7. 7. Ref.	Bishop Chadwick	Old French Carol
8. 7. 8. 7. 8. 7. 8. 7.	John Cawood	Anonymous
C. M.	Isaac Watts	G. F. Handel–arr. Lowell Mason
8. 8. 6. 8. 8. 7. 8. 8. 8.	Philip Nicolai	Philip Nicolai
8. 8. 8. 8. 4.	Zion's Harp	Anonymous
6. 6. 8. 8. 6. 6.	Joseph Mohr	Franz Gruber
C. M. 5L.	Nahum Tate	Geo. F. Handel
7. 7 .7. 7. D.	Chas. Wesley	F. Mendelssohn
C. M.	Anonymous	Harmonia Sacra
P. M.	From Lat. F. Oakley	J. Reading
7. 7. 7. 7. D.	Sir John Bowring	Lowell Mason
6. 6. 6. 6. D.	Th. T. Lynch	John Stainer
7. 6. 7. 6. 6. 7. 6.	St. Germanus	M. Praetorius–arr. W. E. Yoder
L. M. 6L.	Tr. J. M. Neale	Plain Song
8. 7. 8. 7. 7. 7.	Cecil F. Alexander	H. J. Gauntlett
8. 8. 8. 6. Ref.	J. H. Hopkins	John H. Hopkins
7. 7. 7. 7. 7. 7.	Douglas L. Rights	Johann G. Ebeling
L. M.	Henry H. Milman	John B. Dykes
L. M.	Isaac Watts	Arr. Lowell Mason
P. M.	Sidney Lanier	Peter C. Lutkin
7. 6. 8. 6. 8. 6. 8. 6.	Elizabeth Clephane	F. C. Maker
P. M.	Seven Last Words	Theo. Dubois
P. M.	Geo. Bennard	Geo. Bennard
7. 7. 7. 7. 7.	Zion's Harp	Anonymous
L. M.	Frederick Faber	John B. Dykes
8. 7. 8. 7.	John Bowring	Ithamar Conkey
S. M.	Zion's Harp	Anonymous
10. 10. 10. 10.	Anonymous	Anonymous
L. M.	Matthias Loy	Cantionale Germanicum
9. 8. 9. 8.	Reginald Heber	J. S. B. Hodges
10. 10. 10. 10.	G. W. Briggs	F. Cunningham
8. 8. 8. 8. 8. 8. 8.	Nic. Grundtvig–tr. Carl Döving	L. M. Lindeman
7. 7. 7. 7. 7. 7. 7.	Geo. Duffield	Arr. Ben. Carr
S. M.	A. R. Wolfe	Arr. Lowell Mason
7. 7. 7. 7.	Chas. Wesley	J. A. Freylinghausen
10. 10. 10. 10.	Horatius Bonar	Edward Dearle
7. 7. 7. 7. Ref.	Michael Weisse–tr. C. Winkworth	Gesangbuch mit Noten
8. 7. 8. 7. Ref.	A. B. Kolb	A. B. Kolb
10. 11. 11. 11. Ref.	E. L. Budry–tr. R. B. Hoyle	Geo. F. Handel
8. 7. 8. 7. D.	Wm. C. Dix	St. Basil's Hymnal
8. 8. 8. Ref.	Tr. J. M. Neale	Melchior Vulpius
8. 7. 8. 7.	E. E. Higbee	I. B. Woodbury
8. 7. 8. 7. 8. 8.	Johann Scheffler–tr. Joanna S. Andres	Hermann Rhein
8. 7. 8. 7.	Mary D. James	John Stainer
7. 6. 7. 6.	J. Stegmann	Melchior Vulpius
C. M.	Reginald Heber	I. B. Woodbury
S. M.	Chas. Wesley	Aaron Williams
C. M.	James Merrick	Este's Psalter
8. 8. 8. 8. D.	J. Franck–tr. C. Winkworth	J. Crüger
L. M. 6L.	F. W. Faber	Hemy–Walton
11. 11. 11. 11.	A. J. Gordon	D. B. Towner
8. 6. 8. 6.	Mary B. Peters	Wm. Arnold

No.	First Line	Tune
116.	I have set watchmen	Watchmen
117.	I'm not ashamed to own my Lord	Azmon
118.	From Greenland's icy mountains	Missionary Hymn
119.	Immortal Love, within whose	Sandon
120.	Join all the glorious names	Culloden
121.	Lord of might	Iliff
122.	Lord, in the fullness	Es ist ein Born
123.	Jesus, my all	Duane Street
124.	Lamb of God, our souls adore Thee	Behold the Lamb of God
125.	Draw us to Thee	Johann
126.	Lord Jesus Christ, with us abide	Selnecker
127.	'Midst the darkness	Tersteegen
128.	Now in the days of youth	Youth
129.	O Master, let me walk with Thee	Maryton
130.	O Thou God of my salvation	Regent Square
131.	Looking upward every day	St. Kevin
132.	O Jesus, Prince of life	Send Me
133.	Rise, my soul, and stretch thy wings	Amsterdam
134.	Rise up, O men of God	Walter
135.	Praise the Saviour	Fellowship
136.	Service is our watchword	Service
137.	Shall I for fear of feeble man	Samson
138.	Soldiers of Christ, arise	Elmswood
139.	Saviour, when in dust, to Thee	Spanish Hymn
140.	Strive aright when God doth call	Ringe Recht
141.	When I can read my title clear	Ninety-Fifth
142.	Thou Power and Peace	St. Vincent
143.	Where cross the crowded ways	Germany
144.	Ye Christian heralds	Missionary Chant
145.	The work is Thine	Die Sach' ist Dein
146.	O Spirit of the living God	Melcombe
147.	O God of mercy! hearken now	Hesperus
148.	Ye servants of the Lord	Old 134th
149.	Thou, whose almighty word	Perkins

CHRIST'S MINISTRY

No.	First Line	Tune
150.	Wake, awake	Wachet Auf
151.	Fierce raged the tempest	St. Aelred
152.	O sing a song of Bethlehem	Bethlehem

CHRIST'S SECOND COMING

No.	First Line	Tune
153.	The King shall come	Jerusalem, Jerusalem
154.	Hosanna to the living Lord	Hosanna
155.	Our God, our help in ages past	St. Anne
156.	Christ is coming! let creation	Neander

THE CHURCH

No.	First Line	Tune
157.	Glorious things of thee are spoken	Austrian Hymn
158.	God of the living church	Ackley
159.	Jesus, from whom all blessings flow	Duane Street

GOD'S HOUSE

No.	First Line	Tune
160.	Unto Thy temple, Lord, we come	Mendon
161.	Within Thy tabernacle	Tallis' Ordinal

HOLY SPIRIT AND TRINITY

No.	First Line	Tune
162.	Eternal Father, when to Thee	Wareham
163.	Breathe on me, Breath of God	Trentham
164.	Hover o'er me, Holy Spirit	Fill Me Now
165.	Lead us, heavenly Father	Dulce Carmen
166.	Holy Spirit, hear us	Wem in Leidenstagen
167.	We all believe	The Apostles' Creed

Meter	Author	Composer
P. M.	Anonymous	Harmonia Sacra
C. M.	Thomas H. Gill	Carl G. Gläser
7. 6. 7. 6. D.	Reginald Heber	Lowell Mason
10. 4. 10. 4. 10. 10.	S. A. Brooke	Chas. Purday
6. 6. 6. 6. 8. 8.	Isaac Watts	Walter E. Yoder
8. 8. 8. 2. 7.	J. S. Blackie	L. B. Longacre
8. 6. 8. 6.	Th. H. Gill	C. E. Miller
L. M. D.	John Cennick	Geo. Coles
8. 7. 8. 7. D.	James G. Deck	James Langran
8. 7. 8. 7.	F. Fabricius—tr. C. Winkworth	Har. J. S. Bach
L. M.	N. Selnecker	Har. J. S. Bach
8. 5. 8. 5. D.	G. Tersteegen	Clara H. Scott
6. 6. 8. 6. D.	W. J. Mathams	Geo. J. Elvey
L. M.	Wash. Gladden	H. P. Smith
8. 7. 8. 7. 8. 7.	Thomas Olivers	Henry Smart
7. 6. 7. 6. D.	Mary Butler	Art. S. Sullivan
8. 6. 8. 6. D.	Anonymous	R. E. Nolte
7. 6. 7. 6. 7. 7. 7. 6.	Rob. Seagrave	James Nares
6. 6. 8. 6.	Wm. P. Merrill	Wm. H. Walter
8. 8. 8. 8.	Th. Kelly	German Melody
6. 5. 6. 5. 6. 5.	Wm. Shaw—John R. Clements	Wm. M. Runyan
L. M.	Chas. Wesley	Geo. F. Handel
S. M. D.	Chas. Wesley	I. B. Woodbury
7. 7. 7. 7. D.	Robert Grant	Spanish Melody
8. 7. 8. 7.	Johann Winkler—tr. C. Winkworth	Gnadauer Choralbuch
C. M.	Isaac Watts	Anonymous
L. M.	C. F. Alexander	James Uglow
L. M.	F. M. North	Ludwig van Beethoven
L. M.	B. H. Draper	Chas. Zeuner
P. M.	Tr. J. Horstmann	Franz J. Haydn
L. M.	James Montgomery	Samuel Webbe
L. M.	E. S. Clark	Henry Baker
S. M.	Phillip Doddridge	Geneva Psalter
6. 6. 4. 6. 6. 6. 4.	John Marriott	E. A. Perkins
P. M.	Philip Nicolai—tr. C. Winkworth	Philip Nicolai
8. 8. 8. 3.	Godfrey Thring	John B. Dykes
C. M. D.	L. F. Benson	G. W. Fink
C. M. D.	Tr. John Brownlie	Thomas Hastings
L. M. Ref.	Reginald Heber	John B. Dykes
C. M.	Isaac Watts	William Croft
8. 7. 8. 7. 8. 7.	J. R. Macduff	Joachim Neander
8. 7. 8. 7. D.	John Newton	Franz J. Haydn
C. M. D.	A. H. Ackley	B. D. Ackley
L. M. D.	Anonymous	Geo. Cole
L. M.	Robert Collyer	Samuel Dyer
C. M.	Scottish Psalter	Thomas Tallis
L. M.	H. D. Ganse	William Knapp
S. M.	Edwin Hatch	Robert Jackson
8. 7. 8. 7. 8. 7. Ref.	E. H. Stokes	Jno. R. Sweney
8. 7. 8. 7. 8. 7.	J. Edmeston	J. M. Haydn
6. 5. 6. 5.	Joseph Mohr—tr. C. F. Hernaman	Fred. Filitz
8. 7. 7. 7. 7. 7.	Tob. Clausnitzer—tr. C. Winkworth	Kirchengesangbuch

COURAGE AND COMFORT

No.	*First Line*	*Tune*
168.	Cast thy burden upon the Lord	Birmingham
169.	Father, to Thee we look	St. Barnabas
170.	Come unto me	Henley
171.	I love to steal awhile away	Lella
172.	How great the goodness	Meribah
173.	God holds my hand	Magines
174.	I need Thee every hour	Need
175.	O Lord, how happy should we be	Meribah
176.	God moves in a mysterious way	Dunfermline
177.	O Love that wilt not let me go	St. Margaret
178.	Jesus, Lover of my soul	Martyn
179.	Lead, kindly Light	Sandon
180.	Rock of Ages	Toplady
181.	O Love divine, that stooped	Quebec
182.	Dear Lord and Father of mankind	Rest
183.	What a friend we have in Jesus	Erie

CONSECRATION

No.	First Line	Tune
184.	Jesus, I my cross have taken	Ellesdie
185.	Am I a soldier of the cross?	Marlow
186.	Saviour, who died for me	I Give Myself to Thee
187.	Sit and pause awhile	Golgotha
188.	It may not be on the mountain height	I'll Go Where You Want Me to Go
189.	Jesus, come, O come to me	Jesus, Come
190.	Just as I am, Thine own to be	Thersa
191.	Take my life, and let it be	Hendon
192.	Loving Jesus, gentle Lamb	Witmarsum

PRAYER AND TRUST

No.	First Line	Tune
193.	Father in heaven, hear us today	Southampton
194.	Saviour, while my heart is tender	Lille
195.	The Lord's my Shepherd	Grant
196.	Abide with me	Eventide
197.	Christ, whose glory fills the skies	Lux Prima
198.	I waited for the Lord	Ballerma
199.	Lord, Thy mercy now entreating	Stockwell
200.	Dear Shepherd of Thy people	Durham
201.	Hold Thou my hand	Trust
202.	For them whose ways	Morwellham
203.	Pray when the morn is breaking	Meirionydd
204.	Pray, O Church, be sanctified	Power of Prayer
205.	My faith looks up to Thee	Olivet
206.	He who would be in God confiding	Wer Nur Den Lieben Gott
207.	In sorrow and pain	Best Refuge
208.	My Spirit on Thy care	Potsdam
209.	Lord Jesus Christ, we seek	Holley
210.	Father, in Thy mysterious	Henley
211.	Teach me to pray	Prayer
212.	Nearer, my God, to Thee	Bethany
213.	Speak, Lord, in the stillness	Samuel
214.	One thought I have	Praetorious

THE WORD

No.	First Line	Tune
215.	I think when I read	Sweet Story
216.	How firm a foundation	Adeste Fideles
217.	God's law is perfect	St. Andrew
218.	O the unsearchable riches	Unsearchable Riches
219.	Thy Word is like a garden	Seraph
220.	Shine Thou upon us, Lord	Broughton
221.	How I love Thy law	Thy Law

EVANGELISM

No.	First Line	Tune
222.	Come, ye sinners	Jeremiah
223.	Amazing grace! how sweet the sound	McIntosh

Meter	Author	Composer
P. M.	Psalm 55:22; 25:3	F. Mendelssohn
11. 10. 11. 10.	Fred. Hosmer	John B. Dykes
11. 10. 11. 10.	Cath. Esling	Lowell Mason
C. M.	Phoebe Brown	Chas. E. Pollock
8. 8. 6. 8. 8. 6.	Psalm 31:16-19	Lowell Mason
4. 6. 4. 6. 4. 6.	Rose Magines	Sidney Zook
6. 4. 6. 4. 7. 6. 7. 4.	Annie S. Hawks	Robert Lowry
8. 8. 6. 8. 8. 6.	Jos. Anstice	Lowell Mason
C. M.	Wm. Cowper	Scottish Psalter
8. 8. 8. 8. 6.	Geo. Matheson	Al. L. Peace
7. 7. 7. 7. D.	Chas. Wesley	S. B. Marsh
10. 4. 10. 4. 10. 10.	John Newman	Chas. Purday
7. 7. 7. 7. 7. 7.	A. M. Toplady	Thomas Hastings
L. M.	O. W. Holmes	H. W. Baker
8. 6. 8. 8. 6.	J. G. Whittier	Fred. C. Maker
8. 7. 8. 7. D.	Jos. Scriven	Chas. C. Converse
8. 7. 8. 7. D.	Henry F. Lyte	Arr. H. P. Main
C. M.	Isaac Watts	J. Chetham
6. 6. 6. 4. 6. 6. 6. 4.	Mary J. Mason	D. B. Towner
8. 7. 8. 7. 8. 7.	Zion's Harp	Anonymous
9. 7. 9. 7. D.	Mary Brown	Carrie Rounsefell
7. 7. 7. 7.	Zion's Harp	Anonymous
L. M.	Marianne Hearn	Thersa Hostetler
7. 7. 7. 7.	Frances Havergal	Ab. H. C. Malan
7. 7. 7. 7.	Chas. Wesley	Mel. from Unparteyisches – har. W. E. Yoder
P. M.	C. G. Ames	Anonymous
8. 7. 8. 7.	John Burton	Old French Melody
C. M.	Psalm 23	David Grant
10. 10. 10. 10.	Henry F. Lyte	Wm. H. Monk
7. 7. 7. 7. 7. 7.	Chas. Wesley	Chas. F. Gounod
C. M.	Psalm 40–Scottish Psalter	Robert Simpson
8. 7. 8. 7.	Scottish Hymnal	Darius E. Jones
C. M.	John Newton	Ravenscroft's Psalter
11. 10. 11. 10.	Lina Z. Ressler	Thersa Hostetler
8. 6. 8. 6. 8. 6.	Rich. Roberts	Chas. Steggall
7. 6. 7. 6. D.	Mrs. J. C. Simpson	W. Lloyd
7. 6. 7. 6. 6. 6. 6.	Zion's Harp	Anonymous
6. 6. 4. 6. 6. 6. 4.	Ray Palmer	Lowell Mason
9. 8. 9. 8. 8. 8.	Geo. Neumark–tr. J. J. Voth	Geo. Neumark
5. 5. 9.	Zion's Harp	Anonymous
S. M.	Henry F. Lyte	Johann S. Bach
8. 8. 8. 8.	Alexander Stewart	Geo. Hews
11. 10. 11. 10.	Sam. Johnson	Lowell Mason
P. M.	Lina Z. Ressler	Thersa Hostetler
6. 4. 6. 4. 6. 6. 6. 4.	Sarah Adams	Lowell Mason
6. 5. 6. 5.	E. May Grimes	H. Green
C. M.	Fred. L. Hosmer	Harmonai Hymnorum
P. M.	Jemima Luke	Har. Winfred Douglas
11. 11. 11. 11.	Geo. Keith	J. Reading
C. M.	Scottish Psalter	Tans'ur's New Harmony of Zion
10. 7. 10. 7. Ref.	Fanny Crosby	Jno. R. Sweney
C. M. D.	Edwin Hodder	Old English Melody
6. 6. 6. 6. D.	John Ellerton	Thomas Hastings
7. 7. 7. 7. Ref.	Psalm 119	Arr. Ben. Carr
8. 7. 8. 7. D.	Joseph Hart	Jeremiah Ingalls
C. M.	John Newton	Arr. E. O. Excell

Meter	Author	Composer
8. 8. 8. 8. 8. 8.	Chas. Wesley	Jeremiah Ingalls
L. M.	August Crull	Geo. J. Elvey
8. 7. 8. 7. D.	S. T. Francis	T. J. Williams
8. 7. 8. 7. 6. 7.	Eliz. Codner	Wm. B. Bradbury
8. 4. 8. 4. 5. 4. 5. 4.	W. H. Parker	F. A. Challinor
C. M. D.	Wm. Cowper	Anonymous
7. 6. 7. 6. 8. 8. Ref.	W. S. Walton	A. J. Gordon
9. 7. 9. 7. Ref.	J. M. Gray	W. Owen
S. M.	J. S. B. Monsell	J. Barnby
8. 7. 8. 7.	Jas. Montgomery	C. M. von Weber
8. 8. 8. 6.	Charlotte Elliott	Wm. B. Bradbury
C. M.	Rich. Burnham	Anonymous
10. 9. 10. 9. Ref.	H. R. Palmer	H. R. Palmer
7. 6. 7. 6. 7. 7. 7. 6.	Priscilla Owens	Wm. J. Kirkpatrick
11. 7. 11. 7. Ref.	Anonymous	A. Hull
10. 10. 10. 10. Ref.	A. H. Ackley	A. H. Ackley
C. M. Ref.	Lidie Edmunds	Wm. J. Kirkpatrick
9. 9. 9. 9. Ref.	Julia Johnston	D. B. Towner
S. M.	Horatius Bonar	Geneva Psalter
8. 7. 8. 7.	Dora Greenwell	Wm. J. Kirkpatrick
C. M. Ref.	Jennie Hussey	Wm. J. Kirkpatrick
8. 7. 8. 7. Ref.	Psalm 43	Wm. O. Perkins
8. 8. 8. 6. Ref.	Charlotte Homer	Chas. Gabriel
8. 7. 8. 7. D.	Jas. G. Small	Arthur Sullivan
8. 7. 8. 7. Ref.	David Nelson	Geo. F. Root
8. 9. 8. 11.	Zion's Harp	Anonymous
8. 7. 8. 7. 7. 7.	Zion's Harp	Anonymous
5. 4. 5. 4. 5. 4.	Horatius Bonar	Alfred R. Gaul
7. 6. 7. 6. 7. 6. 7. 6. Ref.	Tr. J. M. Neale	Geo. F. Le Jeune
6. 6. 8. 6.	Alfred Tennyson	Geo. F. Root
7. 6. 7. 6.	W. W. How	Gesangbuch mit Noten
L. M.	G. E. L. Cotton	Arr. S. Dyer
L. M.	Alfred Tennyson	Henry Lahee
C. M.	Anonymous	Flora H. Good
7. 6. 7. 6.	John Kebel	Melchior Vulpius
7. 6. 7. 6. D.	Zion's Harp	Anonymous
6. 6. 6. 6. 6. 6.	Tr. Ed. Caswall	Jos. Barnby
7. 7. 7. 7.	Anonymous	Arr. W. H. Monk
11. 10. 11. 10.	H. B. Stowe	Anonymous
7. 7. 7. 7.	Anonymous	C. M. von Weber
8. 4. 7. 8. 4. 7.	F. R. L. von Canitz	Franz J. Haydn
L. M.	Isaac Watts	Harmonia Sacra
7. 7. 7. 7. 4. Ref.	Mary Lathbury	Wm. F. Sherwin
C. M.	Anonymous	Damon's Psalmes
8. 7. 8. 7.	J. Edmeston	Geo. C. Stebbins
8. 8. 8. 8. 8. 8.	Sam. Longfellow	Franz J. Haydn
6. 5. 6. 5.	S. Baring-Gould	Jos. Barnby
10. 10. 10. 10.	John Ellerton	Ed. J. Hopkins
S. M.	John Fawcett	H. G. Naegeli
L. M.	Thomas Ken	Guillaume Franc, Geneva Psalter
P. M.	Numbers 6:24-26	Peter C. Lutkin

Alphabetical Index